A SIGN OF THE TIMES

THE BEST OF THE PENTHOUSE MARQUEE

Leah,
It was so nice to see you.
To say you've been missed is an
understatement. Please give
Griselda the biggest hug and
kiss. I'm looking forward to making
up for lost time
Love always

A SIGN OF THE TIMES

THE BEST OF THE PENTHOUSE MARQUEE

By BENJAMIN JACKSON & AARON CHAPMAN
Foreword by DANNY FILIPPONE

ANVIL PRESS | VANCOUVER

2nd printing: January 2026

Library and Archives Canada Cataloguing in Publication

Title: A sign of the times : the best of the Penthouse marquee / by Benjamin Jackson ; introduction by Aaron Chapman.
Names: Jackson, Benjamin (Bartender), author. | Chapman, Aaron, 1971- writer of introduction
Identifiers: Canadiana 2025027941X | ISBN 9781772142501 (softcover)
Subjects: LCSH: Penthouse Night Club. | LCSH: Neon signs—British Columbia—Vancouver—Pictorial works. | LCSH: Signs and signboards—British Columbia—Vancouver—Pictorial works. | LCSH: Marquees—British Columbia—Vancouver—Pictorial works. | LCSH: Nightclubs—British Columbia—Vancouver.
Classification: LCC GT3911.15.V36 J33 2025 | DDC 971.1/33—dc23

Book design: Derek von Essen
Cover photograph: Dave Worden
Marquee photographers: Justin Filippone, Joshua Coleman and Benjamin Jackson

Represented in Canada by Publishers Group Canada
Distributed in Canada by Raincoast Books
Anvil Press books are available in the United States from Asterism Books (Seattle).

The publisher gratefully acknowledges the financial assistance of the Canada Council for the Arts, the Government of Canada (Canada Book Fund), and the Province of British Columbia through the B.C. Arts Council and the Book Publishing Tax Credit.

British Columbia Arts Council — An agency of the Province of British Columbia
Canada Council for the Arts / Conseil des Arts du Canada
Canadä

Anvil Press Publishers Inc.
P.O. Box 3008, Station Terminal
Vancouver, B.C. V6B 3X5 Canada
www.anvilpress.com

PRINTED AND BOUND IN CANADA

DEDICATED TO THE FILIPPONE FAMILY

And to the mothers of Danny, Ben, and Aaron:
Thanks for letting us stay out late.

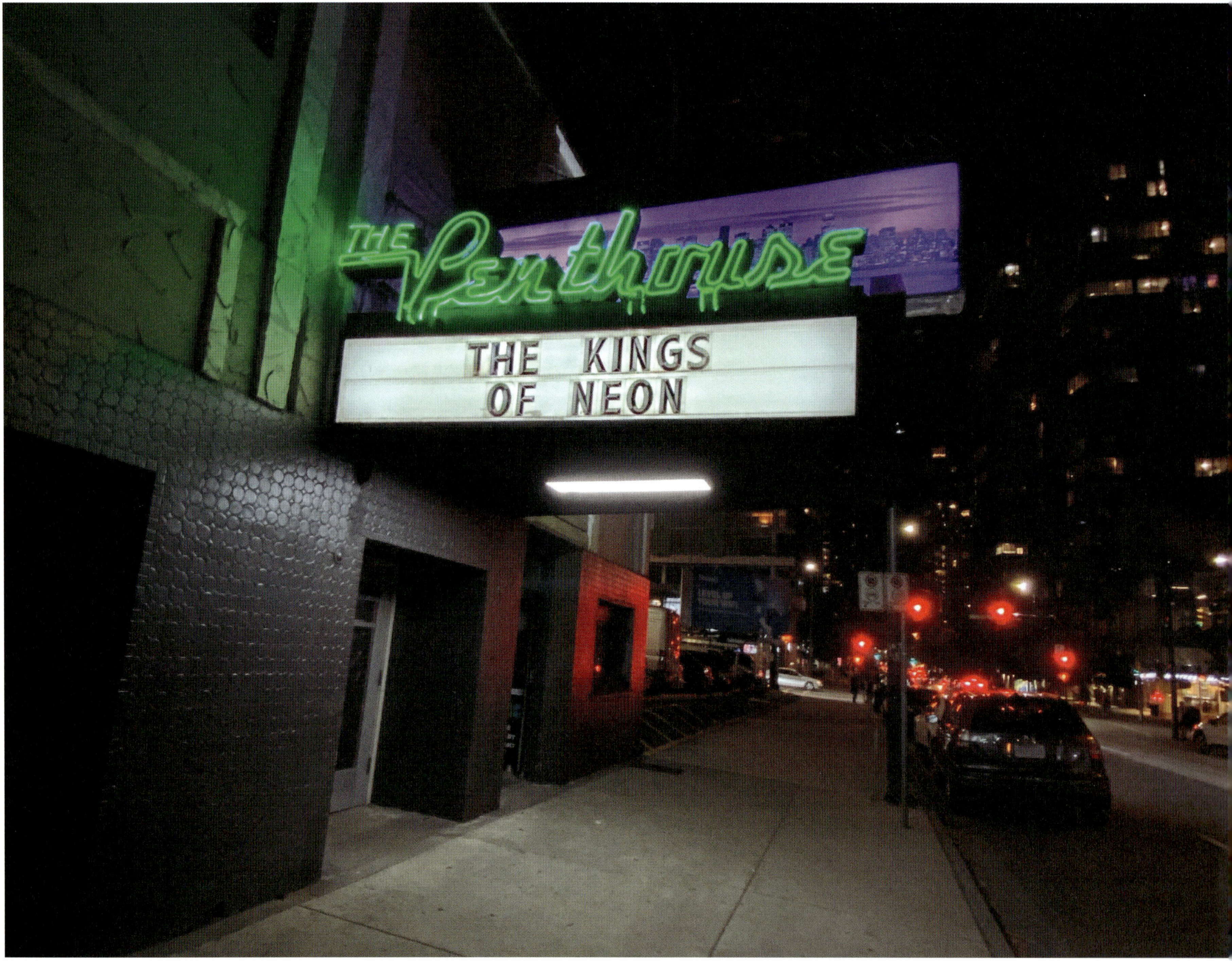
THE Penthouse
THE KINGS
OF NEON

KINGS OF NEON

Foreword by Danny Filippone

VANCOUVER HAS HAD MORE than its fair share of iconic neon signs. Many of them are gone. Some of them like the BowMac sign is half covered up and doesn't even shine anymore. Others, like the Smiling Buddha, are saved in museums or preserved in storage like The Only Seafoods restaurant sign.

But many others are still spread around the city and can be seen at their original locations. The Orpheum, the swinging Helen's neon sign in Burnaby, and many like The Vogue, and the Commodore Ballroom are still around for us to see. Some of them only say so much, like the Sylvia Hotel "S" or the Woodwards "W". I think it's fair to say that the Penthouse nightclub neon sign has said more than any of them.

In the 1930s and 40s, in the days before the nightclub opened, it was just a sign that read TAXI, as we ran the dispatch office for our cab company Diamond Cabs and the courier company Eagle Time Delivery there. Even when the Penthouse neon sign was put up in the 1950s, it didn't have the tile lettering space at the bottom, which was added later in the 1960s.

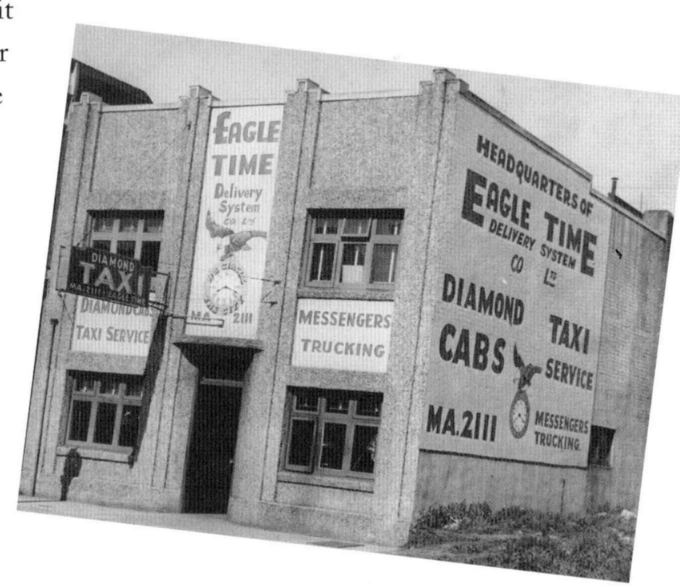

Some of my earliest memories of the nightclub have to do with that sign. I remember in the 1970s, even though the signs would just be announcing exotic entertainment stars that would be featured there, "Coming Soon: Big Fanny Annie", or a musician, or band that was appearing — as a kid, the names and mystery of what went on where my family worked probably stoked my imagination about the nightclub business. But Uncle Joe didn't just let anyone

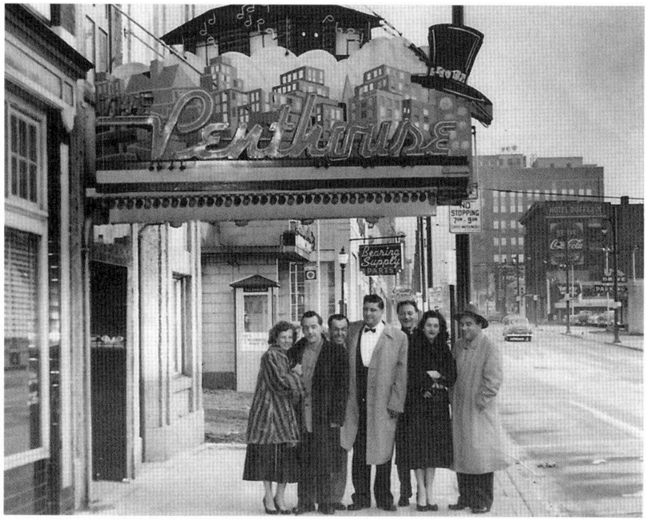

change the letters on the sign. So when I first started working there as an underaged busboy at the age of seventeen, and Uncle Joe told me I was next up to change the letters on the sign, I thought it was a big deal. I perhaps found out why they were so eager to pass it off soon after.

In those days, they kept all the letters in a box up in a shed on the roof. So you had to go up four flights of stairs to get up to the roof and bring them all back down. If you forgot any letters, you had to go all the way back up to get them. So, my first order of business was to find a spot for them down in the old kitchen on the ground floor, and they've been there ever since.

I don't think Uncle Joe, or my dad Ross, had ever thought about doing anything out of the ordinary with the sign. When I took over in 1983, I thought we could have some fun with the sign and I started posting predictions about the Canucks and BC Lions games. One year, when both teams were having a bad year, I put up a sign, "Go Lions Go! And Take the Canucks with You". I was just angry they were losing all the time, but those signs might have been the first ones to raise a few eyebrows.

In 2010, Former US President Bill Clinton was in town to give a keynote speech to the Vancouver Board of Trade. The Monica Lewinsky scandal was still very much in the public mind, and the Clinton visit was a big news story at the time. I put up a sign that read: "President Clinton — Our Lips Are Sealed". I thought it was cheeky and funny, and figured the Presidential motorcade coming in from the airport might take Seymour Street as they came in downtown. But three days later, I got a letter from a local contact of the US Secret Service asking me to take it down. I thought it was a joke at first, but they said they didn't think it was in good taste, and asked us if we could kindly remove it. I hummed and hawed, and I did take it down. I was at the Penthouse the day he arrived, and I stood outside for a while to see if the motorcade would come by, but they took another route into town. I thought, maybe

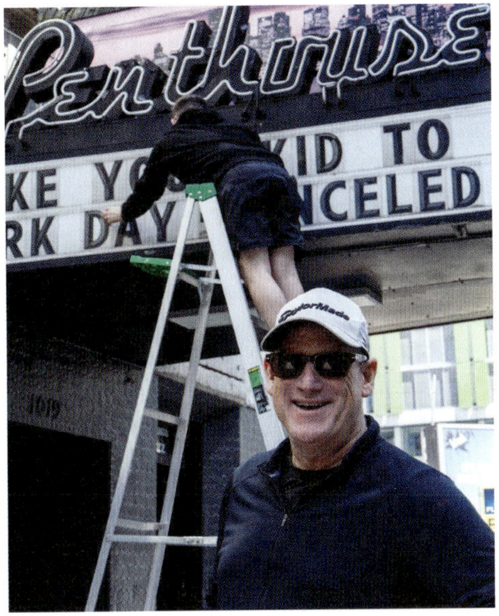

they thought I hadn't taken the sign down yet? I guess even then I should have considered the power of the Penthouse sign!

After the Penthouse had a fire in November 2011, in the months afterwards when we were repairing and renovating, we also wanted to do a makeover with some rebranding. Logos, and internet engagement was becoming prominent, and we were stuck with a bit of nostalgic old top hat and cane representation. I had weekly meetings with a marketing company that helped us with rebranding the Penthouse and its history as 'the original strip club'. But one thing we discussed was that the sign was iconic and we ought to do more with it — use the sign as an arm of the business — and do more with its messages. We should embrace it, embrace that it was "ok" to be a strip bar — and we could even poke fun at ourselves with a new sign every week. It was around that time that Ben and his friends came forward.

Over the last ten years, there's been much mystery and speculation about the sign — with many people asking, "Who does your sign?" For a long time, we were tight-lipped and didn't want to reveal the person behind the sign. In a way, it's aways been a team effort. Sometimes Ben bounces an idea around the bar, sometimes I see something in the news that I think he should tackle. But the growing popularity of the sign, along with several posts going viral on social media, and Ben's success, and the sign being featured in the local news, inevitably lured Ben out of the shadows. And now more and more people know (even more so with this book!) that Benjamin Jackson is the "Sign Guy."

I sometimes wonder if there's now added pressure on Ben? Some days he comes to me and says he's got nothing. But then a couple of days later he comes up with a winner. Sometimes we all think that after a sign gets a lot of notice, he'll never come up with one as big as it again. But then Ben outdoes himself and a sign goes viral around the world. Either way, the secret is out.

I consider the Penthouse sign to be a piece of art, with its green neon and pink arrows. There's only a couple of neon sign maintenance businesses left in town, and we regularly have to do repairs. It's a lot of work to keep it going, but we happily do it. It's now part of the legacy of the Penthouse Nightclub.

The sign is where it's always been. But it's only more recently become what seems a part of the city, and water-cooler culture. It's now featured on Tourism BC promotions, and even during Canucks games when a graphic parody of it appears on the Jumbotron announcing to *cheer louder!* It would have been unthinkable in my father's time, when the Penthouse was the subject of so much controversy, as detailed in *Liquor, Lust, and the Law*, Aaron Chapman's best-selling book about the history of the Penthouse.

Yet I often think that the messages on the Penthouse marquee wouldn't work if we were another kind of business. Other businesses have marquee signs and sometimes they try to do what the Penthouse does, but because of our history and the kind of club that we are, we're able to tackle topics that I think a muffler shop or a shoe store couldn't take on — at least not with the same tongue-in-cheek humour. We don't try to pretend we're something exclusive or arrogant, we're just what we are, an entertainment spot that's been here for eighty years.

I sometimes wonder what my father would say today if he saw the news about the Penthouse sign, or what the sign has become. I don't think he could have imagined it. It's just another wild chapter in the history of the place he helped create.

In 2025, after over forty-five years of working at the Penthouse Nightclub, I had the deep honour of being inducted into the BC Entertainment Hall of Fame. I join my father Ross, and my Uncles Mickey, Jimmy, and Joe who were inducted in 2016. And I couldn't be more proud of what the Penthouse was and has become, and that it's such a part of Vancouver's history. Maybe that old neon sign on Seymour Street might one day join the rest of the family in the Hall.

— Danny Filippone
Owner, Penthouse Nightclub

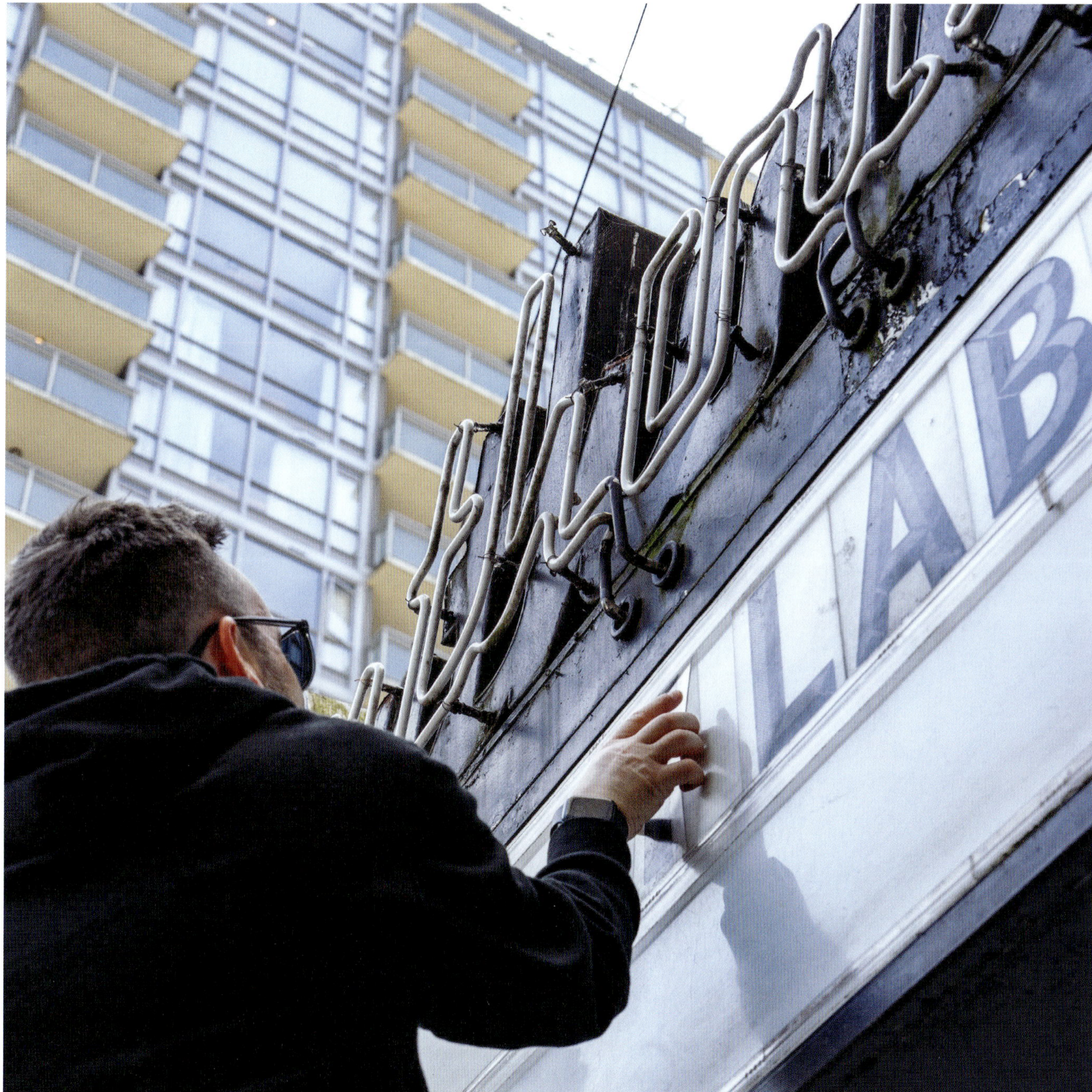
LAB

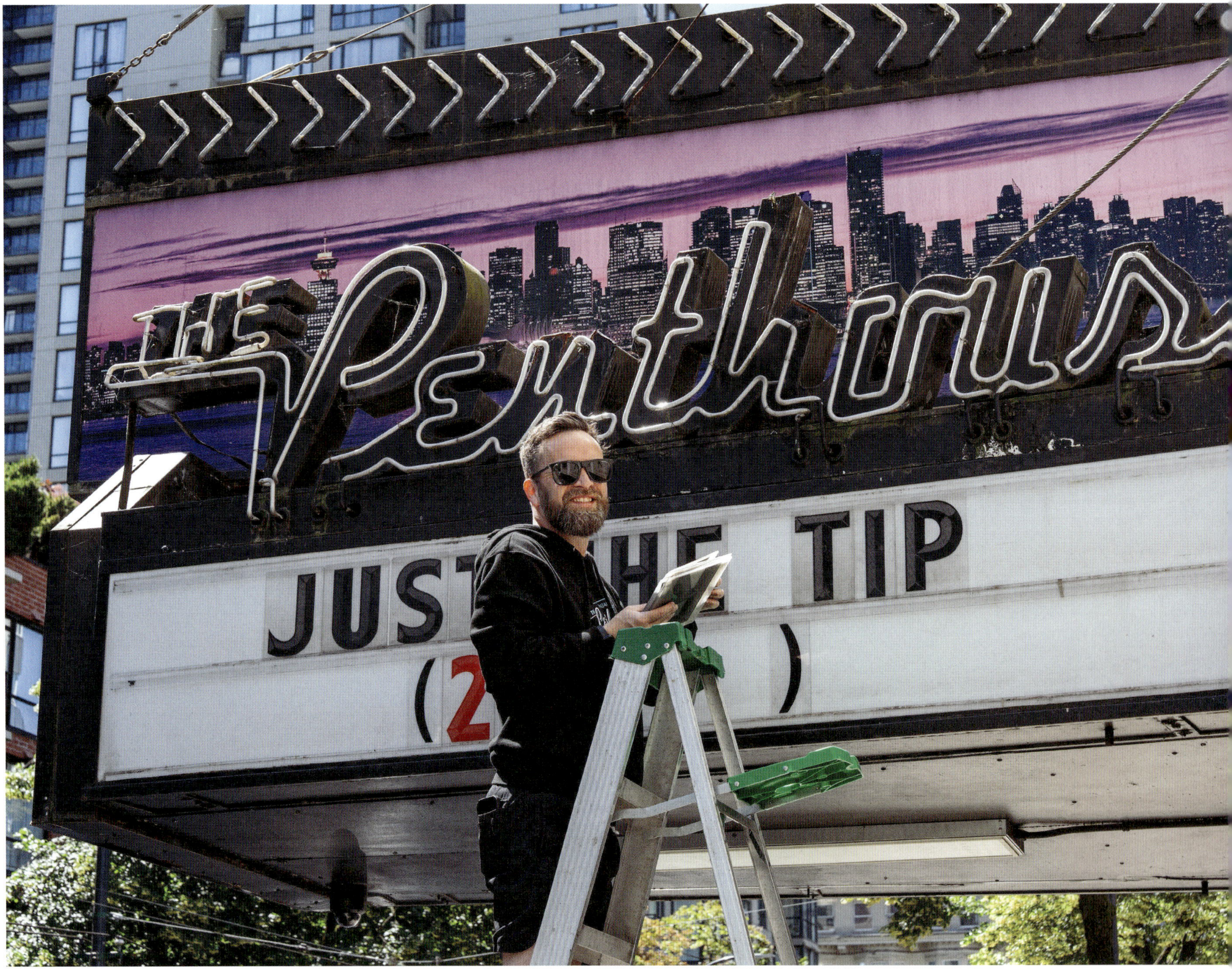
THE
JUST HE TIP
(2)

BENJAMIN JACKSON

Fluent in Sign Language

THE WHOLE THING STARTED with me trying to make my friends at work laugh.

I started working at the Penthouse in June 2015 — I'd never worked in a bar before. My friend, Matt Williamson — also a bartender at The Penthouse — got me the job, and we still work together there today.

I had just moved to Vancouver from Ontario. I didn't know Danny or anybody else in town. I had hung out at the Penthouse many times to visit Matt, see what was happening, and ended up getting hired. My first night there I had to change a keg in the cooler, but I did it wrong and it sprayed beer everywhere. I got completely soaked and tried to mop it all up. It was a disaster and certainly wasn't a great beginning.

A lot of the messages on the Penthouse marquee in the old days were kind of dull. We used to shoot some funny ideas around it at work. I guess I showed the most interest in the sign and started brainstorming at home about it too.

People forget the Penthouse marquee is actually two signs. The south sign faces up Seymour Street, and the north sign faces down it towards Granville Bridge. The first year I was managing the sign, we put jokes on both sides — but I was burning through my material fast! So, we tended to leave our business information — stuff about upcoming events or just the club hours — on the north sign and leave the south one to be the one that people walking and driving past would most often see. Things took off quickly, and soon the Penthouse sign had a reputation of its own — especially on social media. It felt like it was suddenly getting its own momentum.

When owner Danny Filippone started encouraging me to come up with more ideas for the sign, I enthusiastically agreed, but said I wanted to stay away from politics and religion; I didn't want to upset

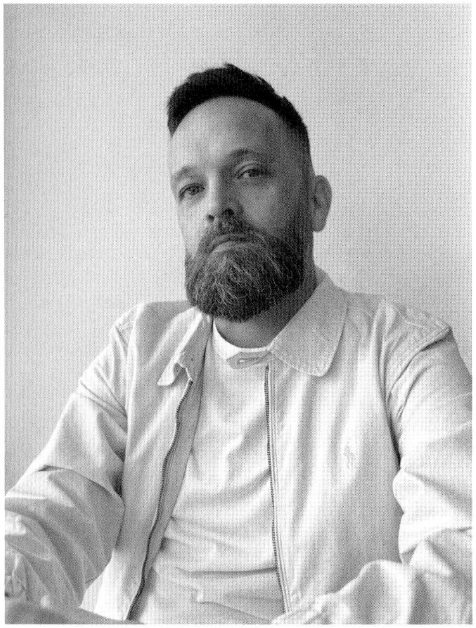

anyone and have them throw a brick through our window. We just wanted to have some fun, get some notice and promo for the club. The dancers had their stage inside, and now we had the marquee as our stage *outside* on Seymour Street!

The COVID lockdown was a big turning point. A few months in, I was worried we might never get back to work — I suppose a lot of people felt that way. But we began to get a lot of different reactions to the signs. Even though we were in this dark period, we tried to stay positive and kept up the humour. There were lots of people who had set foot in the bar before that were enjoying the posts. The club would get all sorts of phone calls and emails saying the Penthouse was keeping them smiling through that tough time. It felt like it had become its own little voice for the city, especially on social media.

I rarely respond to direct messages I'm sent, and forward any business ones off to management. I love the feedback from people passing by on the street, and I regularly post photos of the signs on Instagram and Facebook — but I don't like taking too much of the credit. When a sign goes over big, I like sending photos of them off to friends or family out of town. But I also kind of like hiding my personal persona behind the marquee. It's okay if people don't know my name, or just call me "The Sign Guy." In the early days, on Reddit, they referred to me as "The Marquee Boy." I just like making the city laugh through that sign — and that's the point in the end. The sign speaks for itself!

— Ben "The Sign Guy" Jackson
September 2025

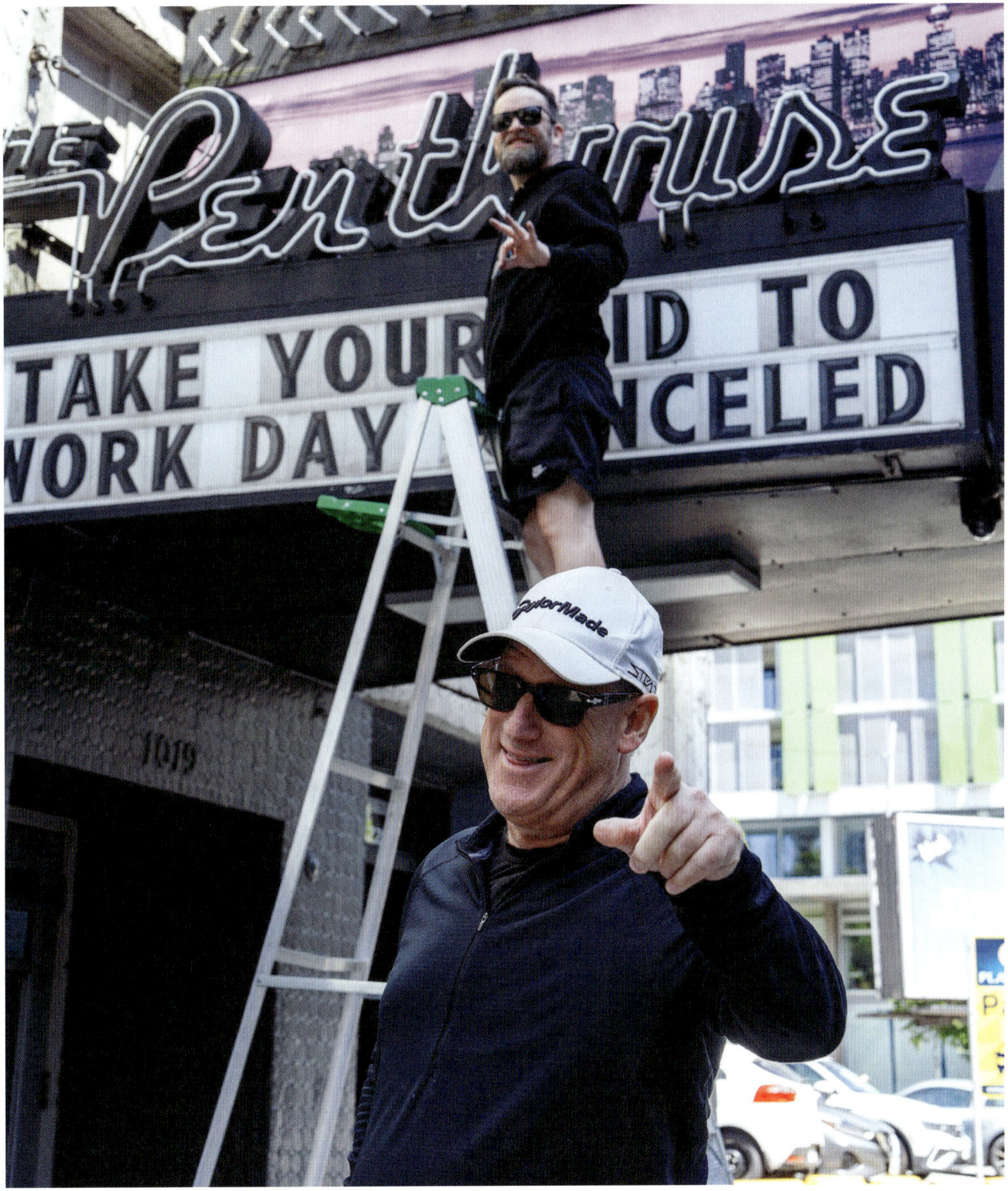
Penthouse
TAKE YOUR ID TO
WORK DAY NCELED
TaylorMade
1019

RARE POKEMON INSIDE

Aaron Chapman: *For Ben, it really all started back in 2016, with the coming news that the Pokémon GO mobile phone game — which uses augmented reality and the phone's GPS to allow you to find, catch, and battle Pokémon in the real world — which was already popular in the USA, would be coming to Canada. Little did Benjamin or the Penthouse know that the club was entering a new era:*

Benjamin Jackson: I had the initial idea for it — but I had never suggested a sign before at work. I mentioned it to our old General Manager — but he didn't want to do it. I begged him for a few days, and when he finally relented, I put it up the day the game was available in Canada — so the timing was perfect.

Next thing we know, the phone is ringing off the hook. People are knocking on the door during the day, begging to come in when only the cleaning staff was there. When I was working my shift that night, the Doormen — who had no idea what Pokémon was — kept grabbing me at the bar to come outside and talk to people who were standing there with their phones. Some parents even came by with their young daughter, asking if the mother stayed outside with their daughter, could her husband run and catch the Pokémon — it was nuts! Local media really latched onto it. Even I started playing the game for a while.

That first marquee sign went viral on its own. People sent me photos of other strip clubs across the continent who used it. I'd get sent photos of people who even used the message on abandoned cars and derelict buildings.

I couldn't imagine what was to come. But it was a turning point for me and the sign together. I started to hear people talking about it on the street. If I happened to meet somebody and I told them I worked at the Penthouse, and I was the guy making up the signs, they thought I was lying. Back then, I didn't have a phone that was full of all the signs to show them, and for the next few years the identity of who was making them would remain a mystery.

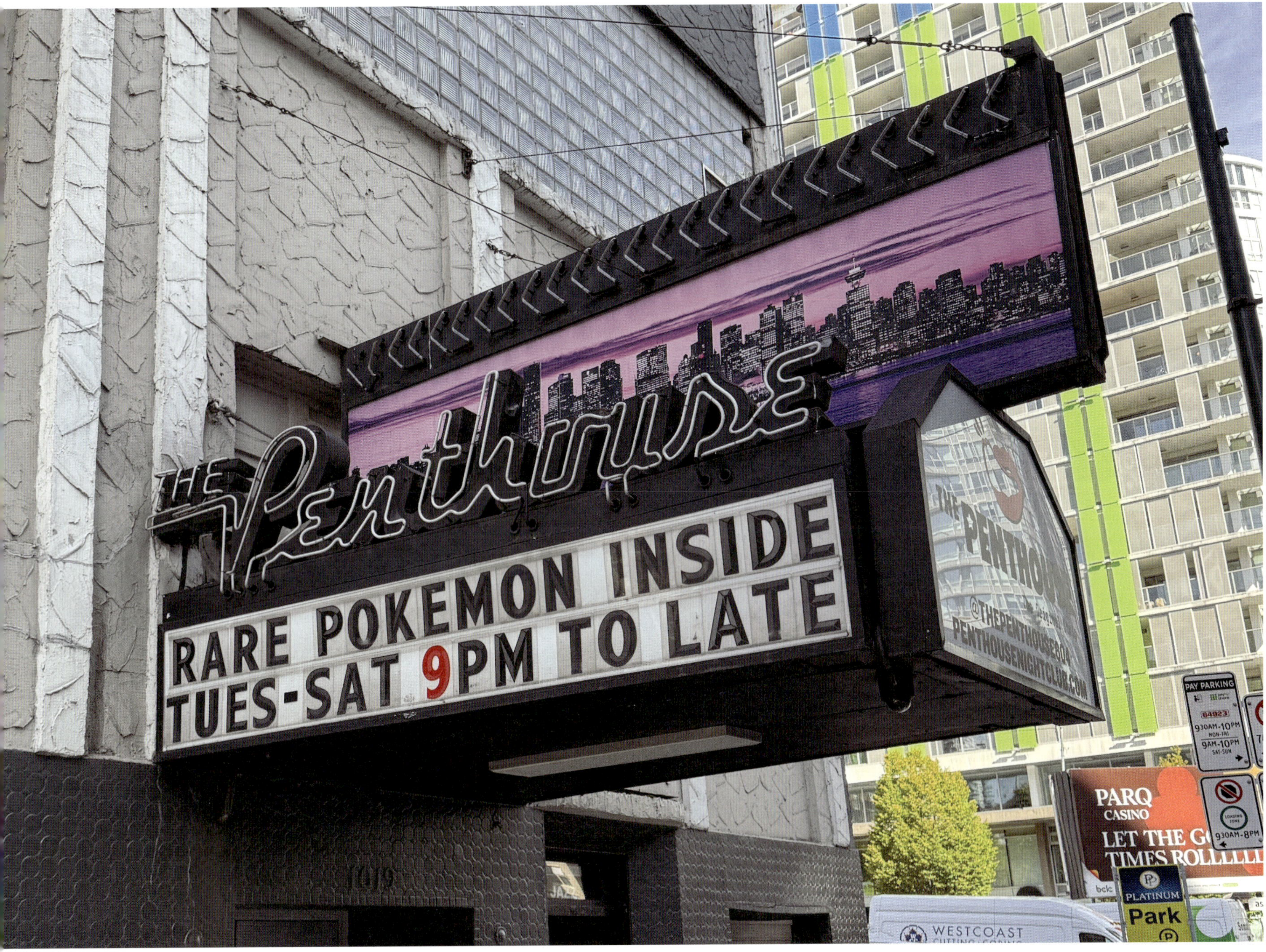
THE Penthouse
RARE POKEMON INSIDE
TUES-SAT 9PM TO LATE
THE PENTHOUSE
@THEPENTHOUSE604
PENTHOUSENIGHTCLUB.COM
PAY PARKING
PARQ
CASINO
LET THE G
TIMES ROLLLLLL
PLATINUM
Park
WESTCOAST

THE WRECK BEACH OF NIGHT CLUBS

The beginnings of the Penthouse Nightclub go back to the 1930s when Joe Philippone founded the Eagle Time Athletic Club, a private club and sports association. This was around the same time that Vancouver's Wreck Beach was acknowledged as the city's only "clothing optional" beach.

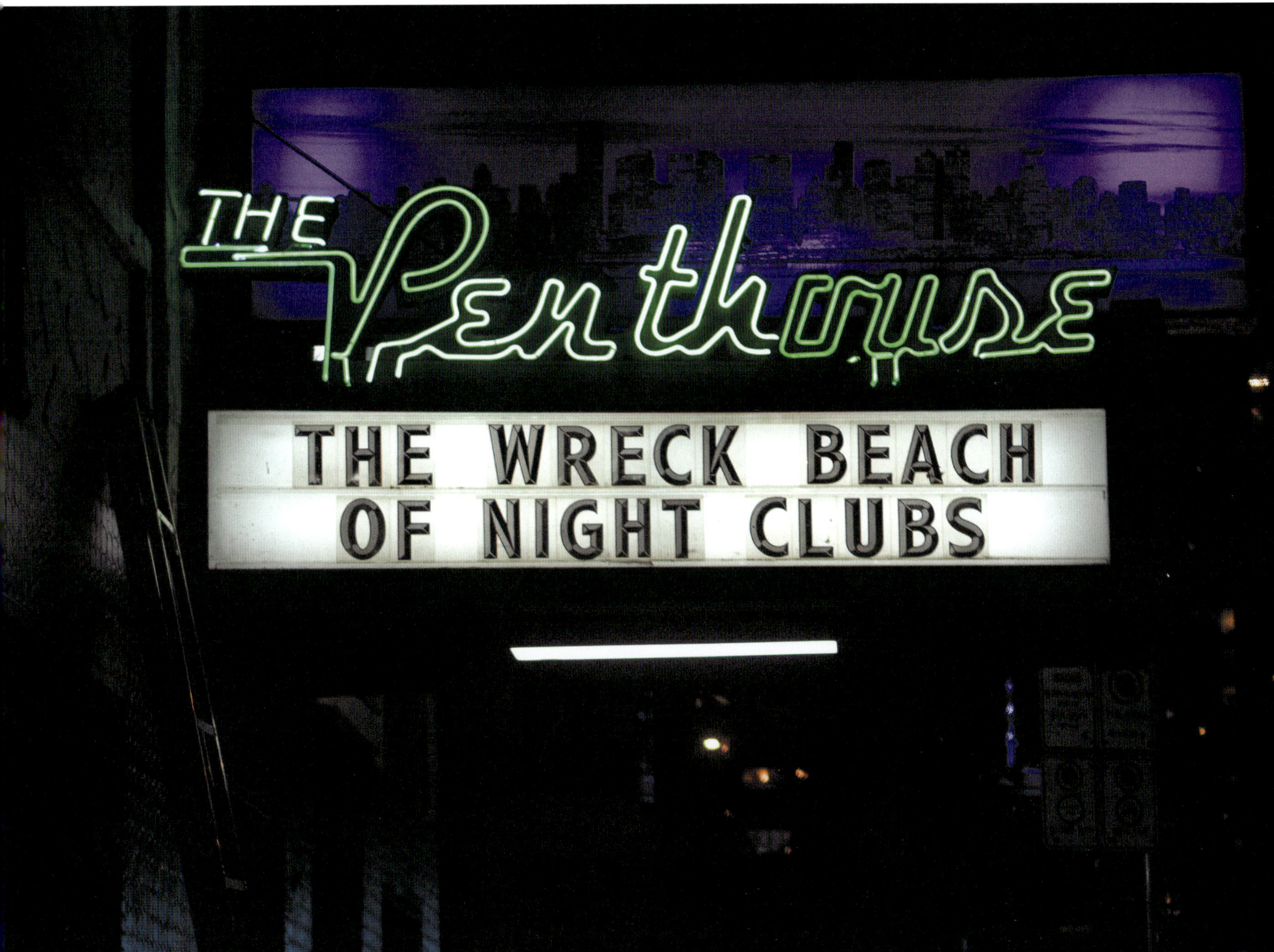
THE Penthouse
THE WRECK BEACH
OF NIGHT CLUBS

LITERALLY FREEZING OUR PANTS OFF

During a period when Vancouver was hit with very cold weather. Images of this sign garnered over 103,000+ Google views when first shared.

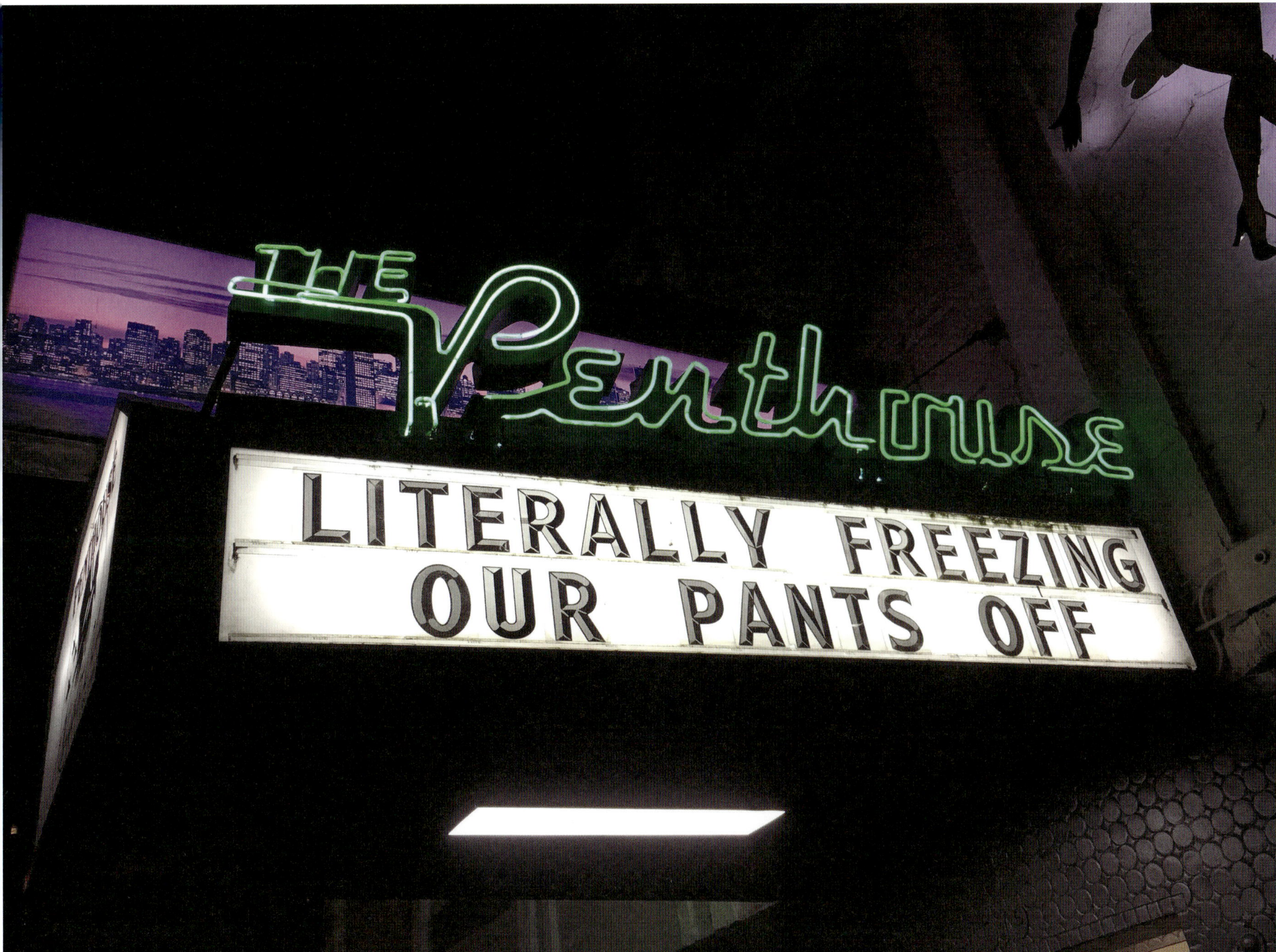
THE Penthouse
LITERALLY FREEZING
OUR PANTS OFF

MAKE IT RAIN (INSIDE)
WE'RE GOOD OUT HERE

The city gets its fair share of rain throughout the year. So does the Penthouse.

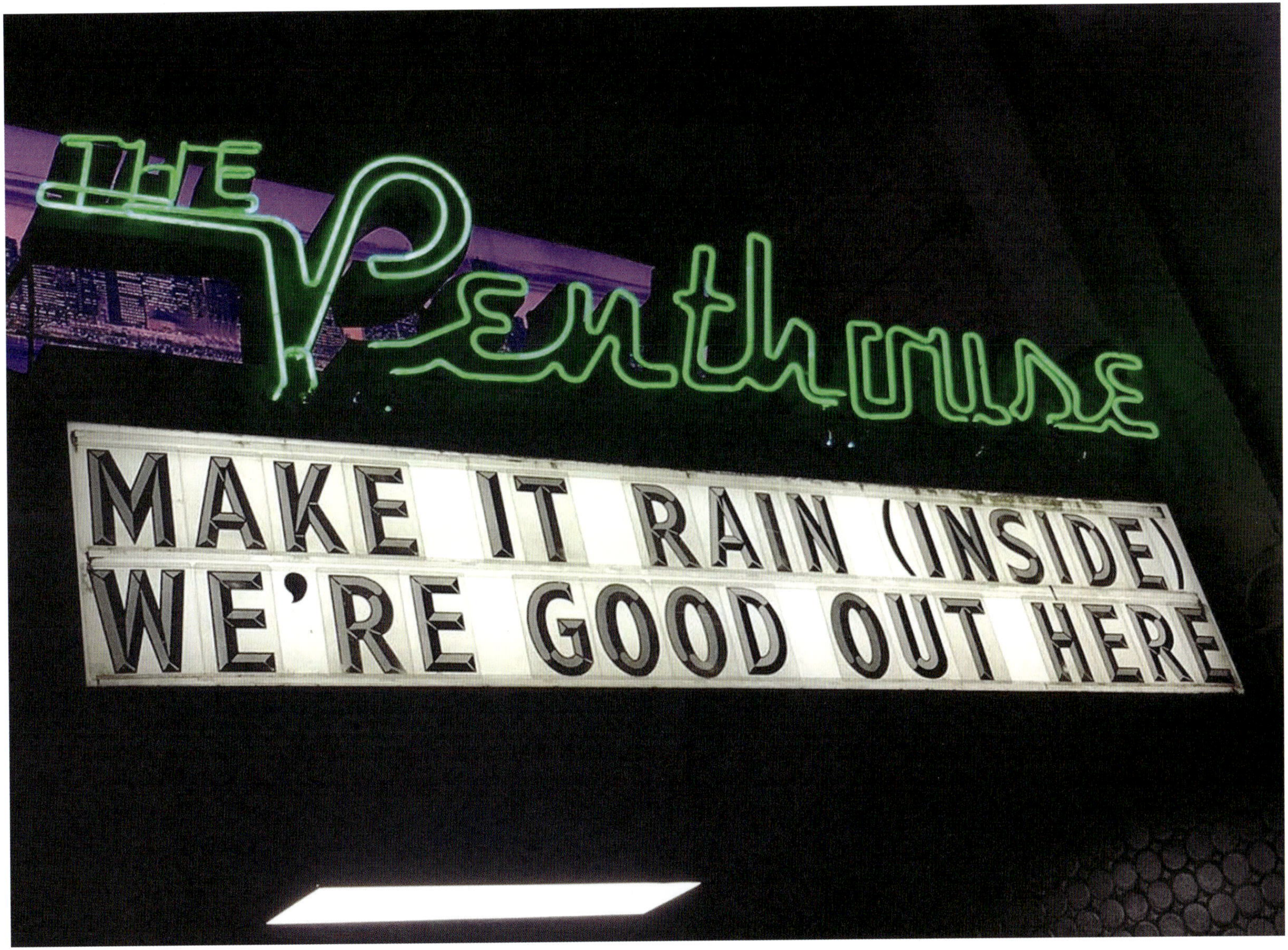
THE Penthouse
MAKE IT RAIN (INSIDE)
WE'RE GOOD OUT HERE

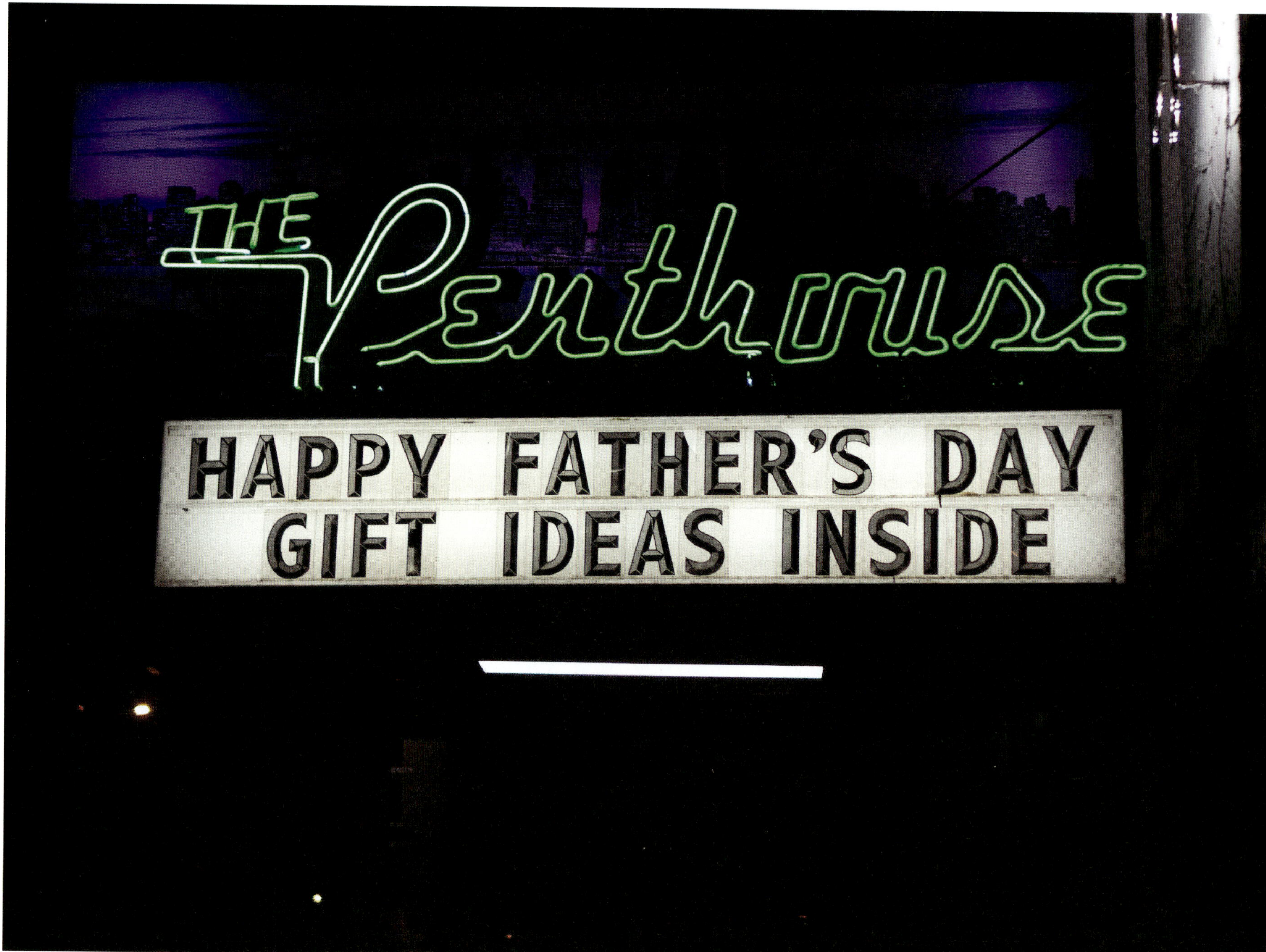
THE Penthouse
HAPPY FATHER'S DAY
GIFT IDEAS INSIDE

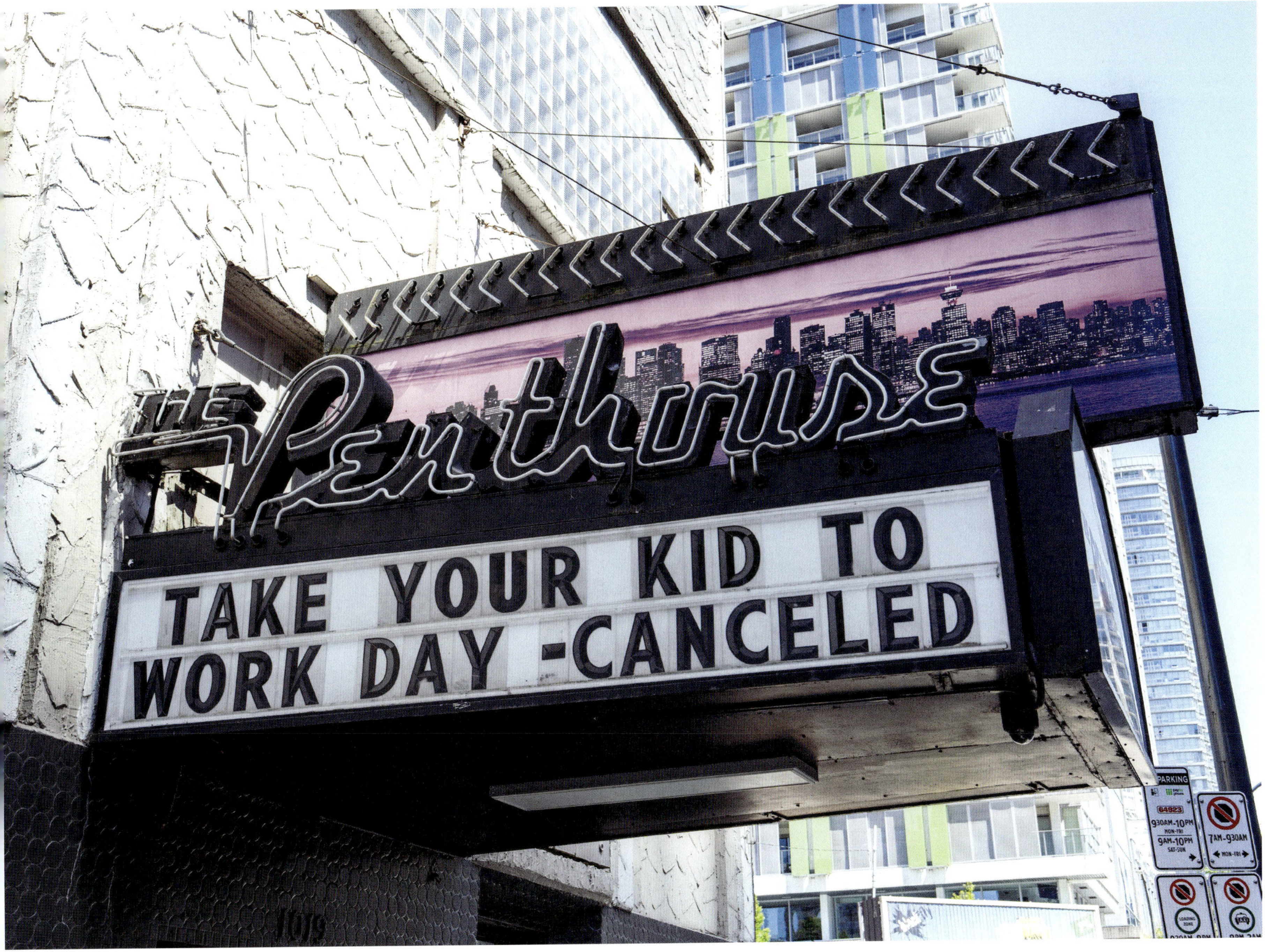
The Penthouse
TAKE YOUR KID TO
WORK DAY -CANCELED

HATE STRIP CLUBS?
TAKE LEFT ON NELSON

A sign that Real Vancouverites got and appreciated — you might only get the joke if you're from the city:

One of my personal favourites. When we put it up, a friend asked me if I was worried people might see it and actually take a left on Nelson, which of course is a one-way street. I told them no, and if they hated strip clubs that bad, and they were taking traffic advice from a strip bar marquee, then they were in more trouble than I could help with. This one got 300,000+ Google views, and there was never an accident, so I think people got the message.

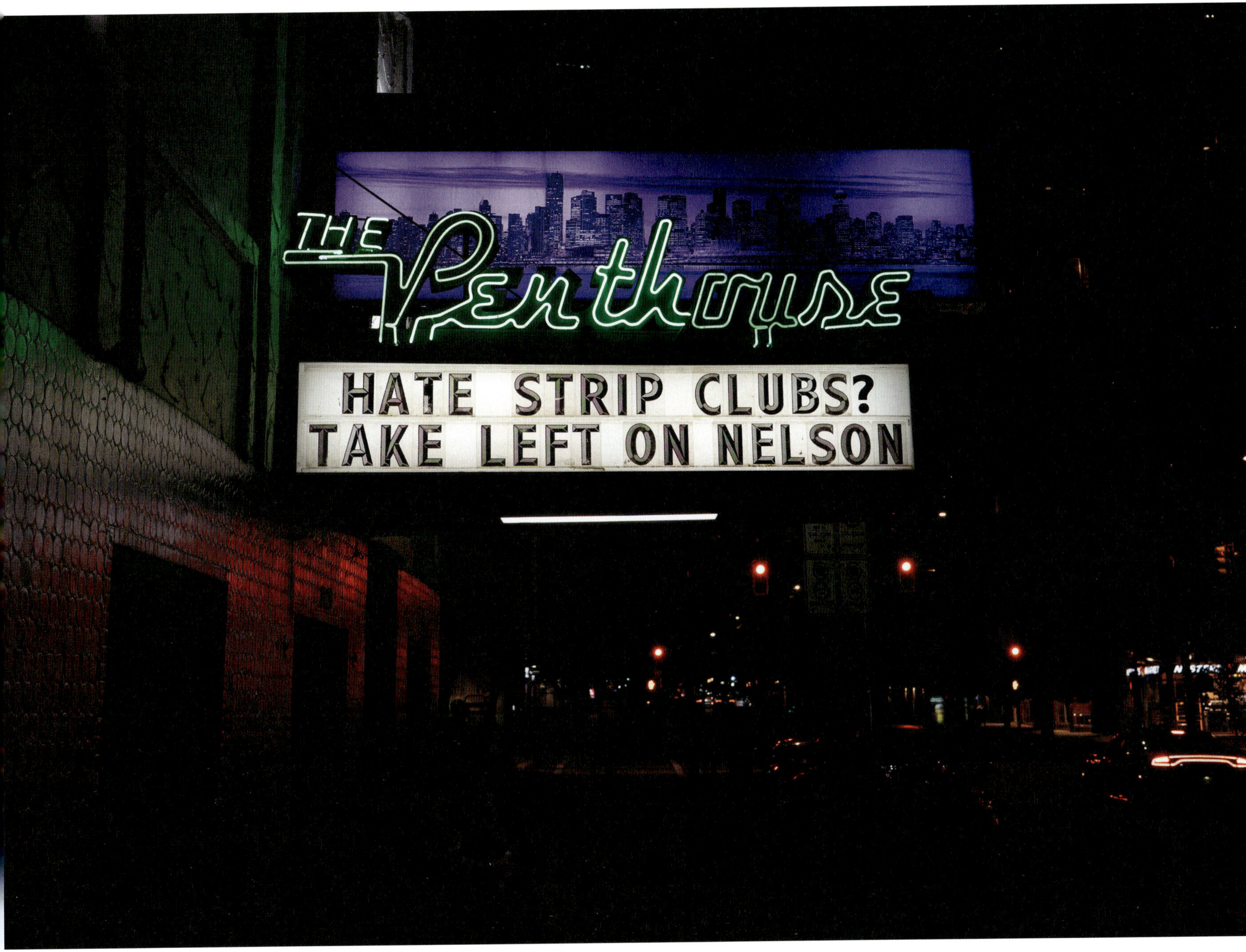
THE Penthouse
HATE STRIP CLUBS?
TAKE LEFT ON NELSON

ONE WAY STREET
TURN AROUND

It's often been the signs that were truly most appreciated by locals that have been the best remembered. Ones where you not only had to be a local, but had to be aware of downtown traffic patters to get the joke:

Sometimes at work if I had a moment, I'd step outside for a break, and watch the cars go by on Seymour Street. The doormen and I would be shocked by how many people would turn the wrong way — south — down Seymour. It happens more often than you might think. So, this was my way of letting drivers — who were maybe just realizing their mistake — know about it in their rear-view mirror.

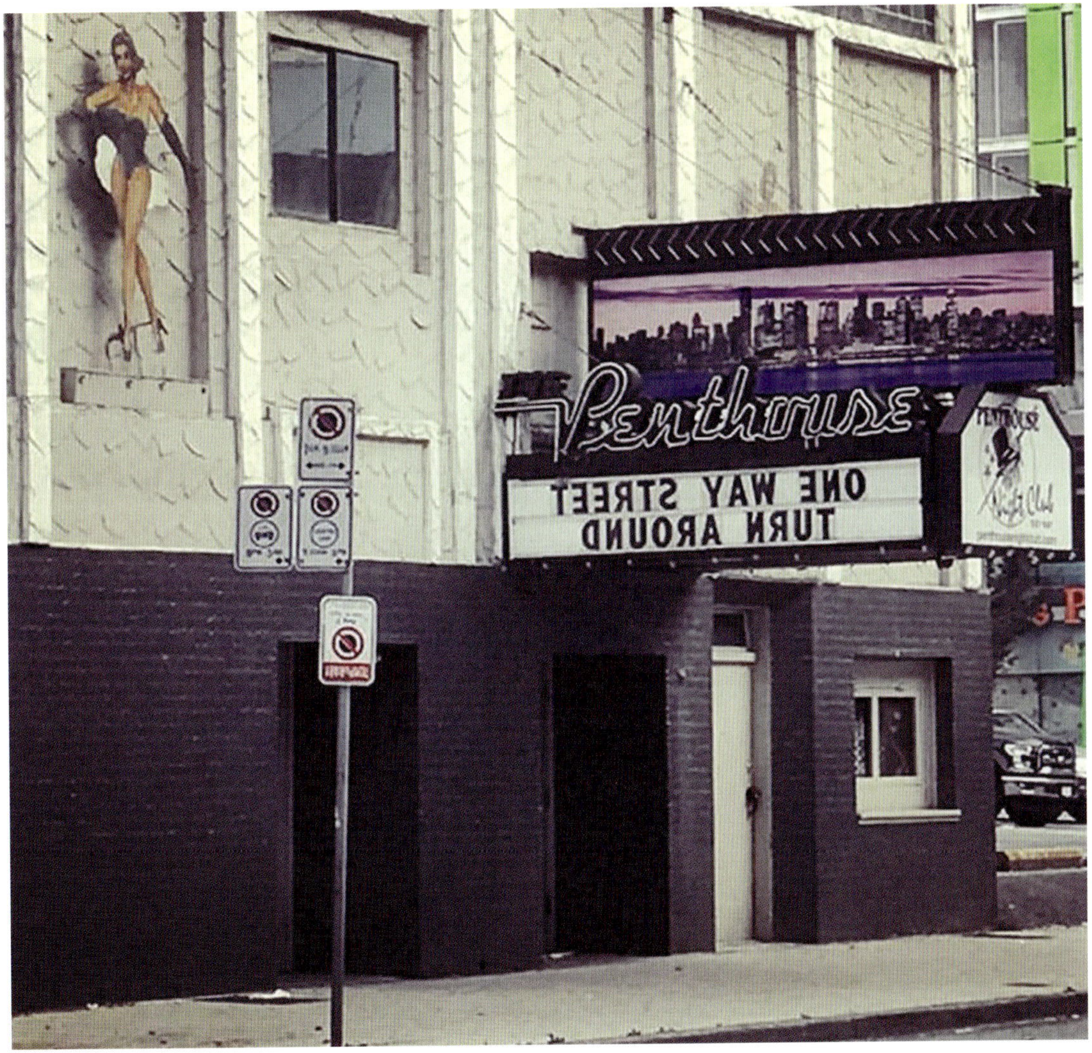

"There's a sly thrill on being in on the joke, when you think how many of your commuting cohorts are also in on the joke. Did they avert their gaze from the audacious public prose on the marquee, or lean into the double-entendres with a wink and a nudge!"

— Pete Fry
Vancouver City Councillor

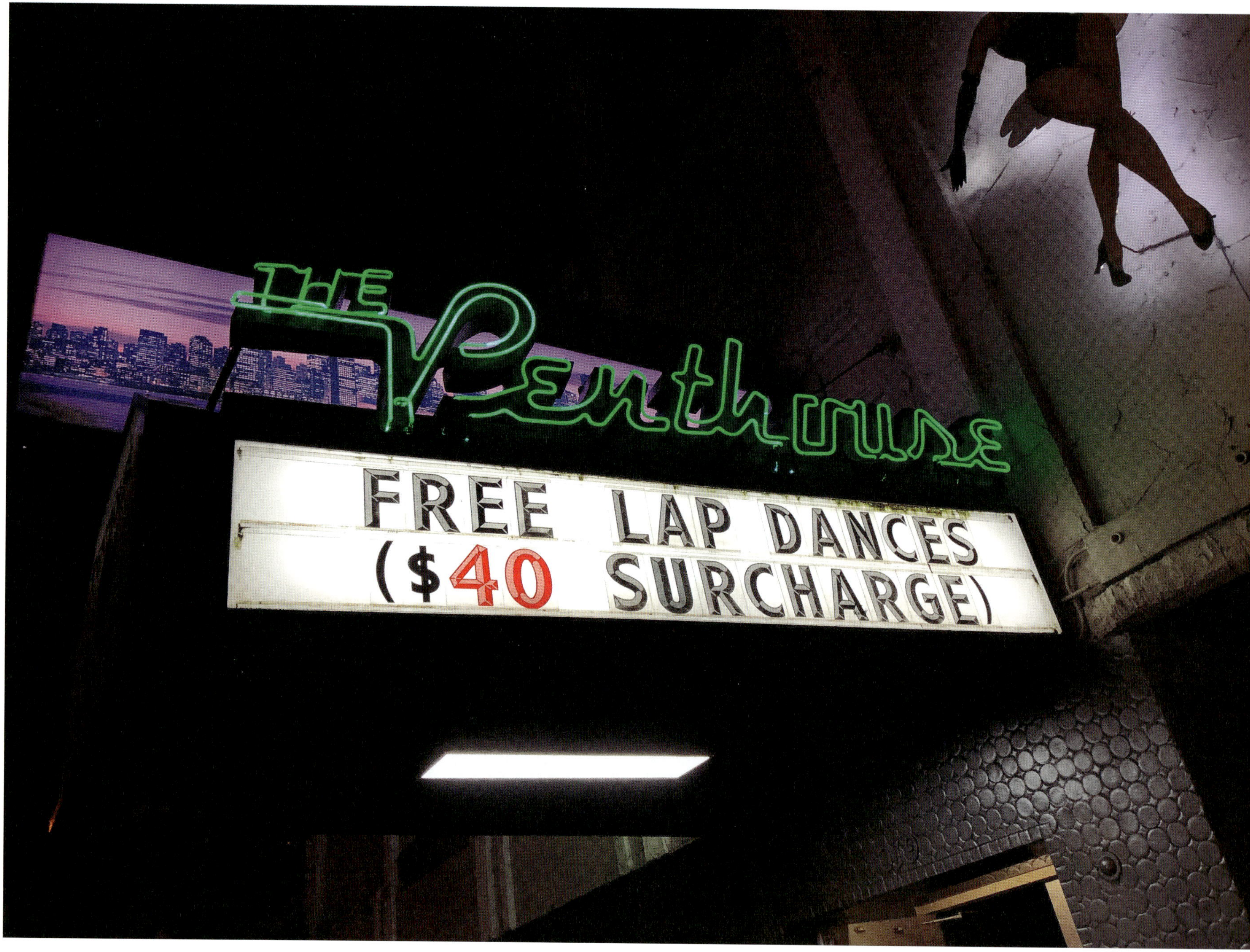
THE Penthouse
FREE LAP DANCES
($40 SURCHARGE)

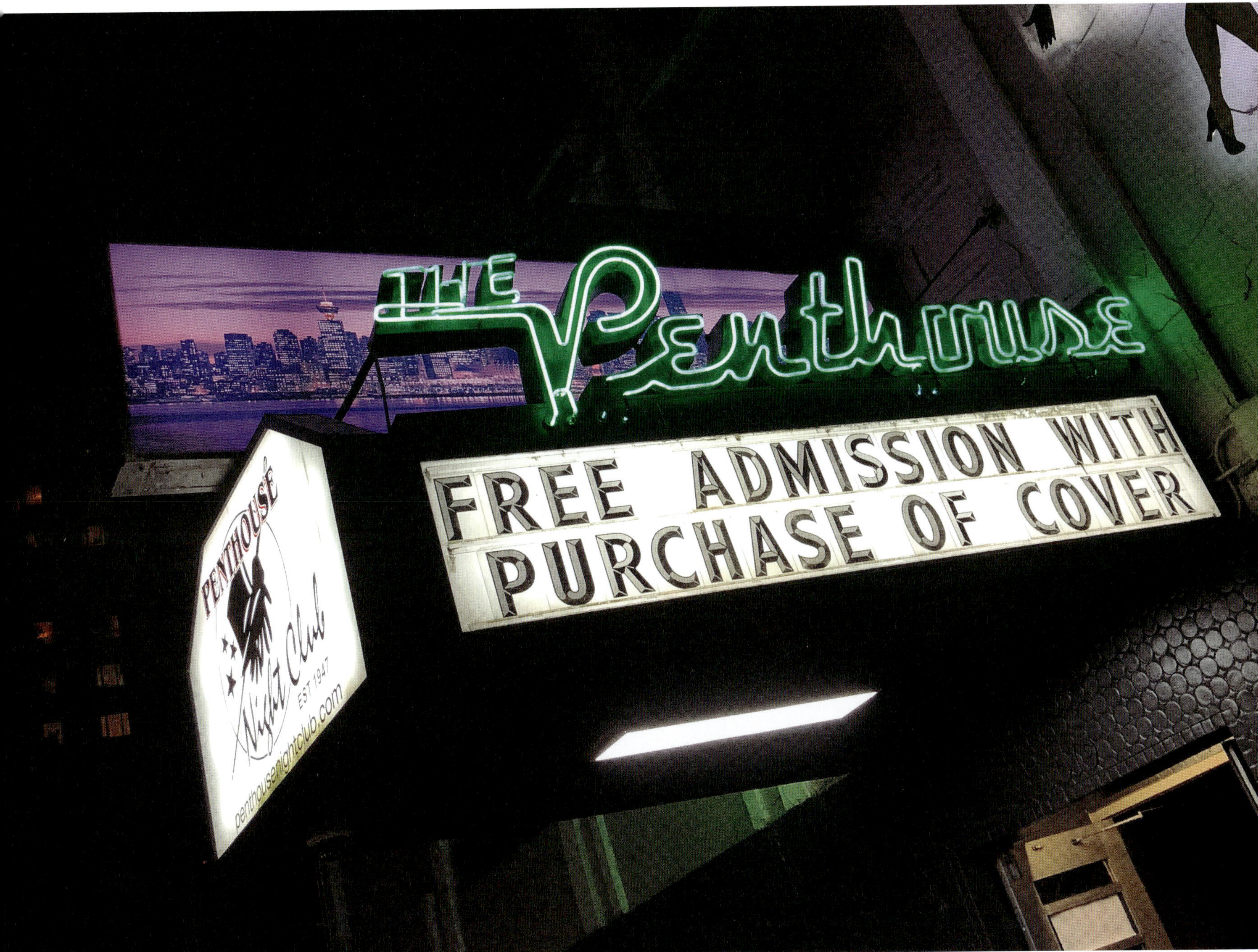
THE Penthouse
FREE ADMISSION WITH
PURCHASE OF COVER
PENTHOUSE
Night Club
EST 1947
penthousenightclub.com

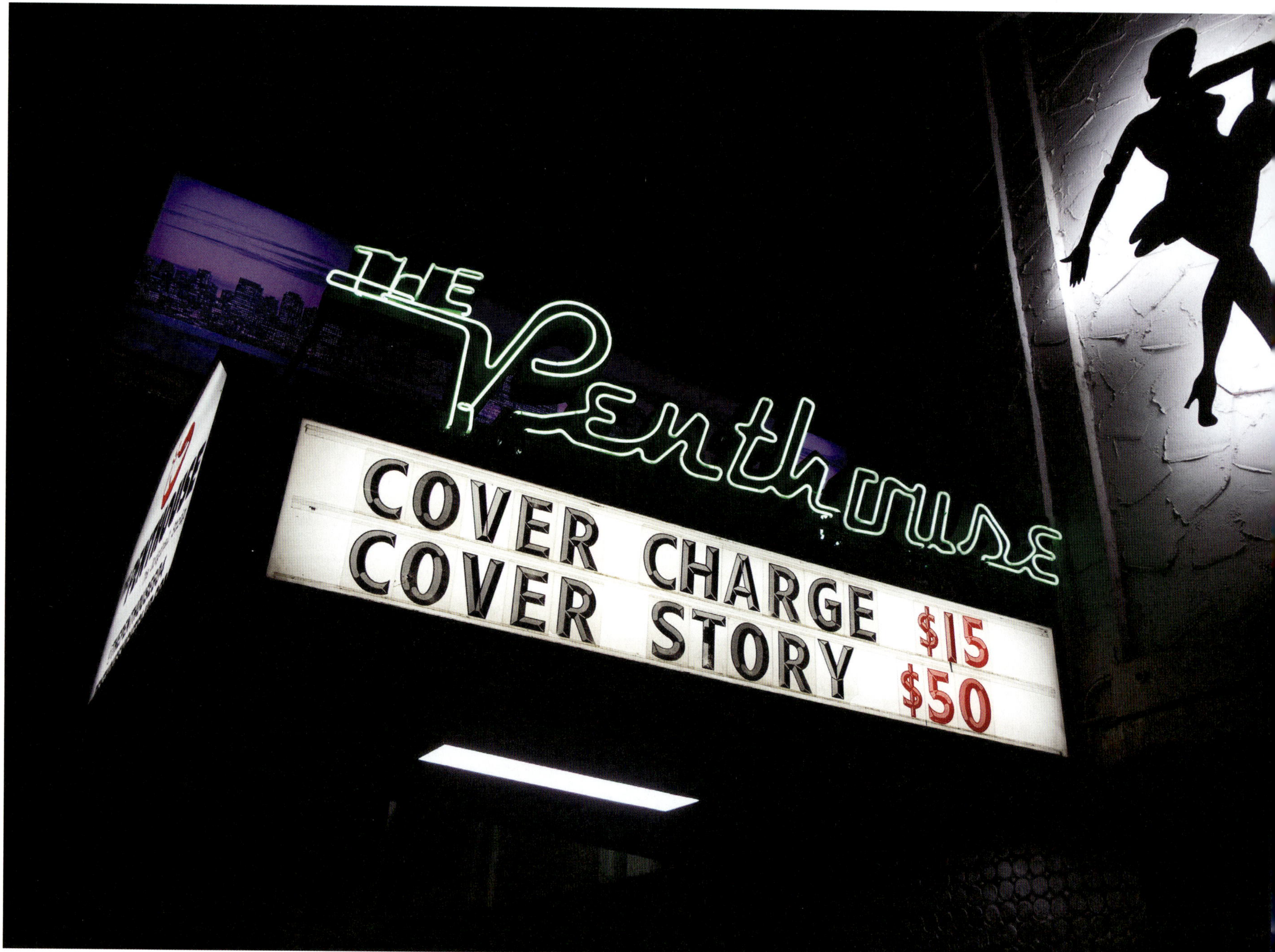
THE Penthouse
COVER CHARGE $15
COVER STORY $50

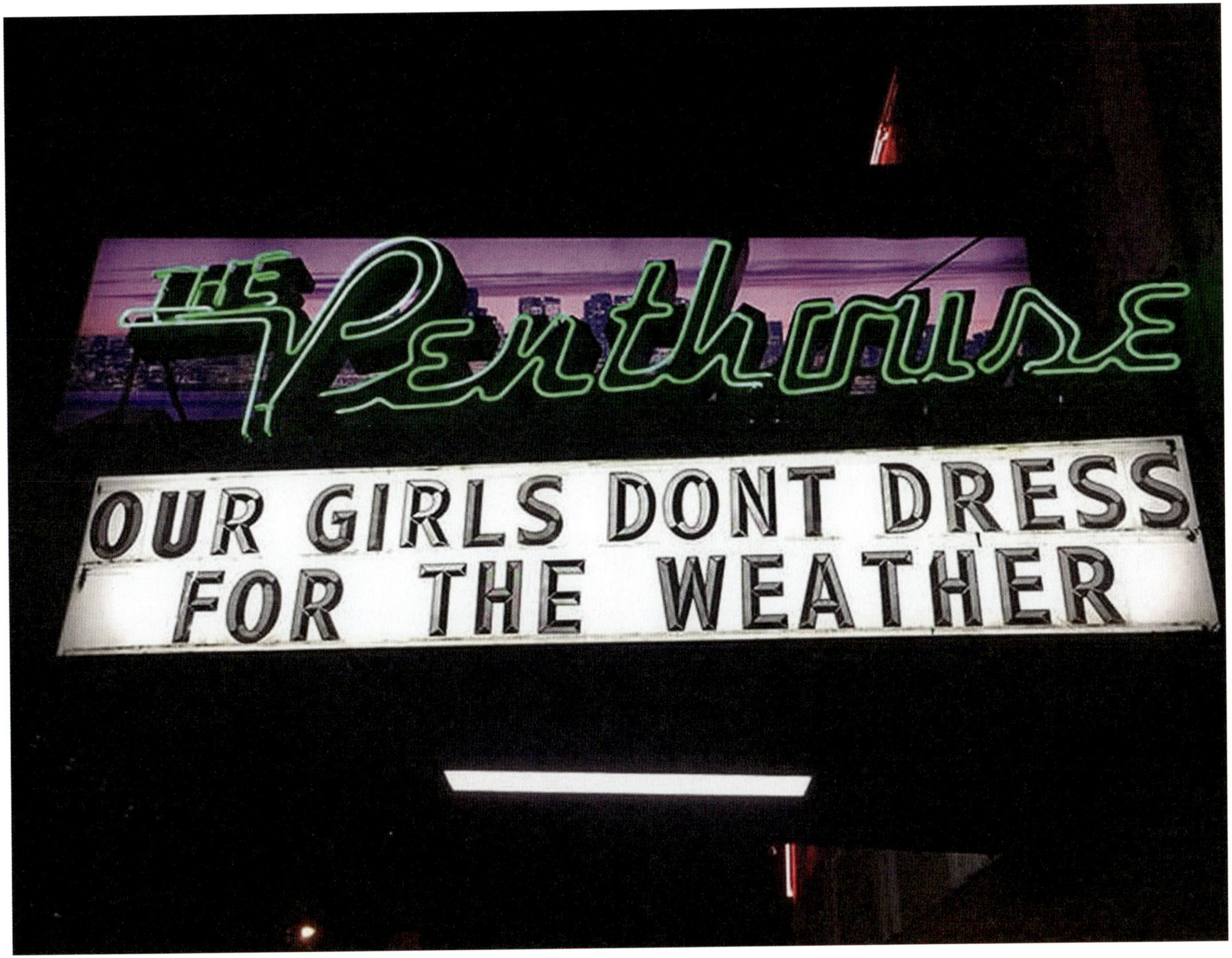
THE Penthouse
OUR GIRLS DONT DRESS
FOR THE WEATHER

POLES MORE RELIABLE THAN CNN PROJECTIONS

U.S. President Donald Trump would inspire a number of signs over the years. But it started November 3rd, 2016 — the morning after Donald Trump's surprise victory over Hillary Clinton in the USA Presidential election:

I remember watching the election results come in that night, and everyone had, of course, been expecting Hillary Clinton to win. It might have been the first politically related sign I did, as we usually — until then — stayed away from politics and religion. But I bounced the idea off Danny, saying, "I know I said I wasn't going to get political ..." but we thought it was funny and clever. I was worried I wouldn't be able to fit in the word "projections", or that you'd have time to read it while driving by. No matter who you might have supported, I think both sides found humour in it.

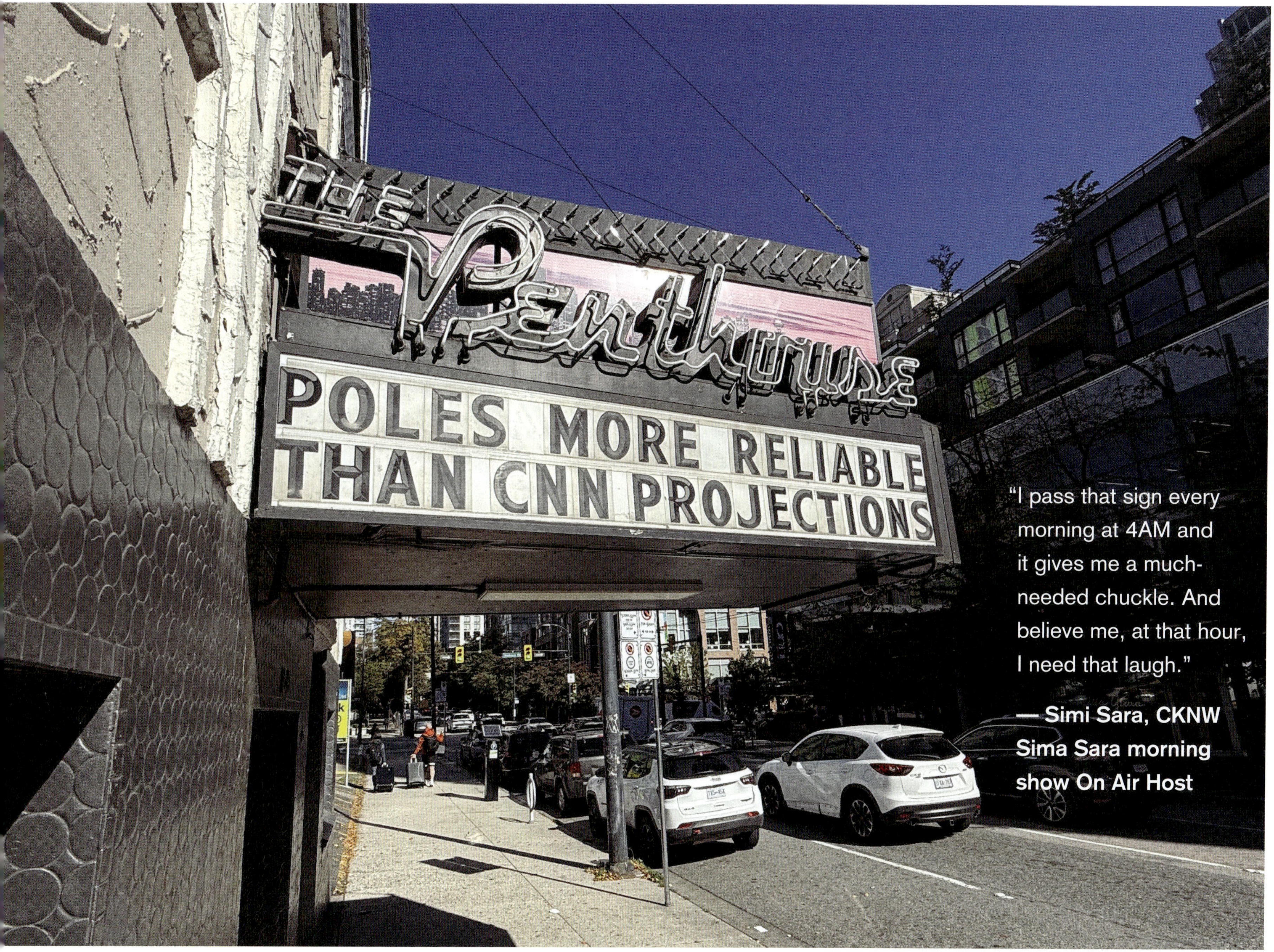

"I pass that sign every morning at 4AM and it gives me a much-needed chuckle. And believe me, at that hour, I need that laugh."

— Simi Sara, CKNW Sima Sara morning show On Air Host

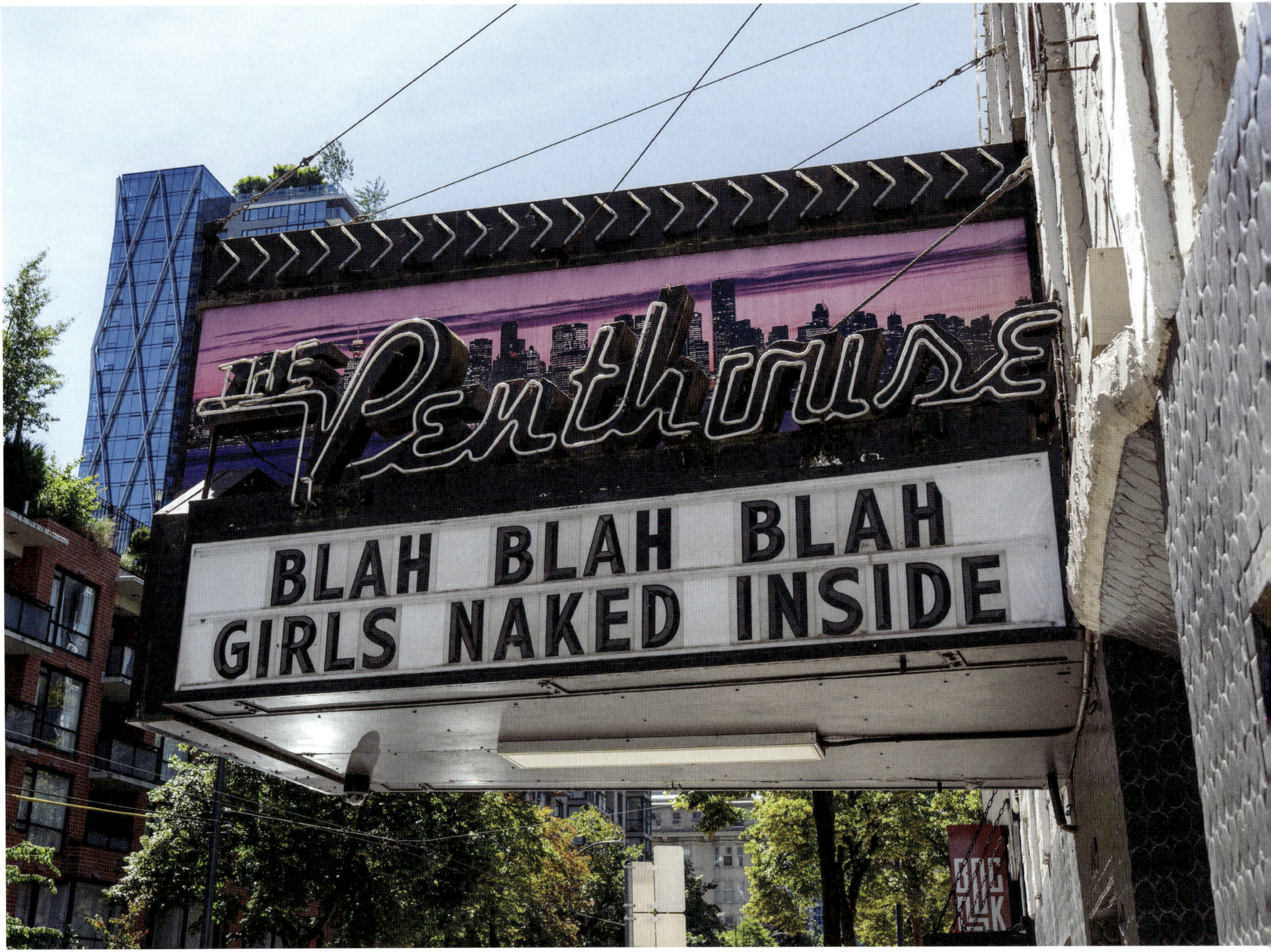
The Penthouse
BLAH BLAH BLAH
GIRLS NAKED INSIDE

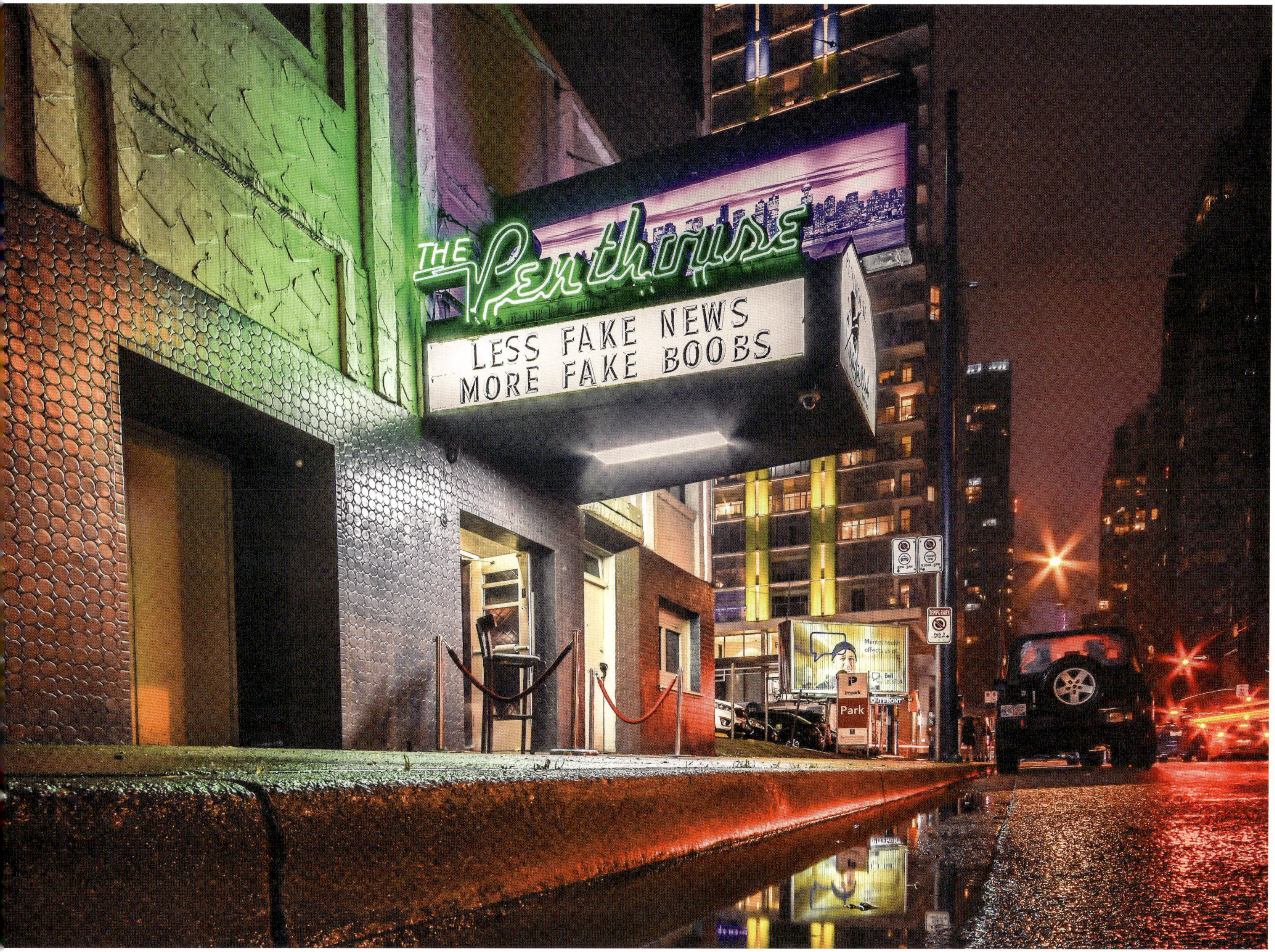
THE Penthouse
LESS FAKE NEWS
MORE FAKE BOOBS
Park

BRALESS SINCE 1947
STRAWLESS SINCE 2018

The Penthouse officially opened in 1947, though it had been running essentially illegally as a private after-hours nightclub in the years prior to that. In 2018, when the City of Vancouver banned plastic straws to reduce single-use item waste, the Penthouse was once again on the front of the issue.

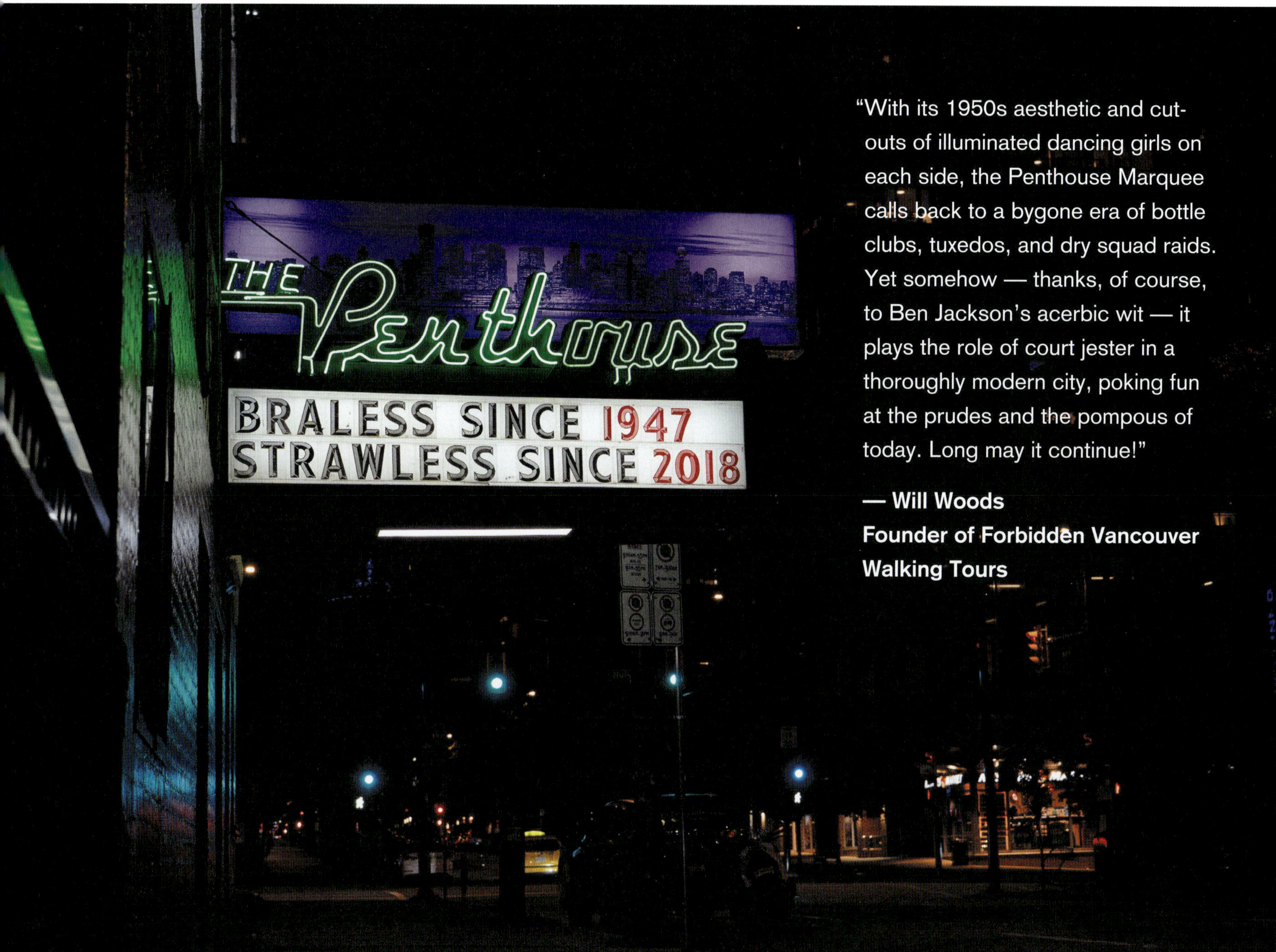

"With its 1950s aesthetic and cut-outs of illuminated dancing girls on each side, the Penthouse Marquee calls back to a bygone era of bottle clubs, tuxedos, and dry squad raids. Yet somehow — thanks, of course, to Ben Jackson's acerbic wit — it plays the role of court jester in a thoroughly modern city, poking fun at the prudes and the pompous of today. Long may it continue!"

— Will Woods
Founder of Forbidden Vancouver Walking Tours

TITS THE SEASON TO BE POLY

IS IT COOL IF WE SAY TITS ON THIS THING?

The Penthouse brought some Christmas cheer in December 2021 — but for Jackson, it was also an early experiment in pushing the boundaries to see if the marquee would get a lump of coal in its stocking:

I was testing the waters with this one. In the beginning of the signs, I often wondered what could I say — or what could I get away with? We never wanted to outright offend anyone — and when I suggested this one to friends around the bar, they said I'd get into hot water for using the word "tits." I thought, I suppose somebody might get upset and complain in an email — but nobody did. All I could hear were people laughing as they drove by on Seymour Street.

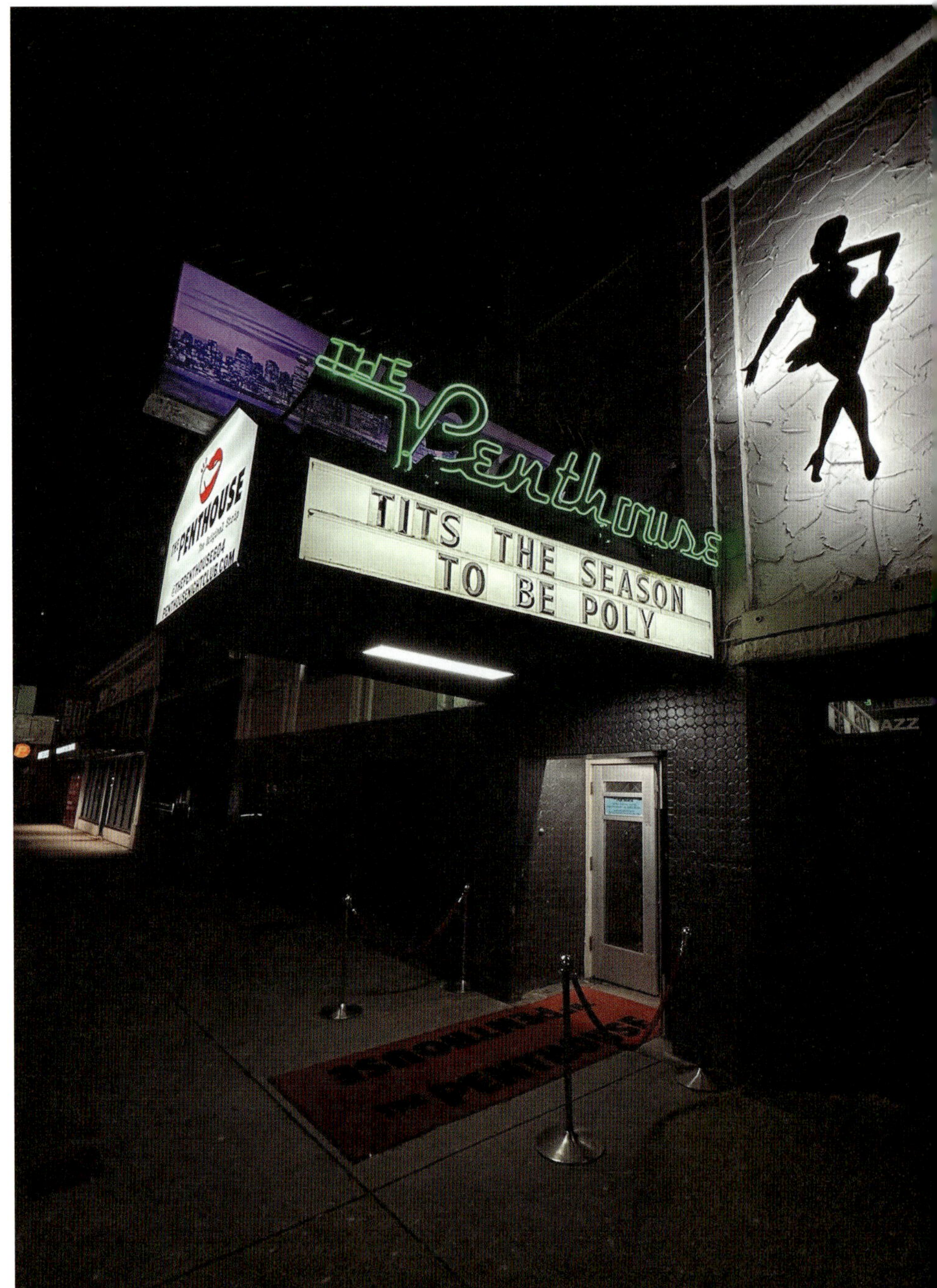

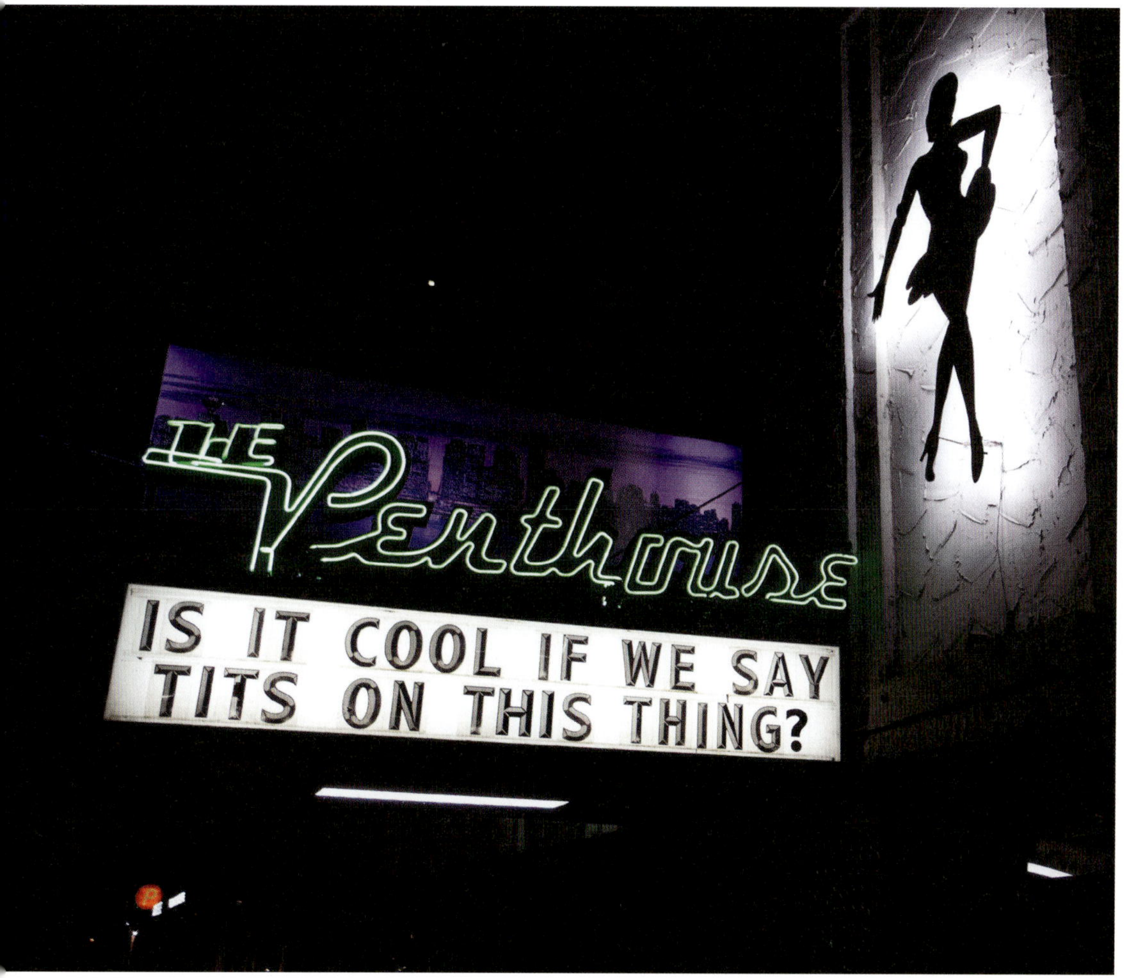

"As a kid growing up, when I saw the Penthouse sign, then the Seymour Billiards sign at Nelson Street, I knew the next stop was either the Orpheum or Pacific Centre — it always meant some kind of adventure as a kid. Later, as I got older, I heard all the lore about the Filippone family, and the stars that passed through the doors of this legendary place. Some seriously historic names! A lot of us drove around during the pandemic, and that was something I did weekly. It broke up the monotony of daily routine. One of the things I appreciated the most driving around a lonely city, was the Penthouse marquee. With the cancelling of Holiday parties in late 2021, "Tits the Season" made me laugh. I still remember seeing it on the Penthouse Instagram page, then driving down to see it with my own eyes. So clever, and those simple messages gave us some humour and wit when we really needed it. It is STILL one of the greatest signs in Vancouver … ever!"

— Jason Manning
Jack FM 96.9 On-Air Host

5318008

While the marquee has become legendary for its epigrams, it also ventured successfully into the world of ambigrams: defined as a word, number, or other figure that can be read upside down.

I was thinking obviously of the old calculator trick that we did as kids in class, where you type some corresponding numbers into the calculator, and turn it upside down to read the word. But it couldn't just say "hello" as with 07734 — it is the Penthouse after all.

"I only ever go to The Penthouse to read the signs."

— Bill Allman, Chairman BC Entertainment Hall of Fame

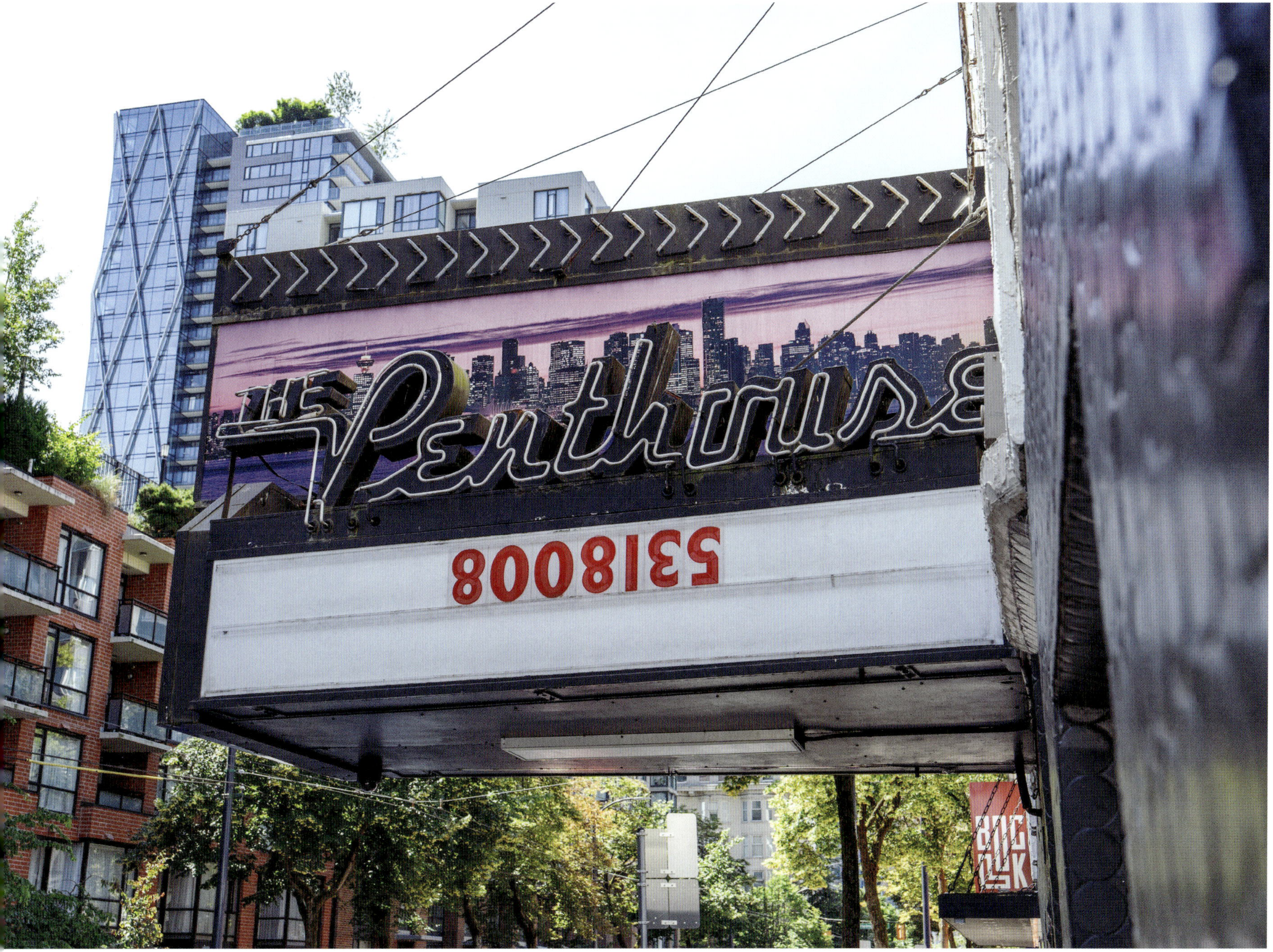
The Penthouse

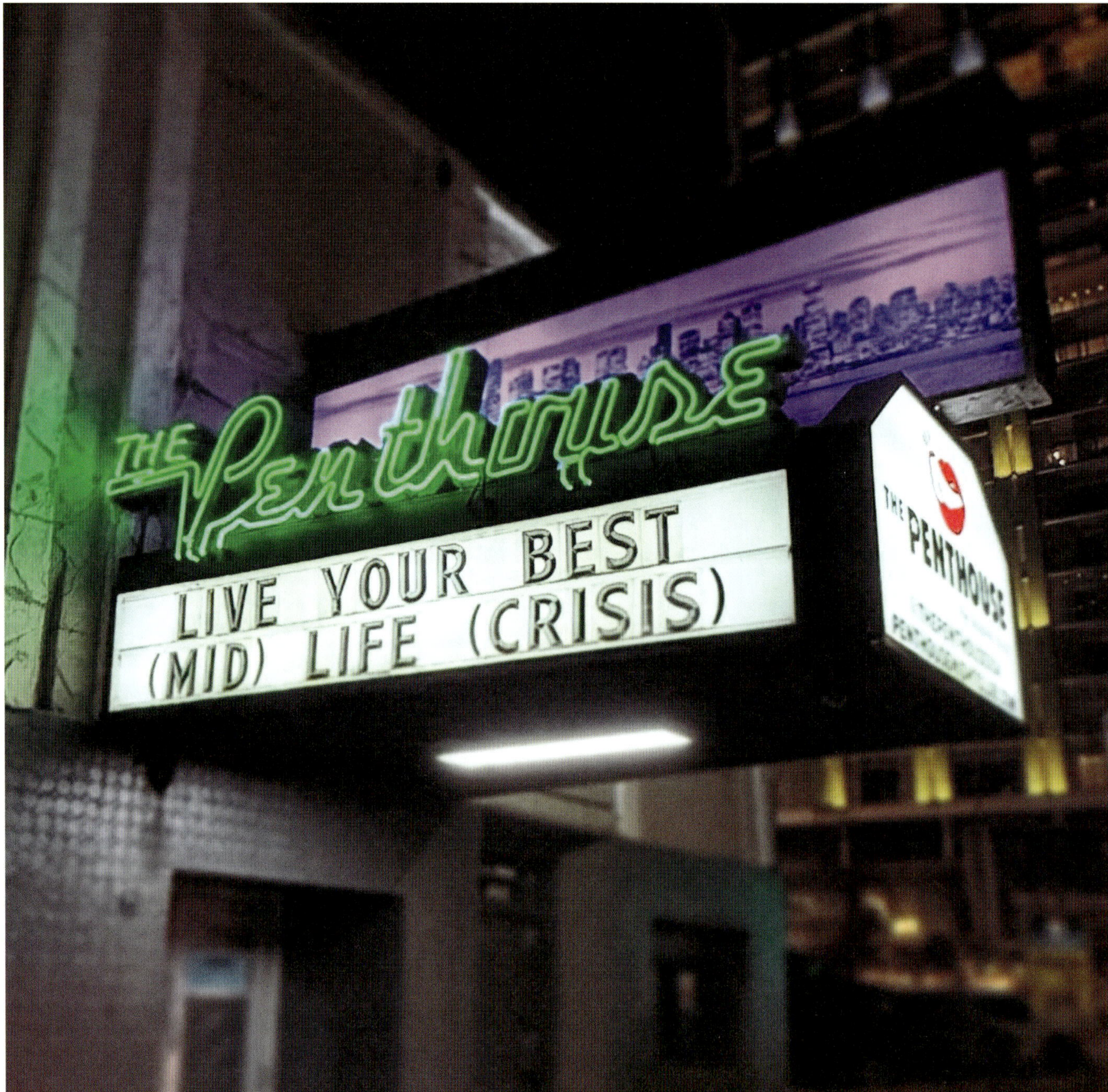
THE Penthouse
LIVE YOUR BEST
(MID) LIFE (CRISIS)
THE PENTHOUSE

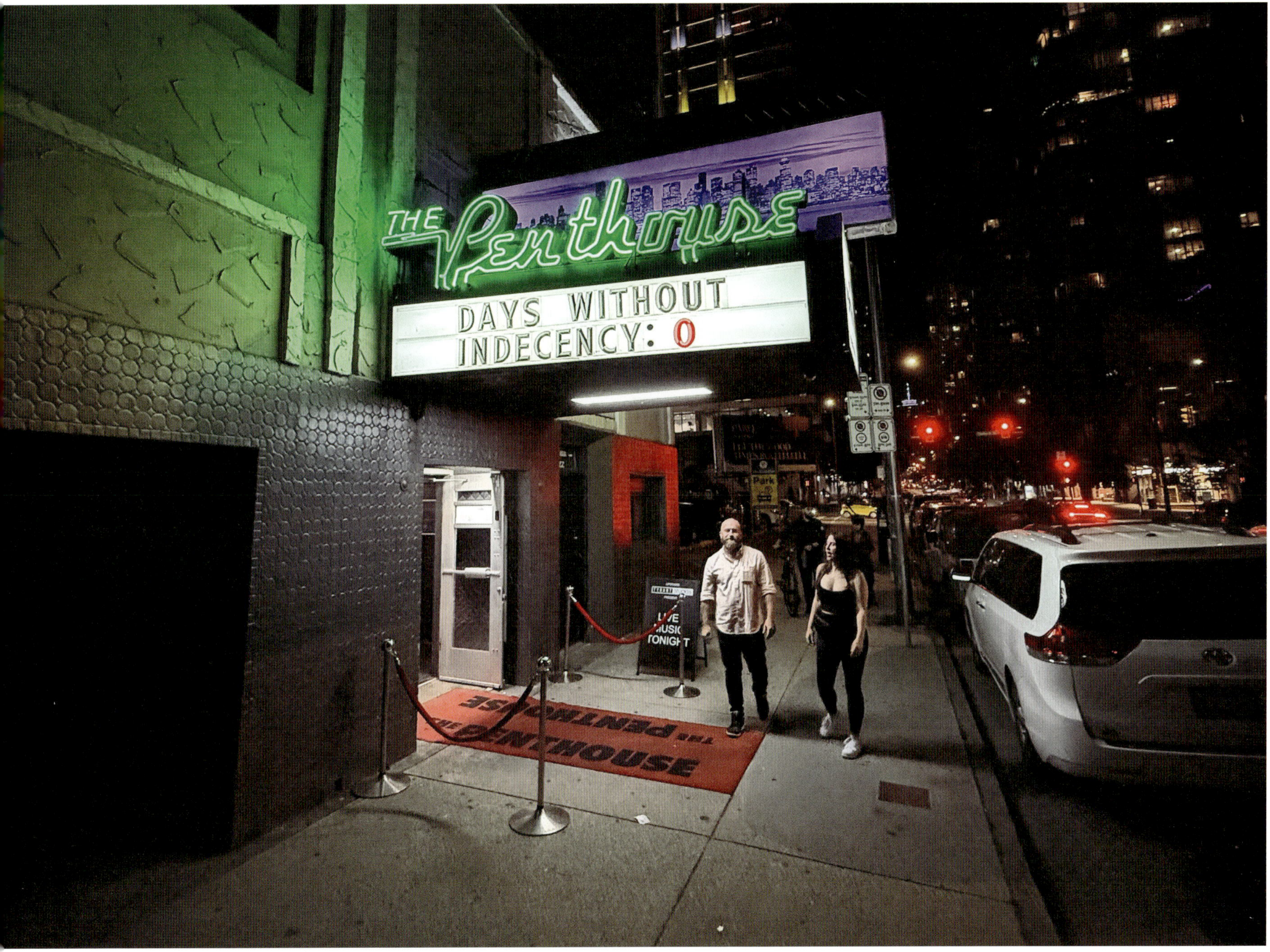
THE Penthouse
DAYS WITHOUT
INDECENCY: 0
LIVE
MUSIC
TONIGHT
THE PENTHOUSE

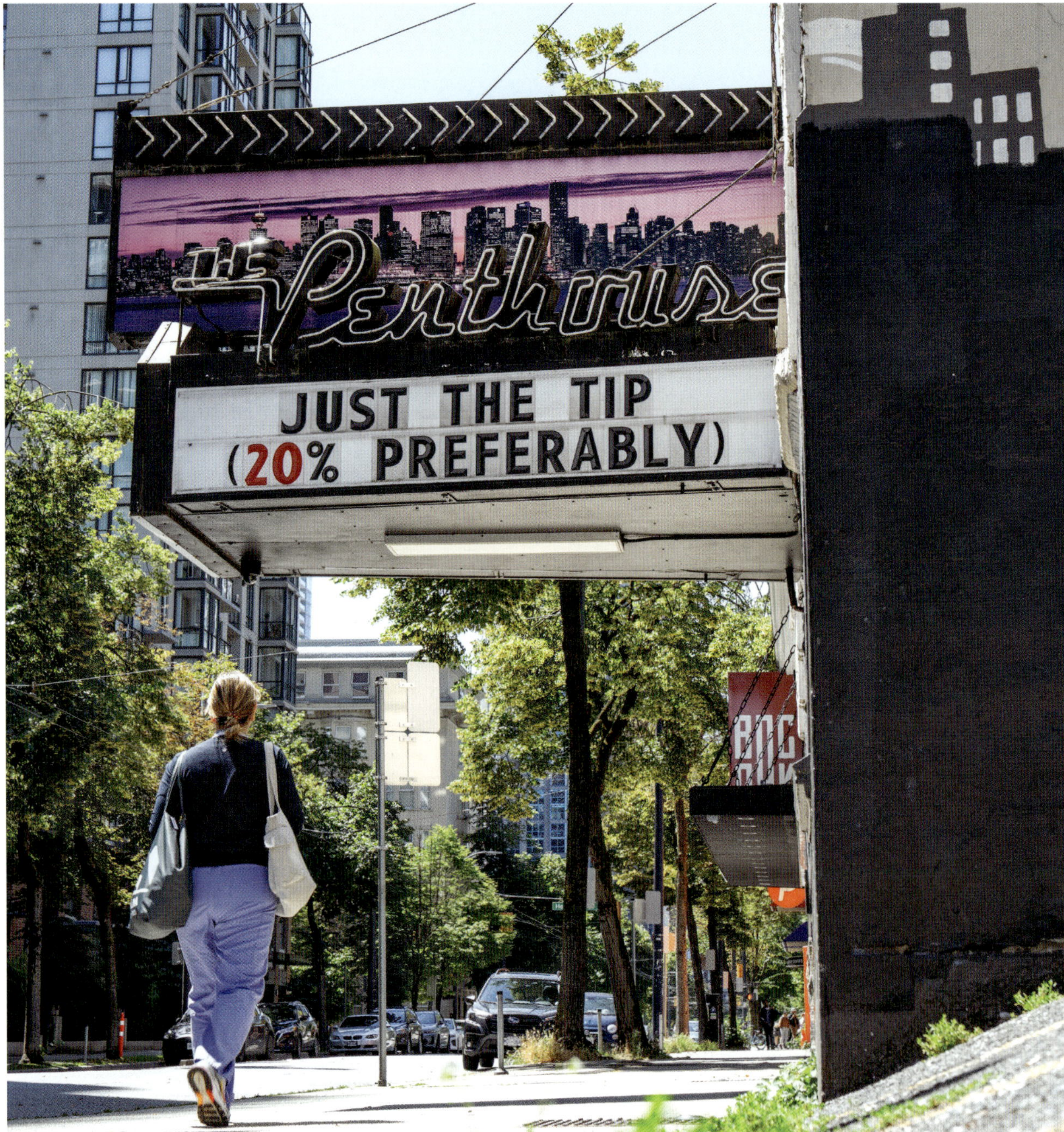
The Penthouse
JUST THE TIP
(20% PREFERABLY)

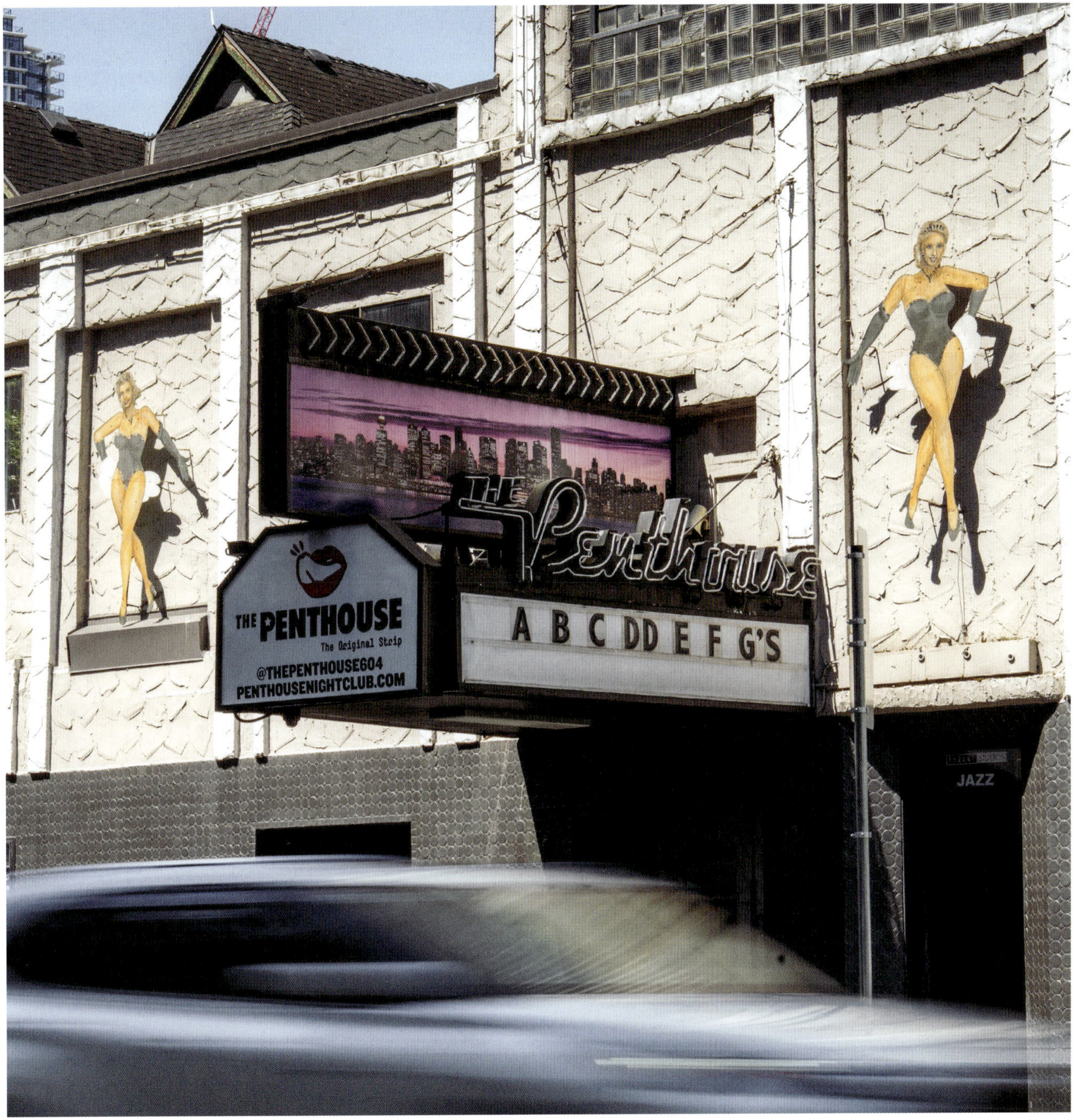
THE PENTHOUSE
The Original Strip
@THEPENTHOUSE604
PENTHOUSENIGHTCLUB.COM
THE Penthouse
A B C DD E F G'S
JAZZ

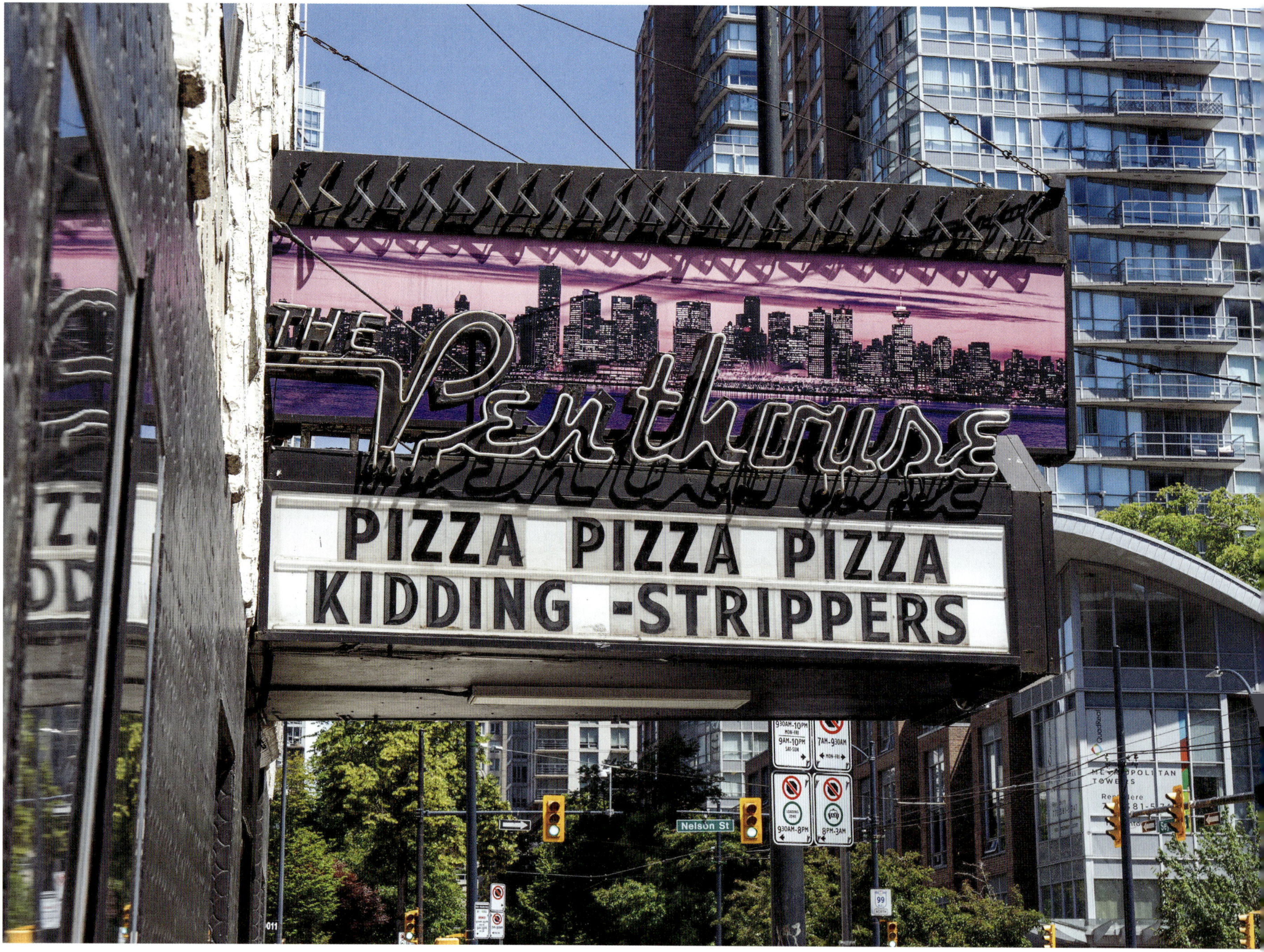
THE
Penthouse
PIZZA PIZZA PIZZA
KIDDING -STRIPPERS
Nelson St

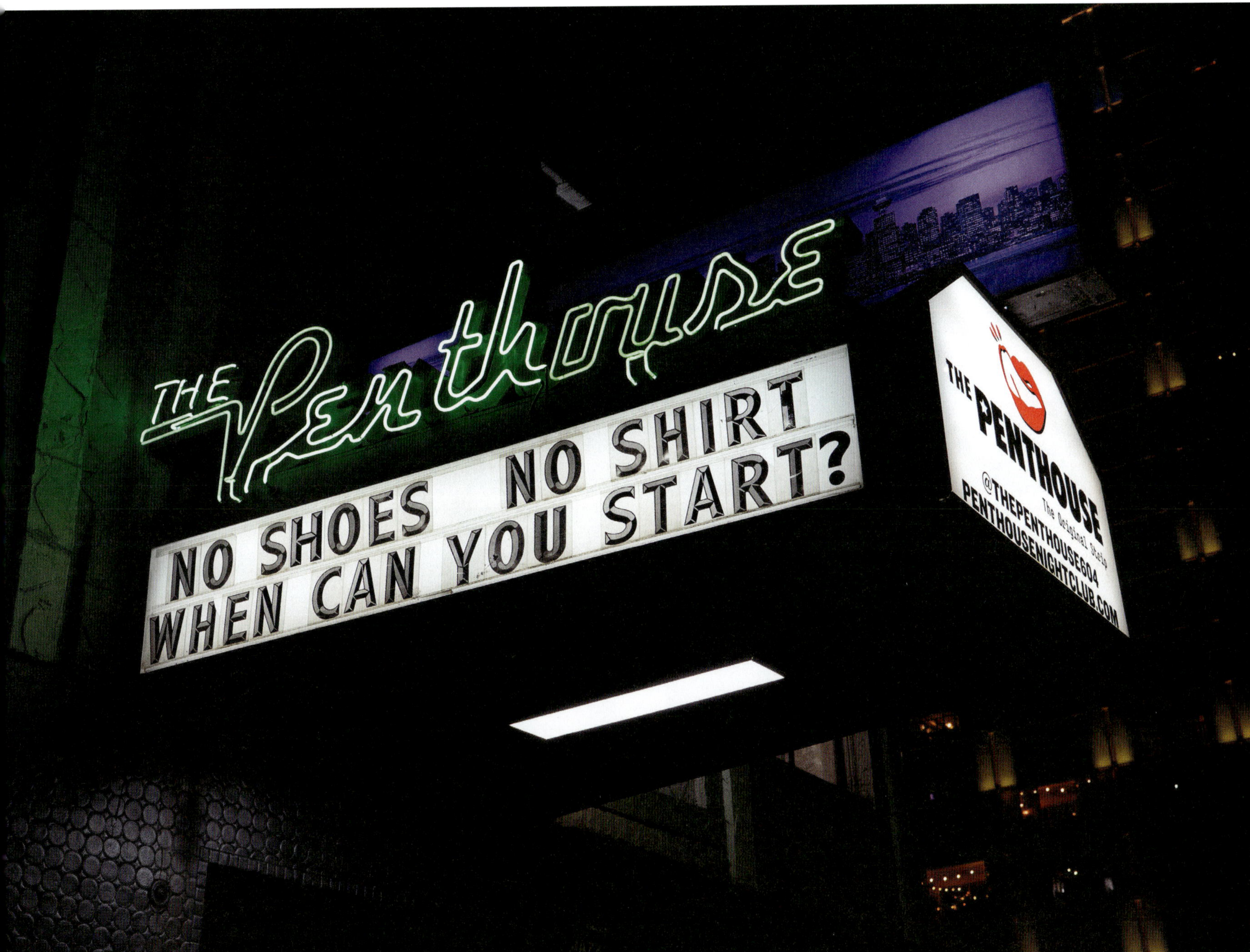
THE Penthouse
NO SHOES NO SHIRT
WHEN CAN YOU START?
THE PENTHOUSE
The Original Strip
@THEPENTHOUSE604
PENTHOUSENIGHTCLUB.COM

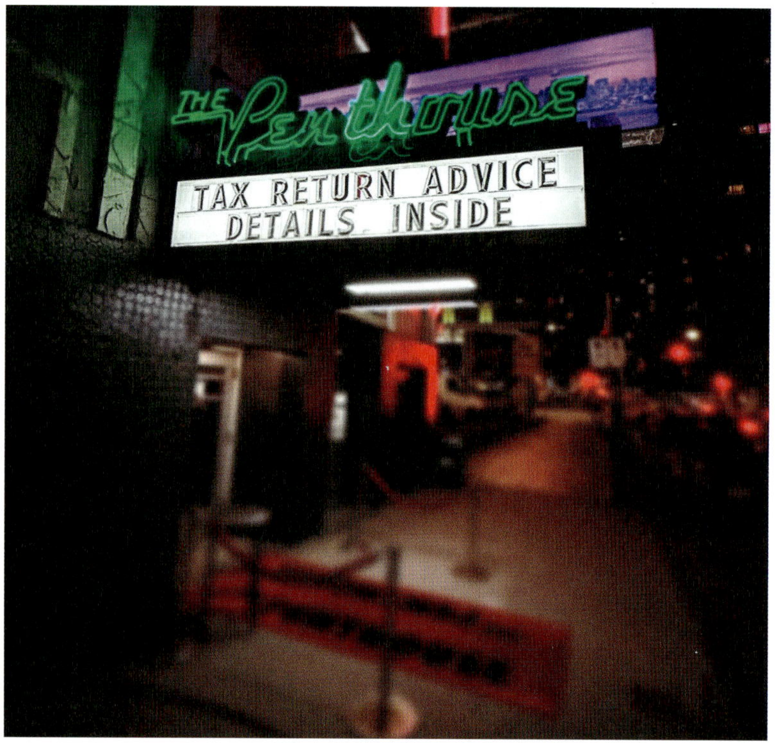
TAX RETURN ADVICE
DETAILS INSIDE

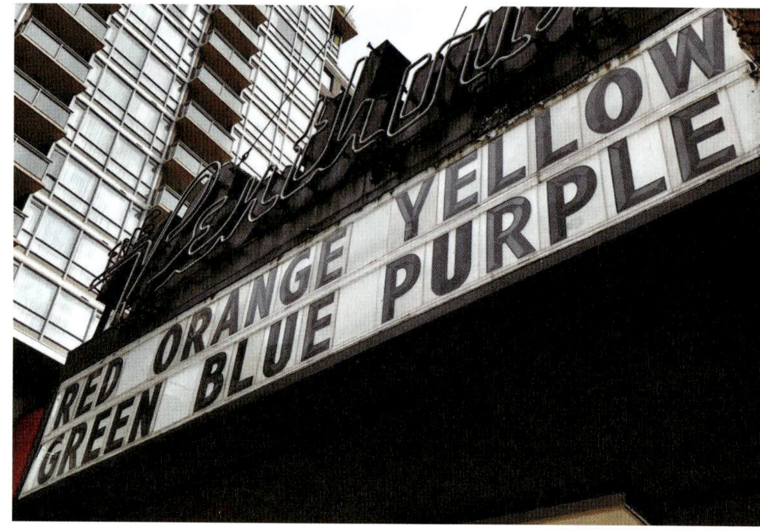
RED ORANGE YELLOW
GREEN BLUE PURPLE

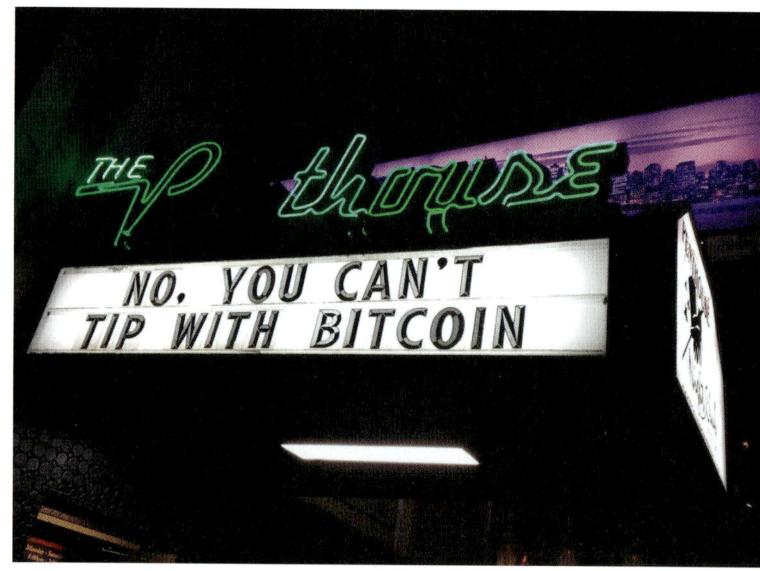
THE thouse
NO, YOU CAN'T
TIP WITH BITCOIN

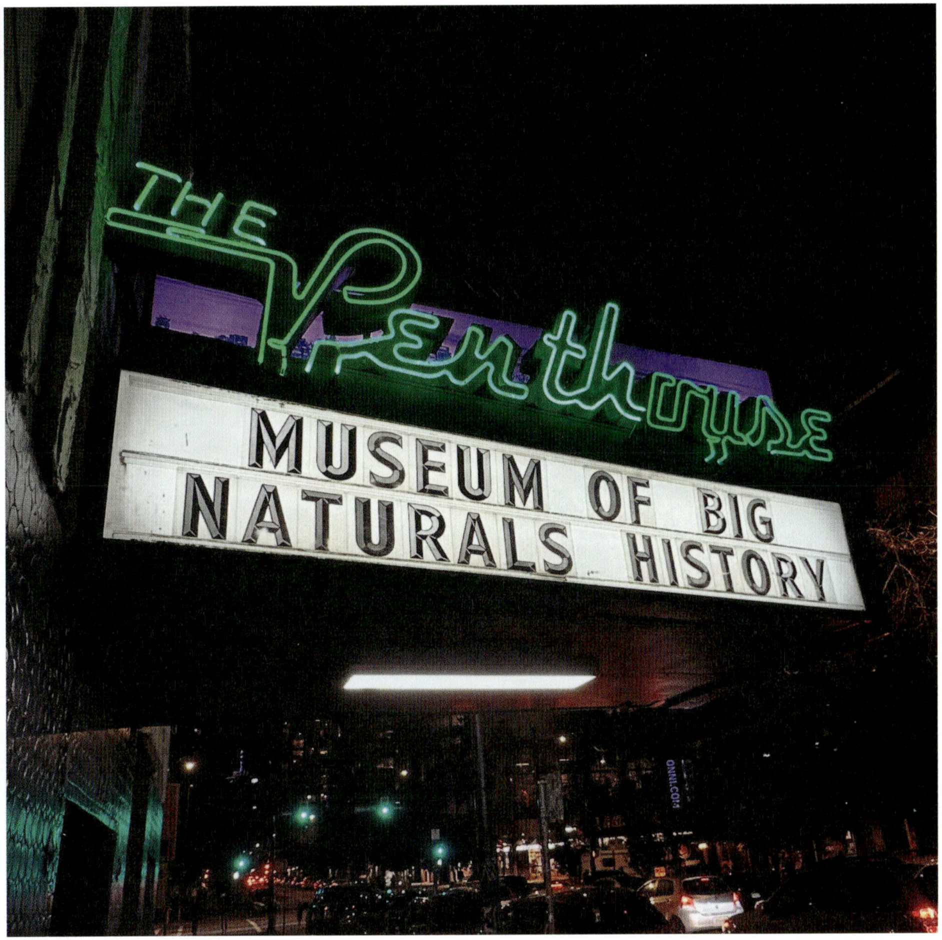
THE Penthouse
MUSEUM OF BIG
NATURALS HISTORY

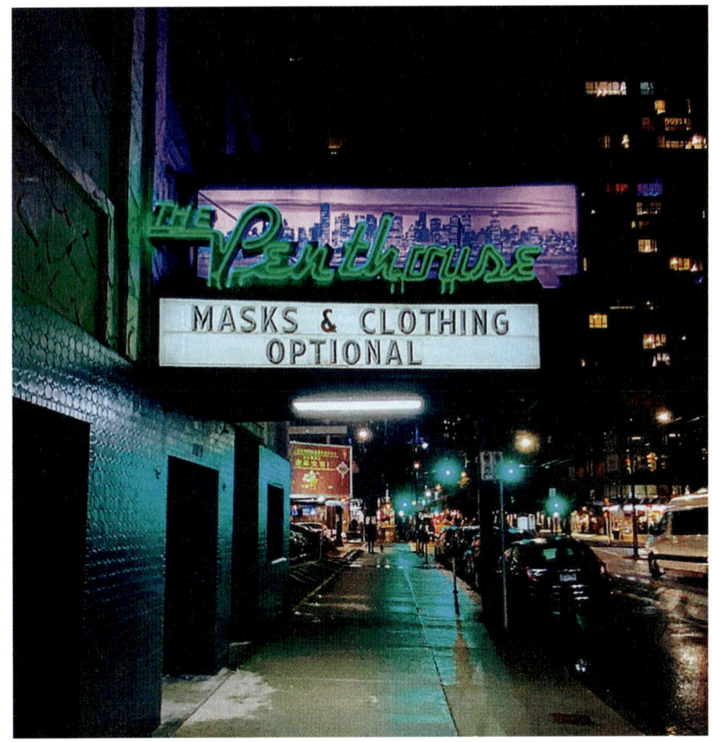
THE Penthouse
MASKS & CLOTHING
OPTIONAL

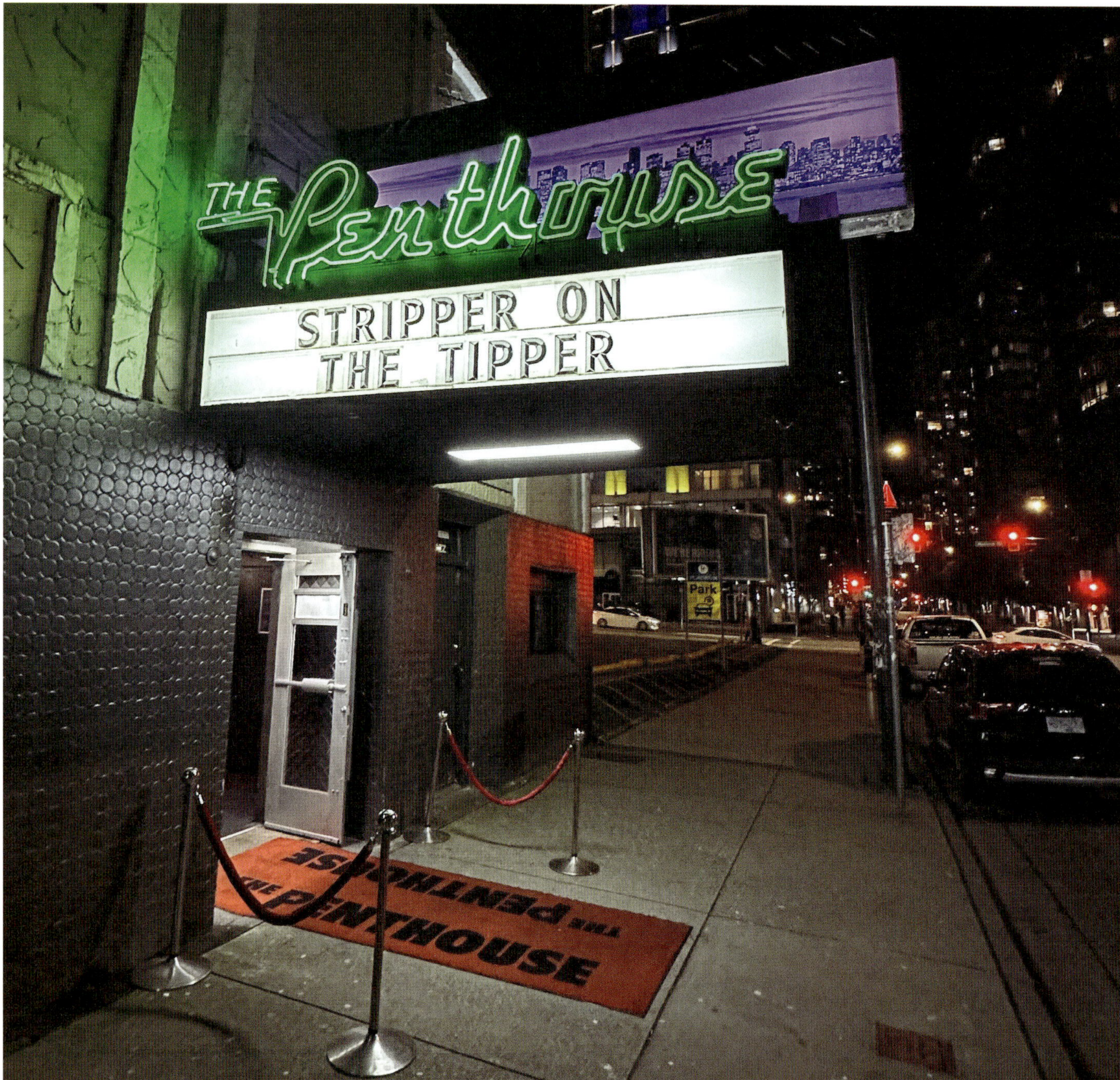
THE Penthouse
STRIPPER ON
THE TIPPER
Park
THE PENTHOUSE

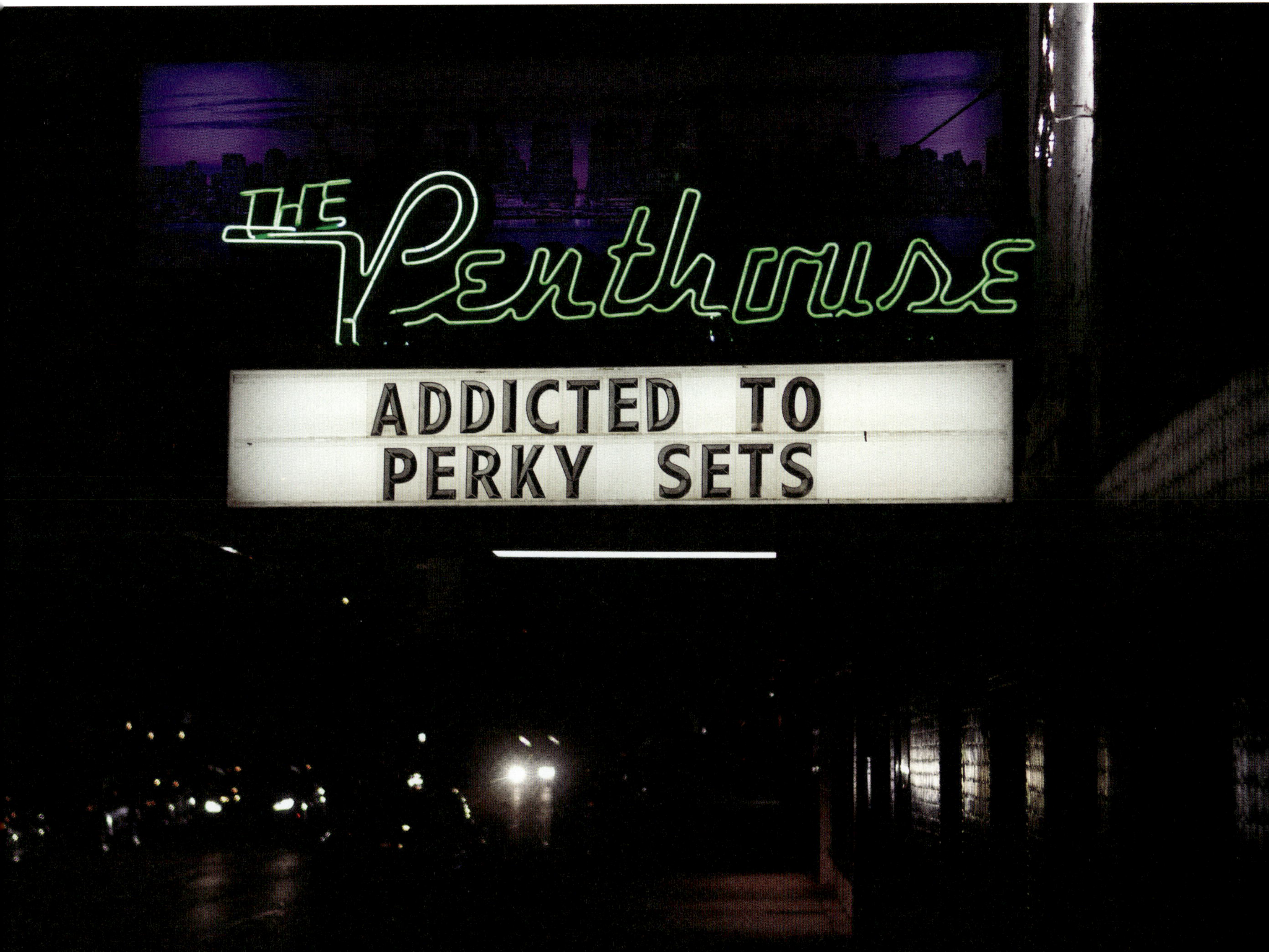
THE Penthouse
ADDICTED TO
PERKY SETS

The dancers at the Penthouse themselves have provided Jackson with inspiration for a number of signs over the years, from "Stripper? I Hardly Know Her", to "Spoiler Alert: They're Naked.", Stripper on a Tipper, and one very popular sign in particular "Girls Just Want to Have Funds".

I get tons of feedback from the dancers when we put up a sign that might relate to them. I even hear from dancers working at other clubs, who message me on Instagram when they've seen the signs and find them funny — they're the biggest fans. I always thought, "Never Voted Best Dressed" would be good on a T-shirt!

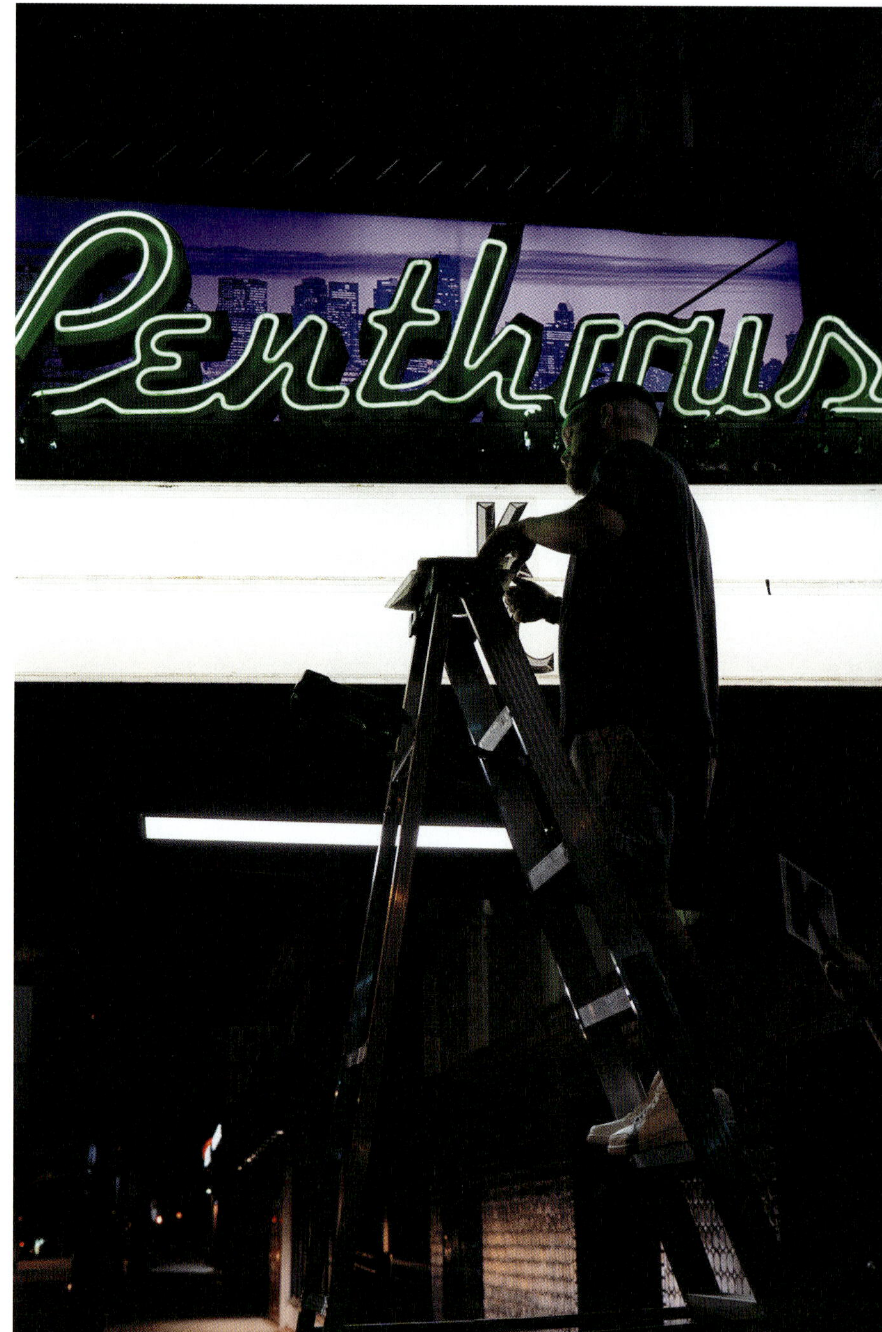

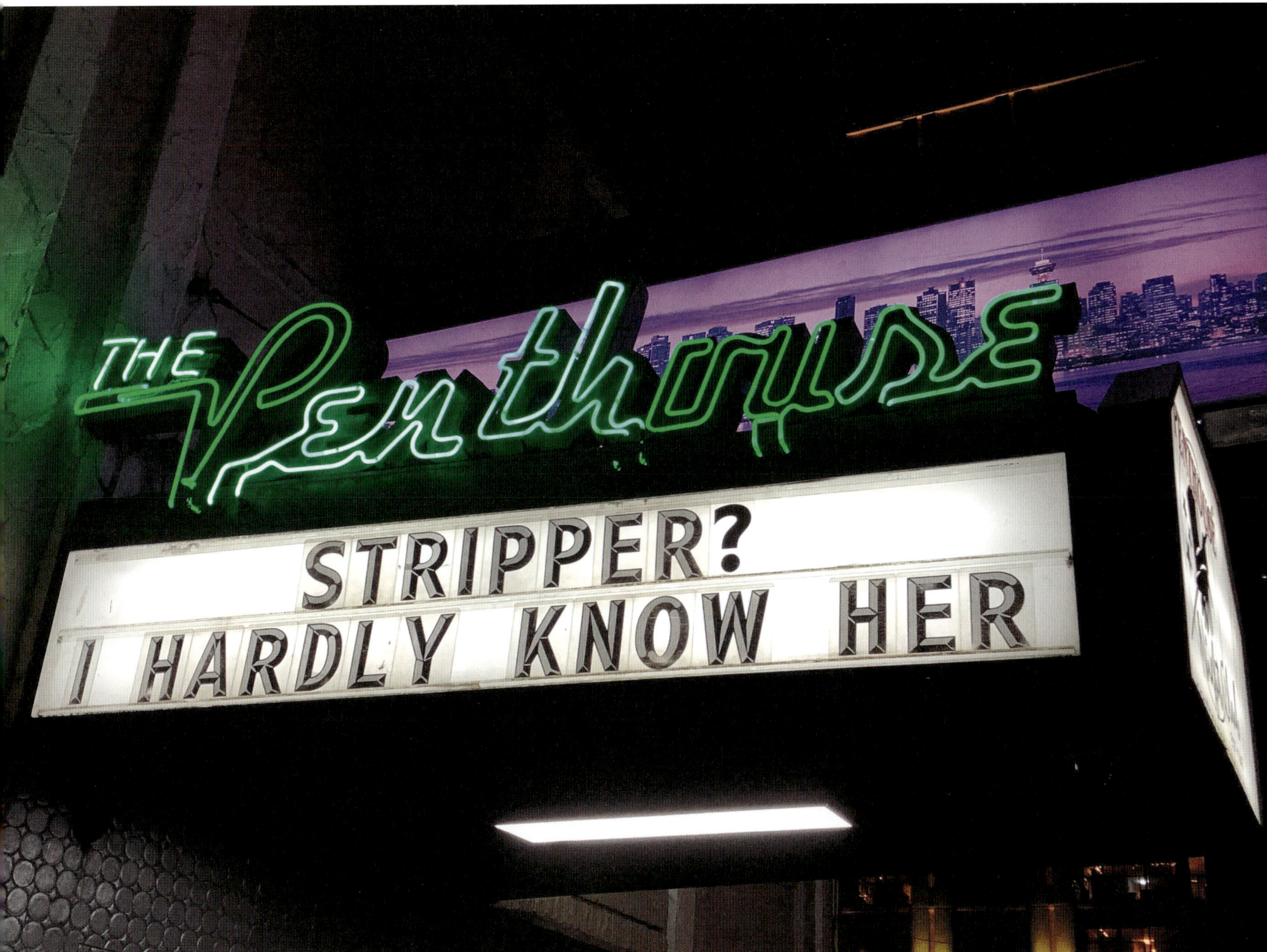
THE Penthouse
STRIPPER?
I HARDLY KNOW HER

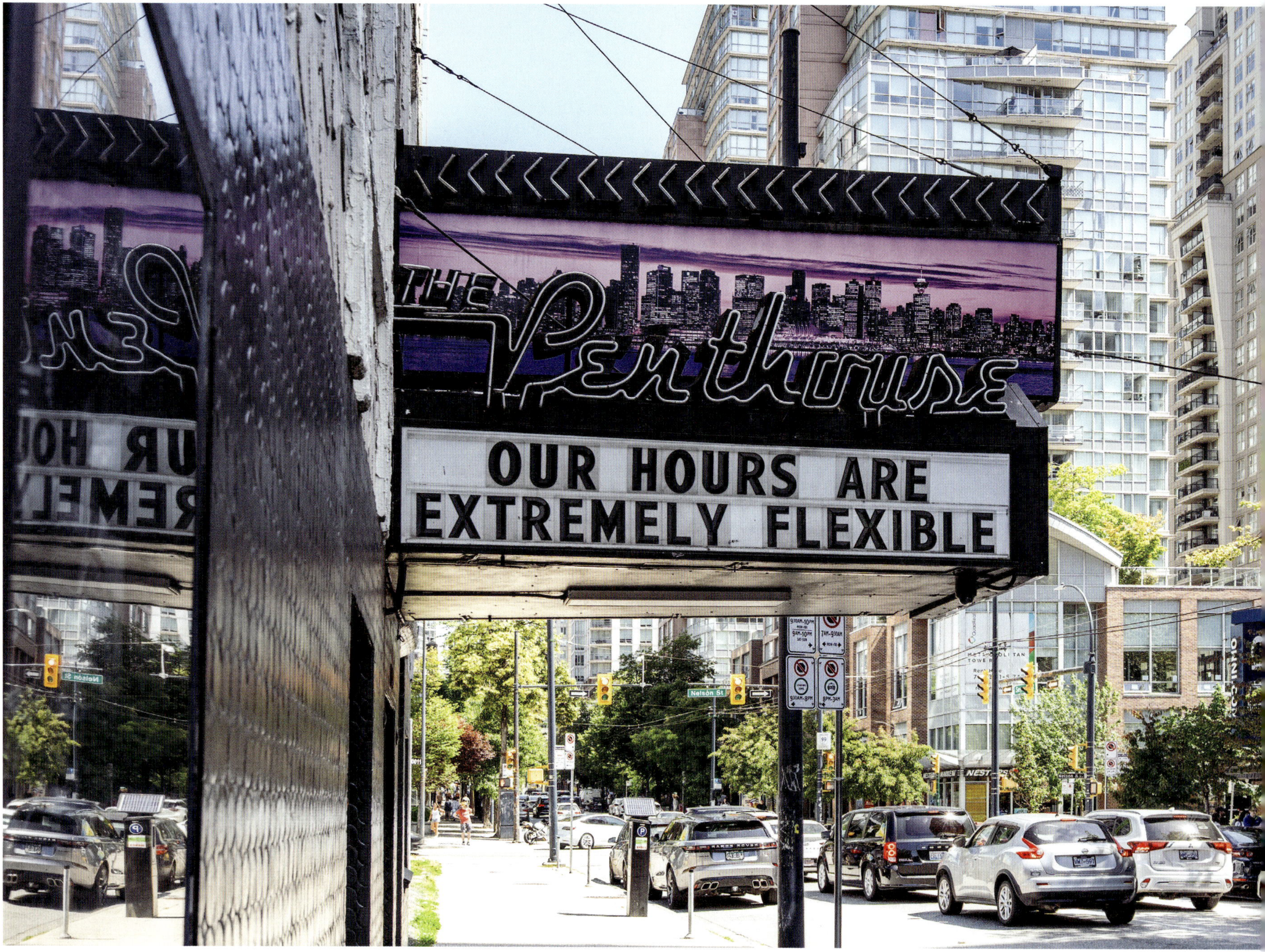

THE Penthouse
OUR HOURS ARE
EXTREMELY FLEXIBLE
Nelson St

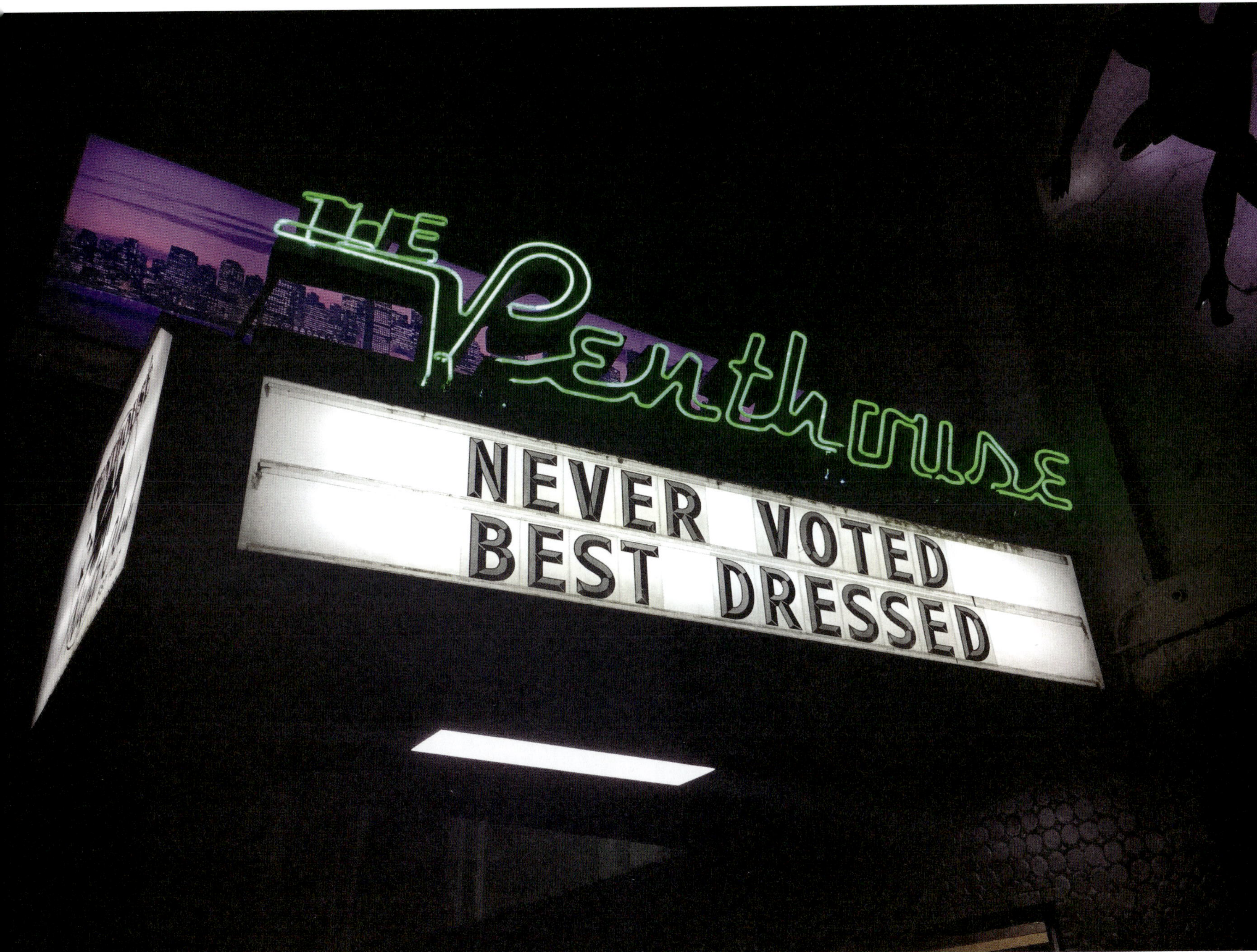
THE Penthouse
NEVER VOTED
BEST DRESSED

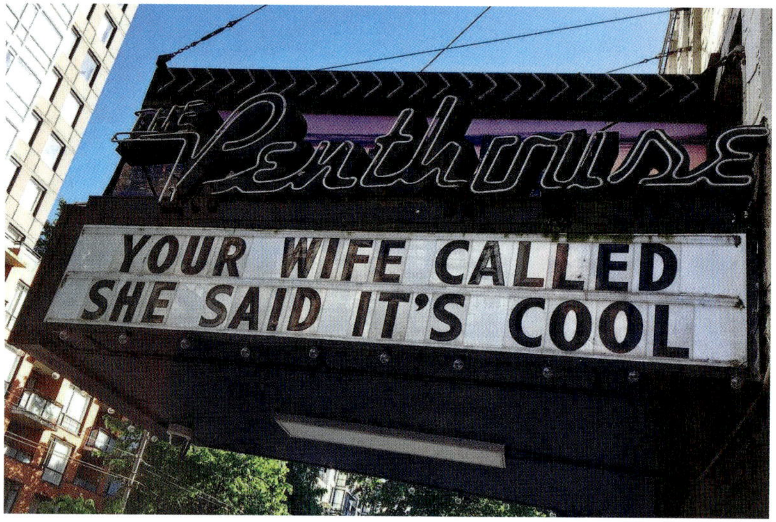
THE Penthouse
YOUR WIFE CALLED
SHE SAID IT'S COOL

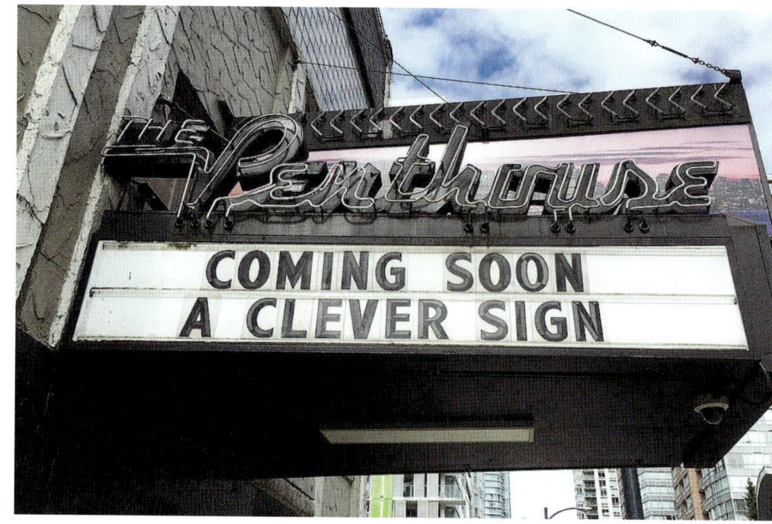
THE Penthouse
COMING SOON
A CLEVER SIGN

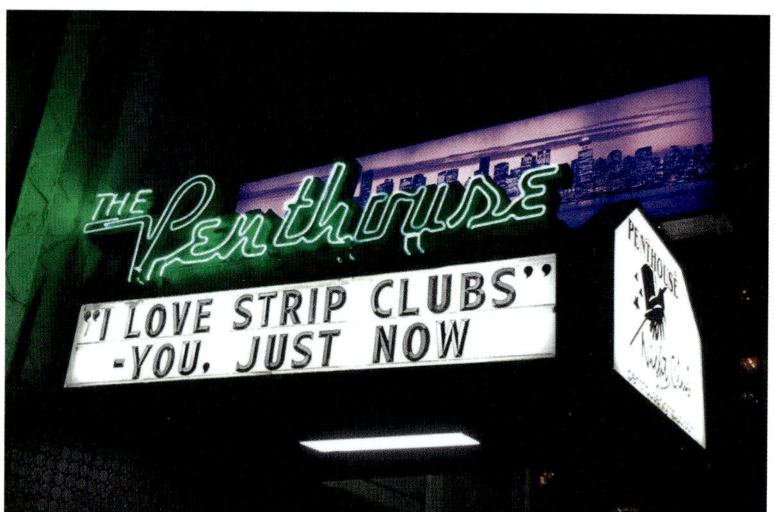
THE Penthouse
"I LOVE STRIP CLUBS"
-YOU, JUST NOW
PENTHOUSE

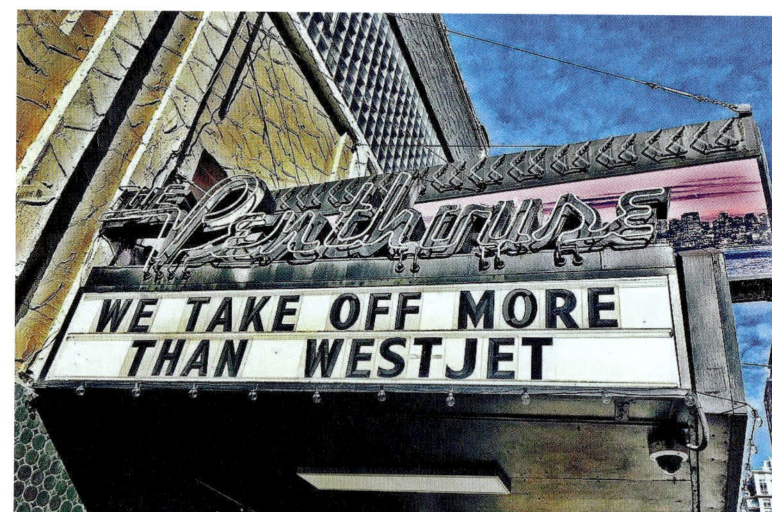
THE Penthouse
WE TAKE OFF MORE
THAN WESTJET

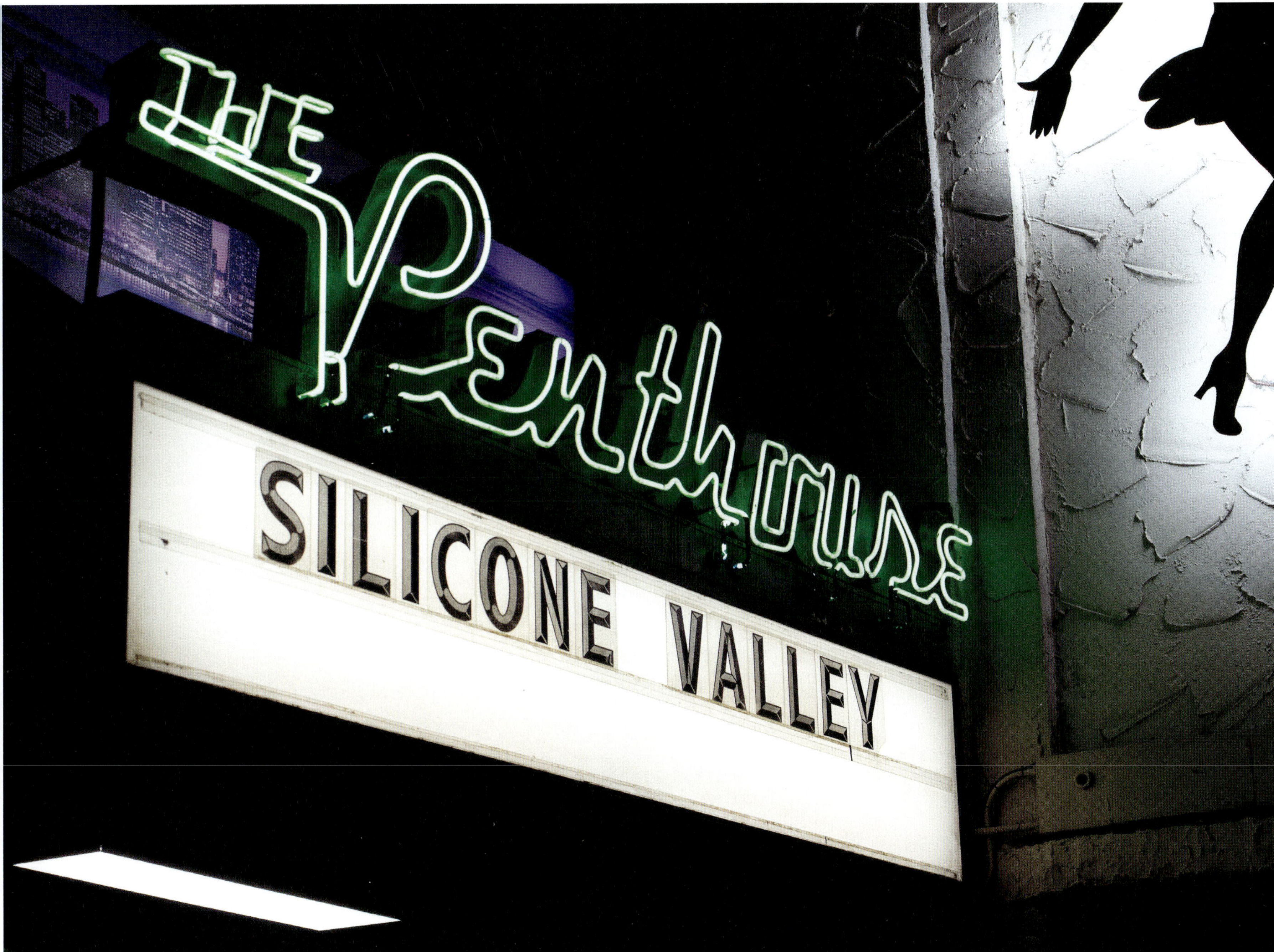
THE Penthouse
SILICONE VALLEY

HONK IF YOU LOVE BJ'S
GO JAYS GO

The Penthouse marquee rarely gives mention to sports teams outside the city, but during the start of a Toronto Blue Jays MLB Playoff run, the marquee had to weigh in.

I remember it was a Saturday night and I changed it that evening. The next day I got a text from an old manager who was in during the day saying I had to take it down. I was surprised, I didn't think the sign was offensive — and they were on a playoff run. But he said no, " ...It's not because it's racy, you have to take it down because people driving down Seymour won't stop honking their cars all day. I can't get any work done!" We left it up as long as we could, but they lost the series they were in and the issue kind of took care of itself.

"Having been on the sports beat in Vancouver for many years, it was this Penthouse Nightclub sign that stands out to me. Not only did myself and a couple of media friends enjoy honking, we damn near smashed into the delivery truck in front of us!"

— Greg Douglas, Sports Columnist/Broadcaster & BC Sports Hall of Fame inductee

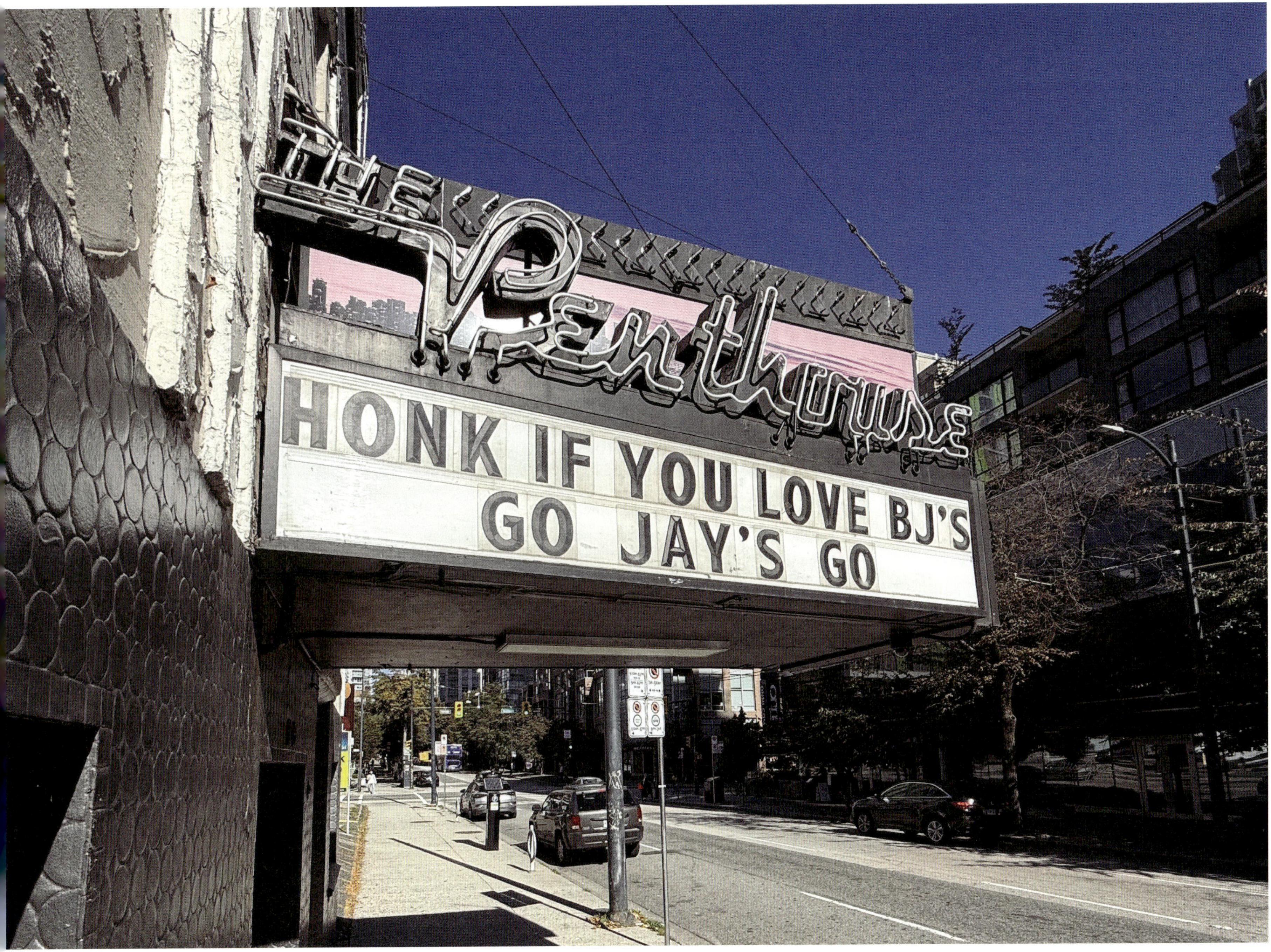
THE
Penthouse
HONK IF YOU LOVE BJ'S
GO JAY'S GO

THE ASTROS STOLE OUR OTHER SIGN

Never fearful of addressing a scandal, the Penthouse marquee weighed in on the notorious "The Houston Astros Sign Stealing Scandal" that broke in November 2019, when members of the team management were suspended and fined for failing to prevent Astros players from illegally using a video camera system to steal pitching signs from opposing teams during in the 2017-2018 baseball seasons.

The whole thing was a black eye on baseball then. We had an old night manager, Larry, who was an Astro's fan, and a pretty serious guy — but even he broke down laughing at it when he came into work the night I put it up.

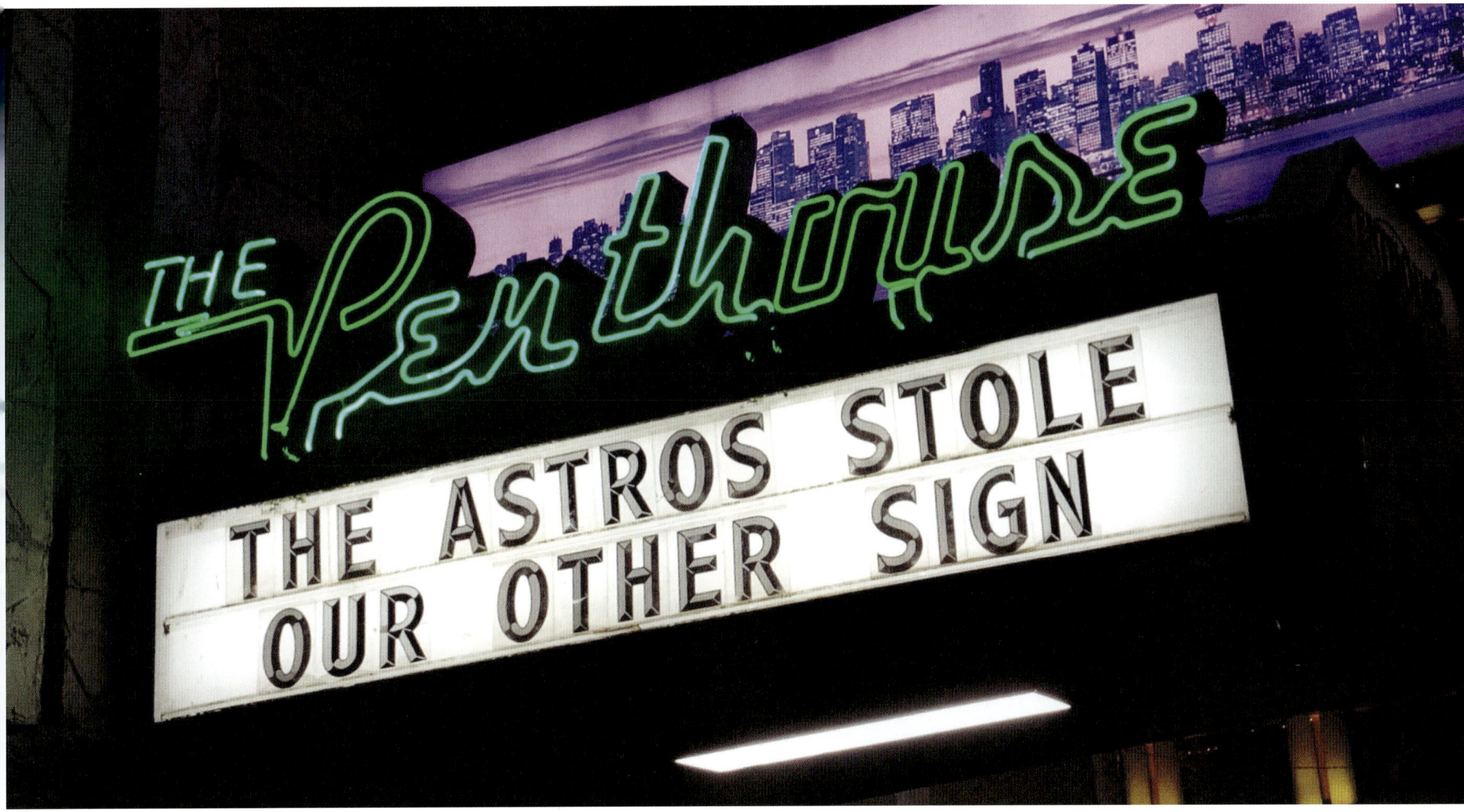
THE Penthouse
THE ASTROS STOLE
OUR OTHER SIGN

"I do appreciate the irony of a strip club using their signage to battle Vancouver's 'No Fun City' reputation."

— Dan Mangan, Musician

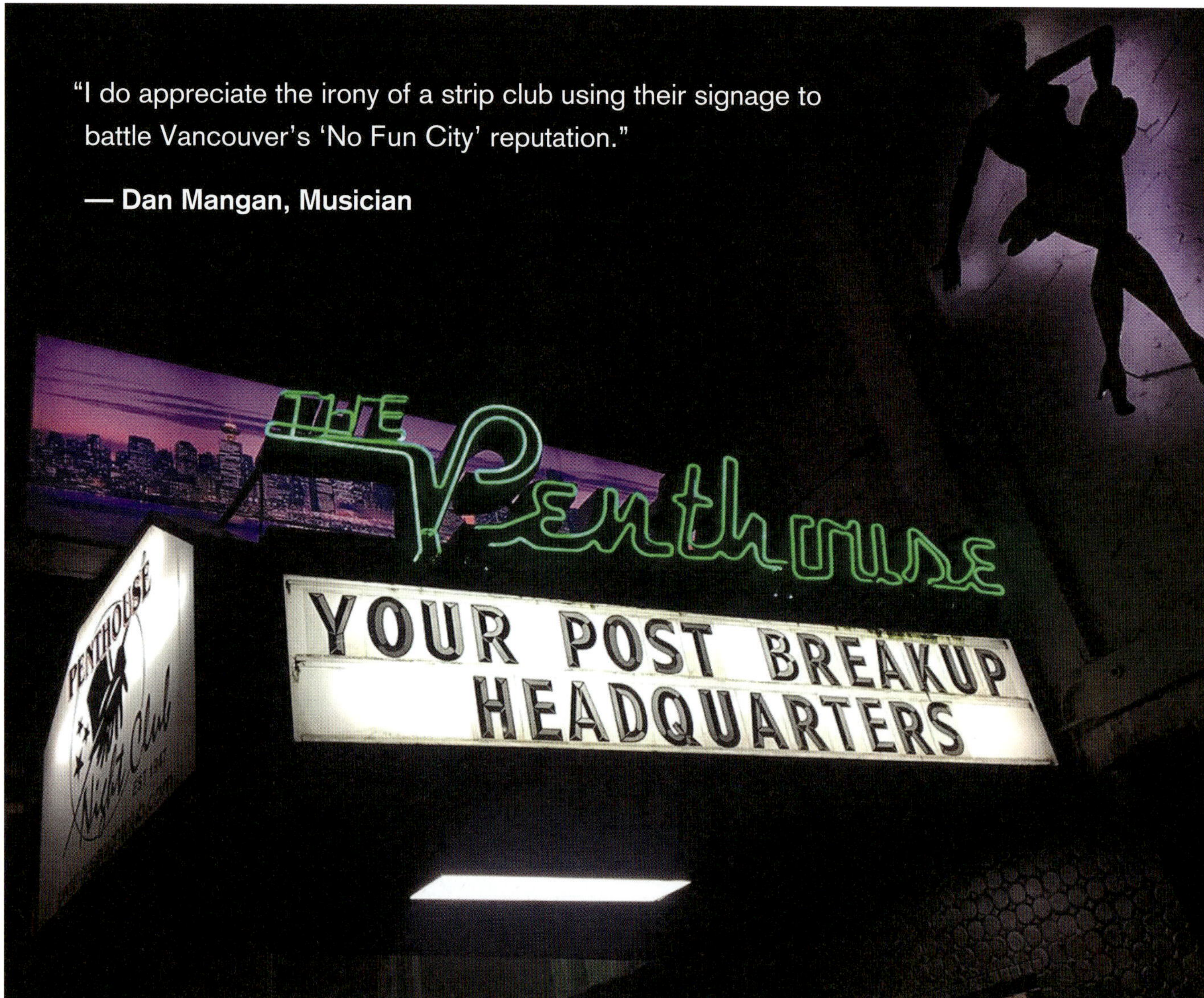

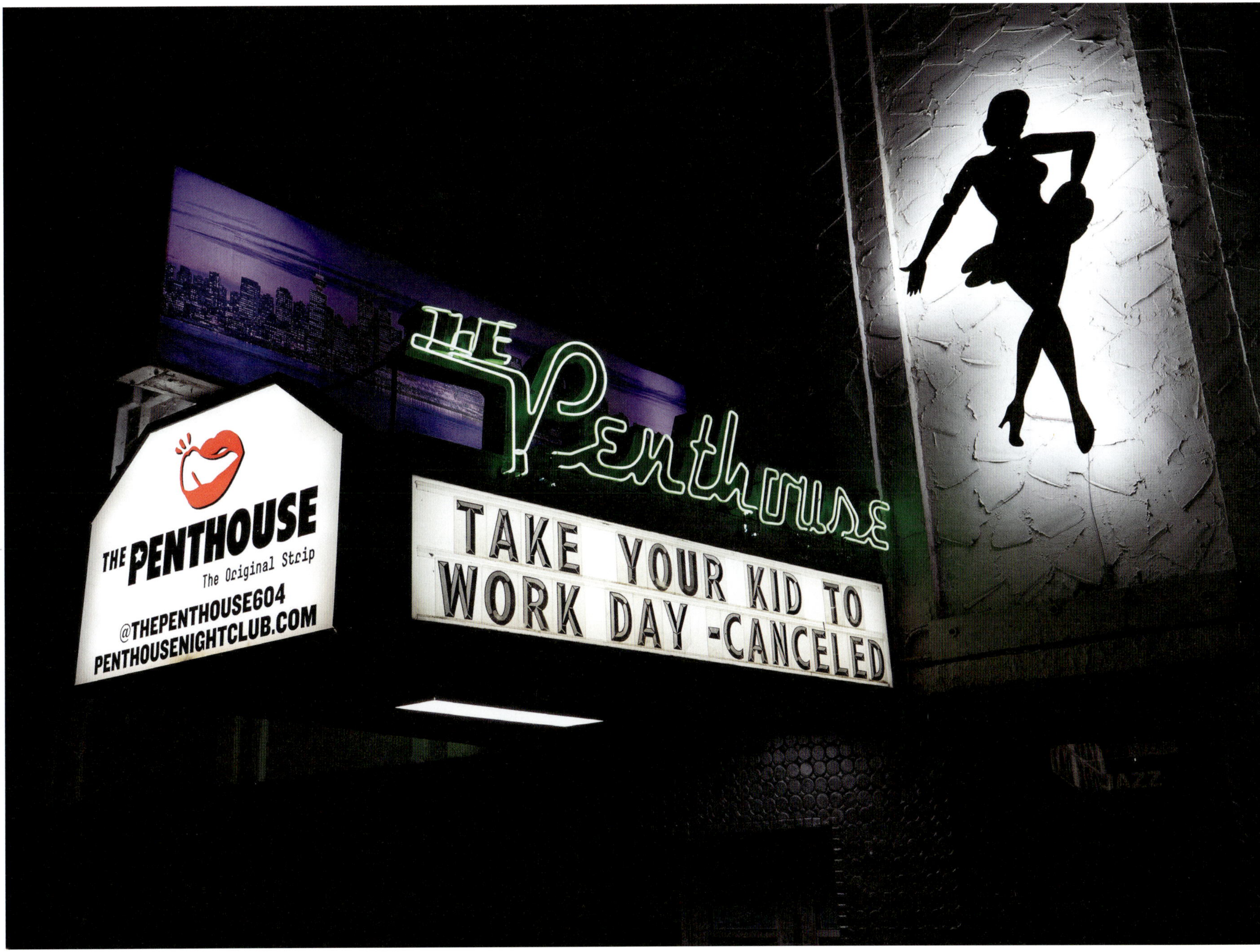
THE Penthouse
TAKE YOUR KID TO
WORK DAY -CANCELED
THE PENTHOUSE
The Original Strip
@THEPENTHOUSE604
PENTHOUSENIGHTCLUB.COM

COMING SOON: PURELL WRESTLING

At the beginning of the pandemic, public health officials were pushing hand sanitizer and regular washing of your hands. It might have been the first COVID related joke I did, because the health authorities were pushing so much hand sanitizer, and Purell was flying off the shelves. But a week or so later — we closed the doors along with every other bar and restaurant. It was supposed to only be for two weeks. A year later, on closure anniversary, I put up another sign: "Longest Two Weeks Ever". A lot of people remembered that marked a year in. We were a ways to go before it was all over.

"I've spent the last decade or so working in Vancouver and it's a city that's become a second home to me. When I'm not here, I miss the people, my favourite poutine spot, and seeing the newest sign above Penthouse. They've always given me a chuckle and have been the topic of conversations many times — not only do you get the odd cheeky pun, but they've provided commentaries on global events, from Brexit to Covid. There's also this attitude behind them that's just so inherently Vancouver in the best possible way."

— Rahul Kohli, Actor
(iZOMBIE/ Midnight Mass/The Haunting/The Fall of The House of Usher)

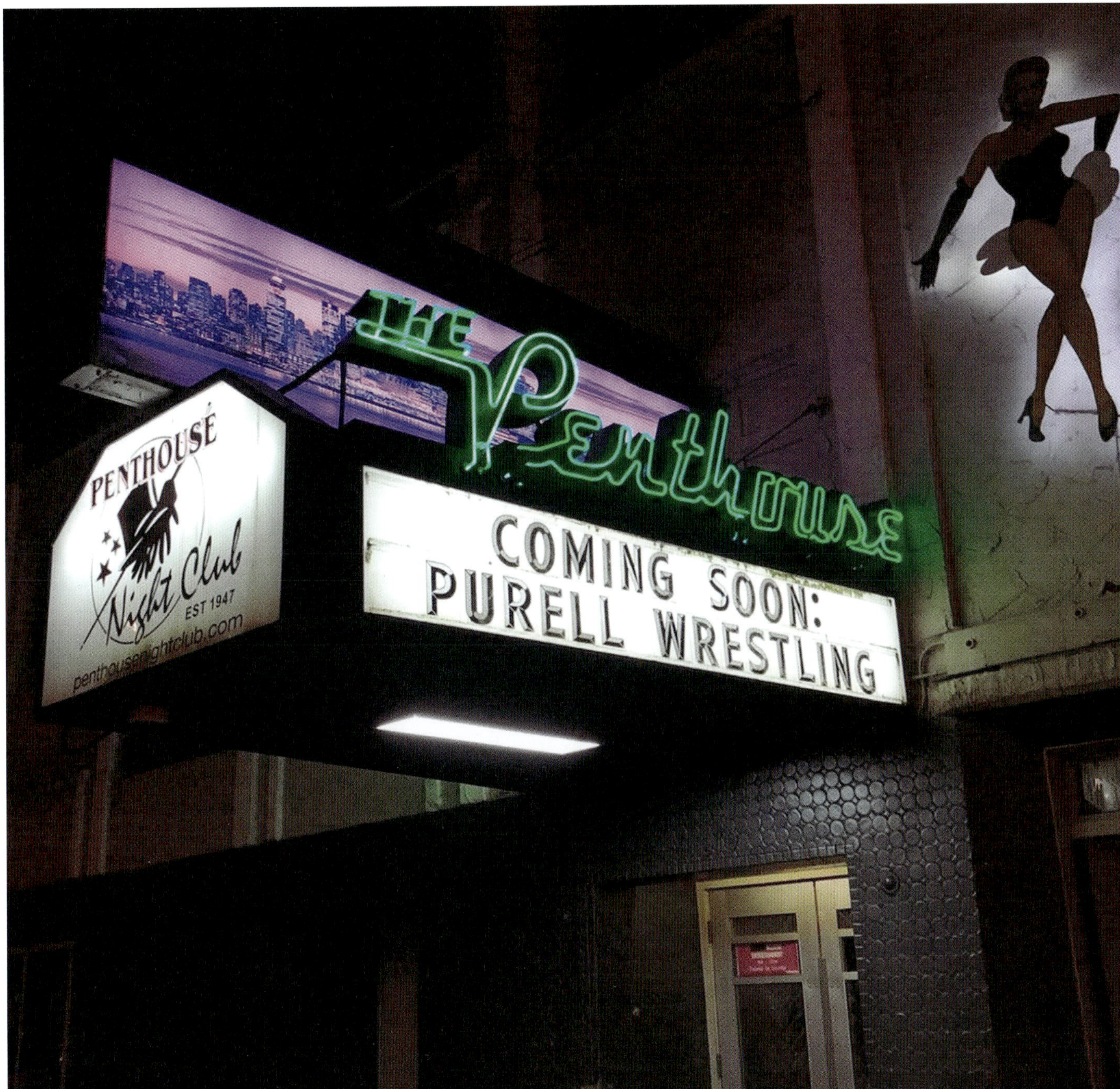

PENTHOUSE
Night Club
EST 1947
penthousenightclub.com
THE Penthouse
COMING SOON:
PURELL WRESTLING

CLOTHED UNTIL FURTHER NOTICE

One had to wonder what David Suzuki thought of the Nature of Things.

The four women underneath the sign in the photo are actually dancers from the club — they were out of work. The club ended up being closed for so long, and without being open to the public, the girls were occasionally coming in to shoot content for Only Fans, using the club stage and booths for photo shoots. This one was featured on the CBC.

“Thanks for today’s sign. It’s the first time I’ve really laughed in months, and it felt good to laugh again.”

— Anonymous caller on the Penthouse Nightclub voicemail, Summer 2020

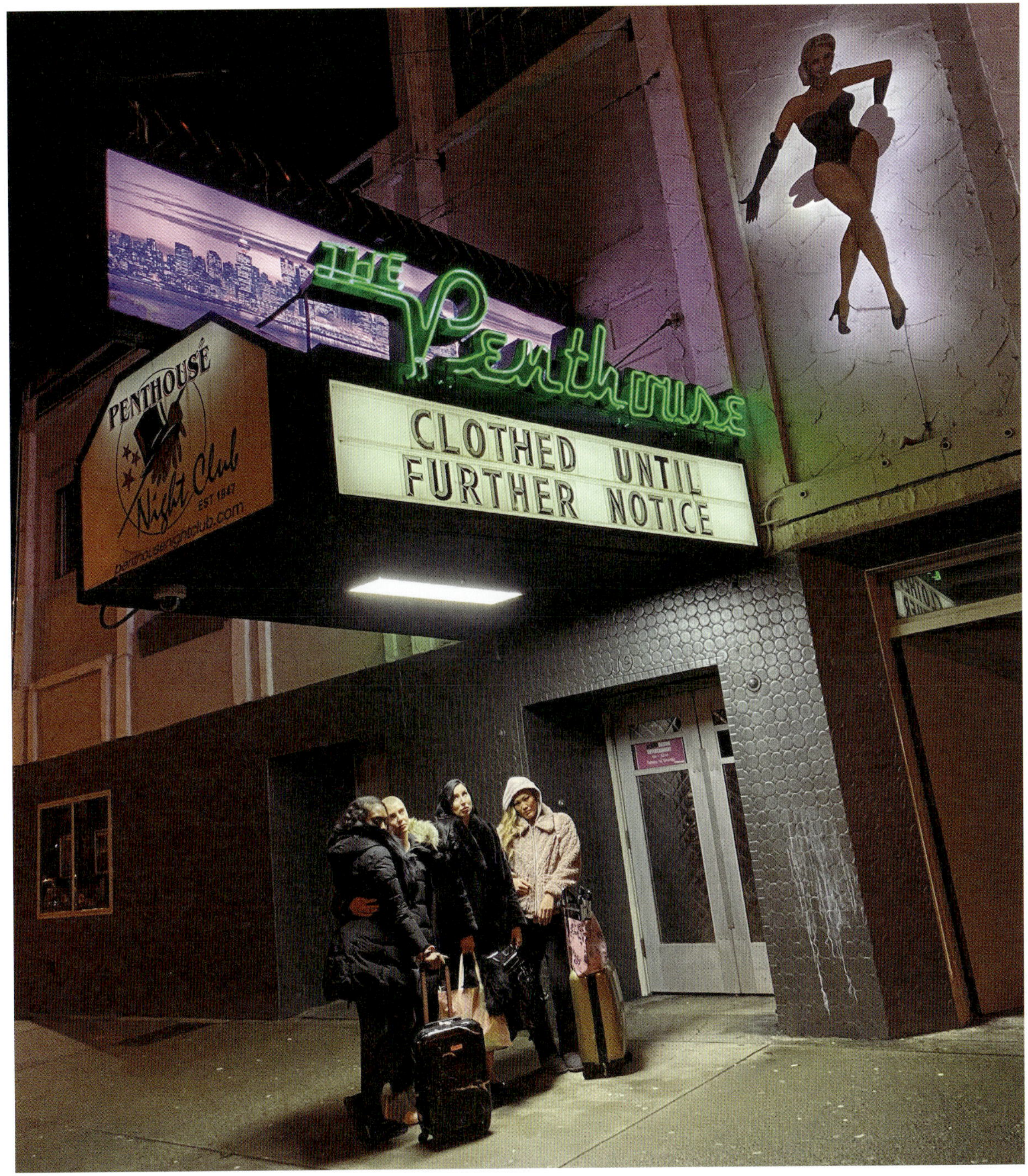

LONGEST 2 WEEKS EVER

Twelve months into the pandemic, without an end in sight, the marquee spoke for many.

At the beginning of COVID we were sort of at a loss for what to say when things closed down. Danny suggested we just put up something simple, "See you in two weeks, stay safe", which we went with. I suppose we didn't have anything very funny to say because nobody knew what was going on at the beginning or how long it would last.

Twelve months later I realized the anniversary of the start of that two-weeks was pending. So, I put this one up on that exact day. Some people remembered that date had been an exact year later. Others said they couldn't believe a year had gone by. I think everybody identified with it.

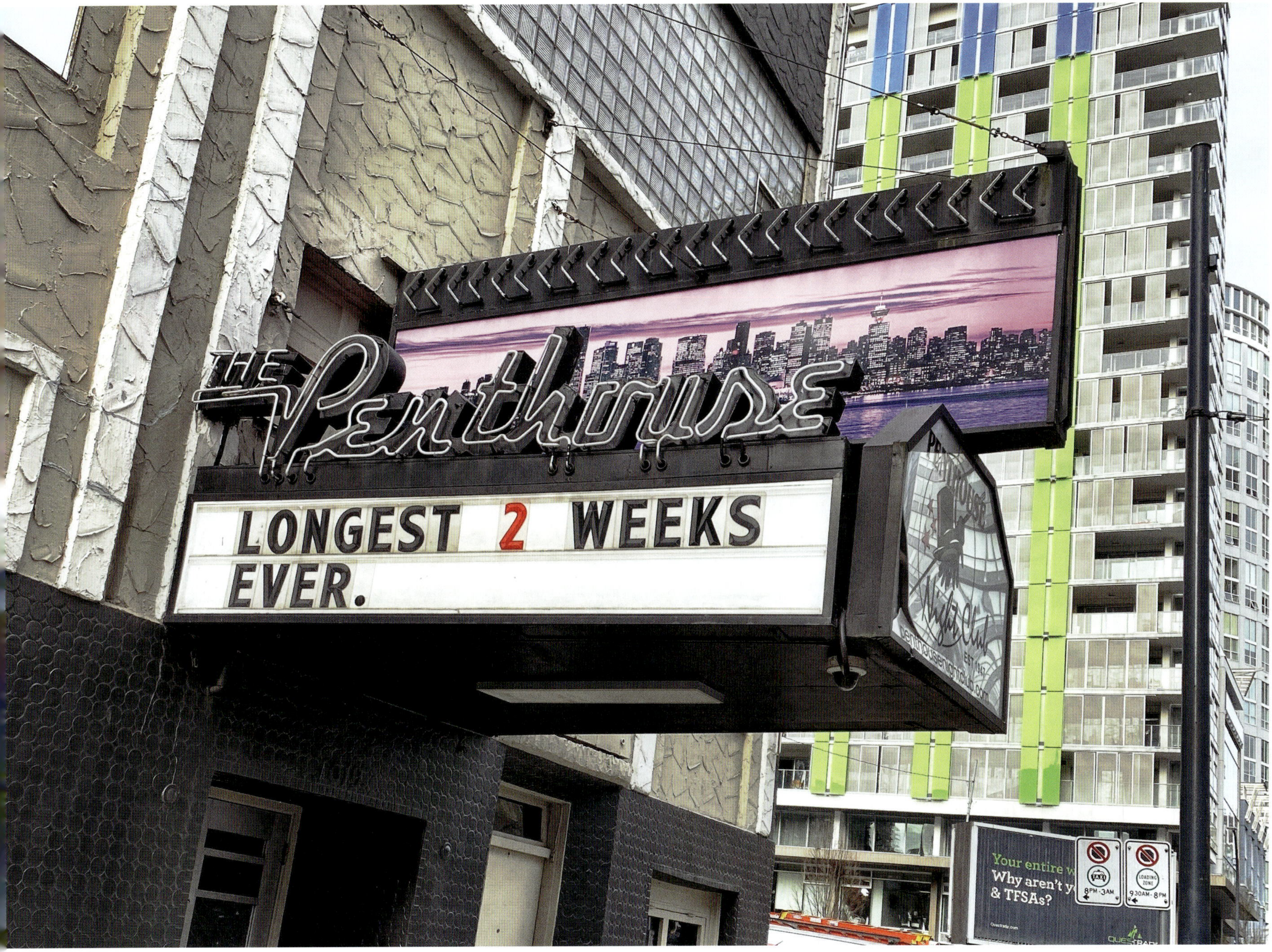
THE Penthouse
LONGEST 2 WEEKS
EVER.
& TFSAs?

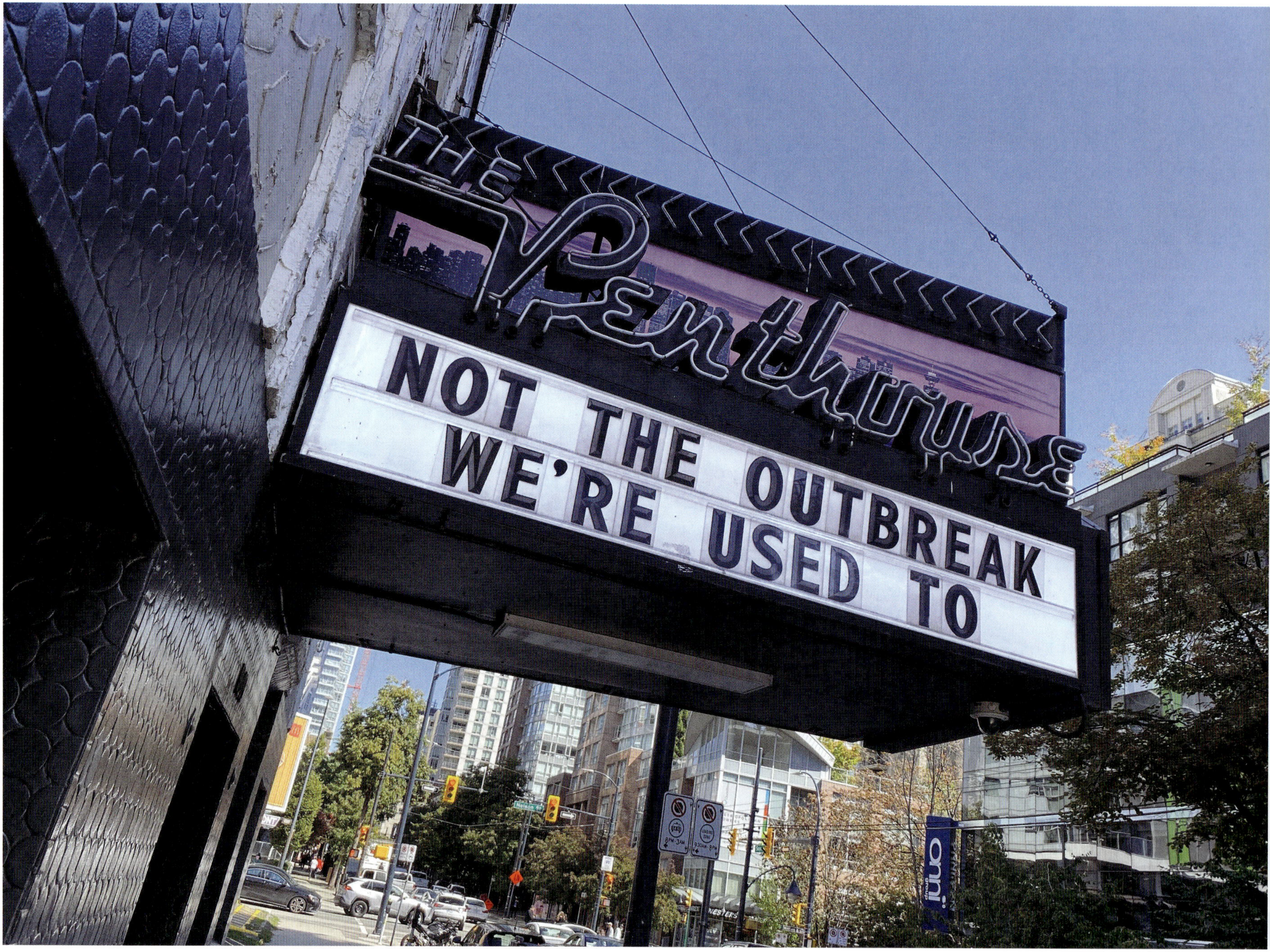
THE Penthouse
NOT THE OUTBREAK
WE'RE USED TO

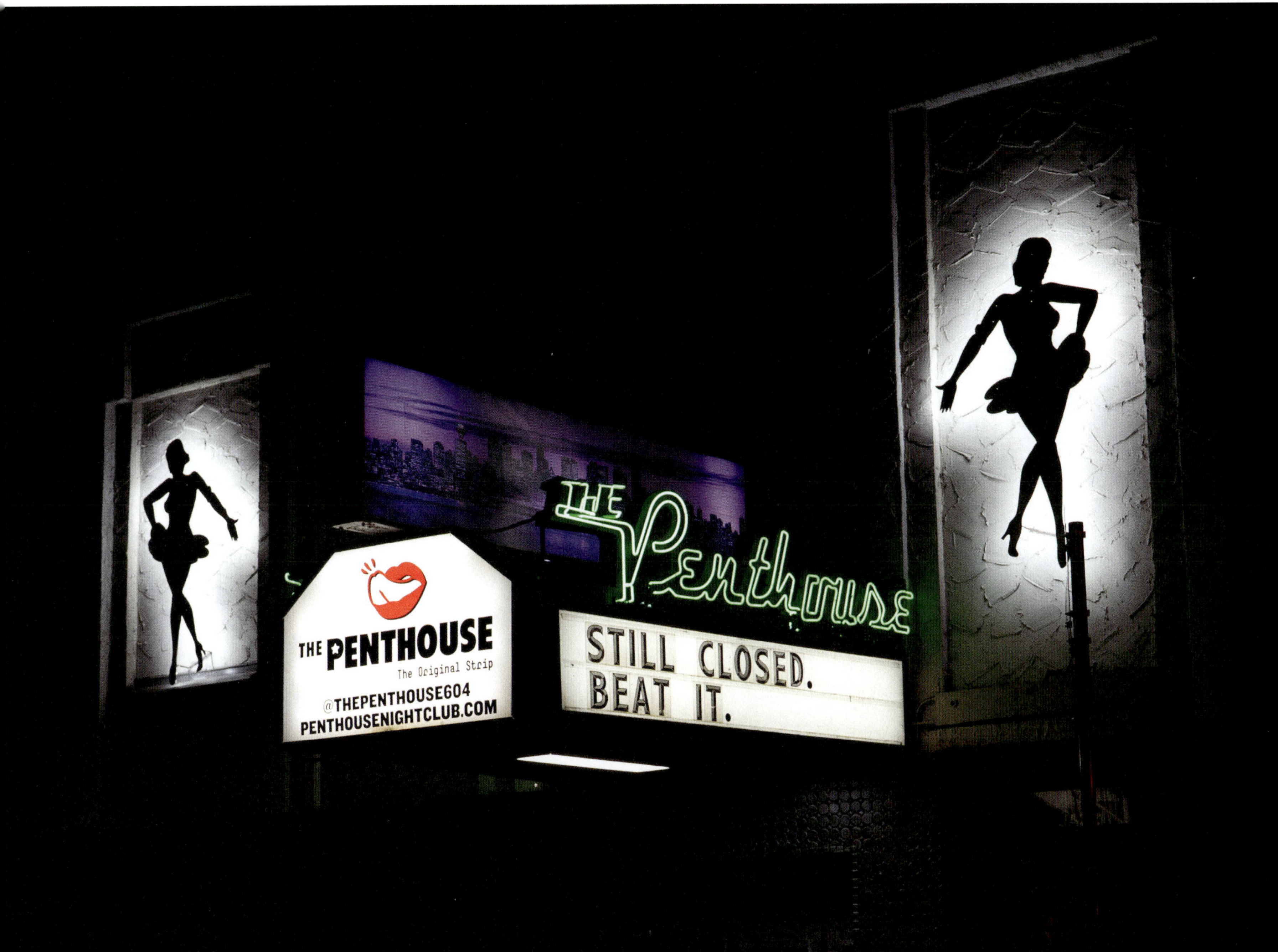
THE PENTHOUSE
The Original Strip
@THEPENTHOUSE604
PENTHOUSENIGHTCLUB.COM
THE Penthouse
STILL CLOSED.
BEAT IT.

NO GLORY HOLES
STOP ASKING

Some months into the pandemic, in July 2020, officials from the British Columbia Centre for Disease Control encouraged wearing masks while having sex, choosing positions that limited face to face contact, and even encouraging the use of "Glory Holes" to prevent the transfer of the coronavirus. The daily press briefings by the urbane and politely spoken Provincial Health officer, Dr. Bonnie Henry, even caused her to blush in detailing the announcement. Neon signs don't blush, and The Penthouse marquee was left to candidly address the latest COVID prevention initiative for itself.

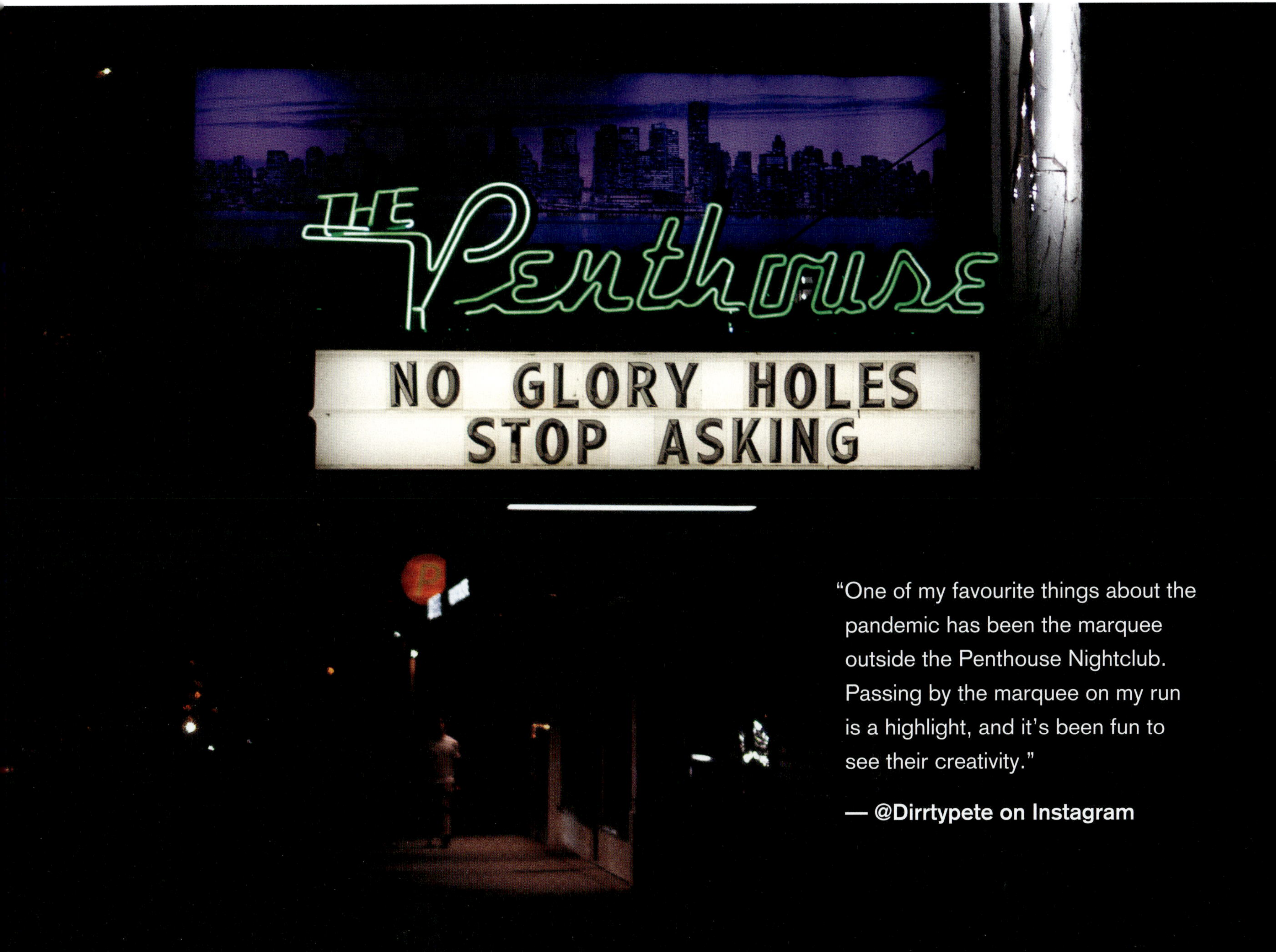

"One of my favourite things about the pandemic has been the marquee outside the Penthouse Nightclub. Passing by the marquee on my run is a highlight, and it's been fun to see their creativity."

— @Dirrtypete on Instagram

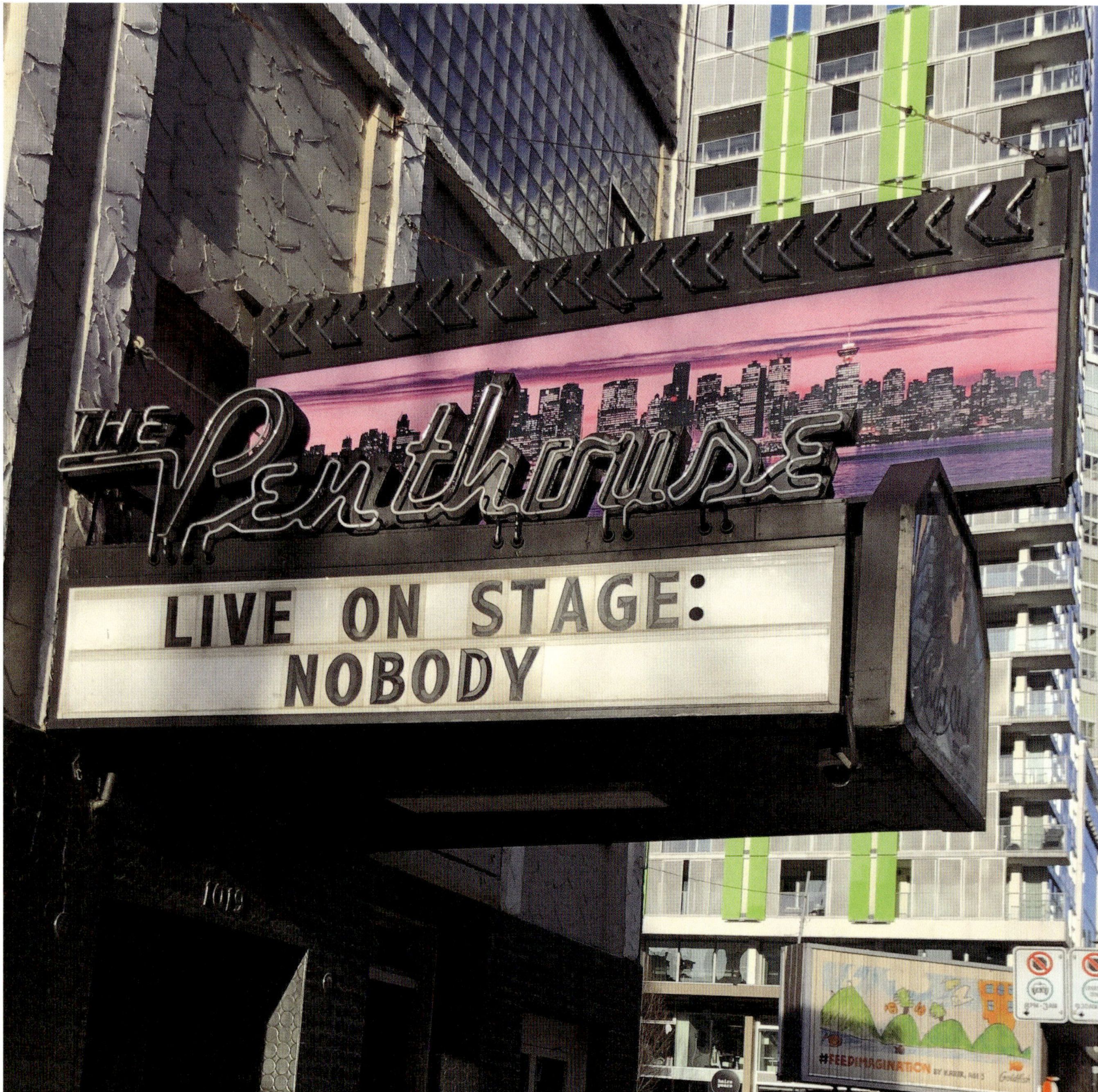
THE Penthouse
LIVE ON STAGE:
NOBODY
1019
#FEEDIMAGINATION

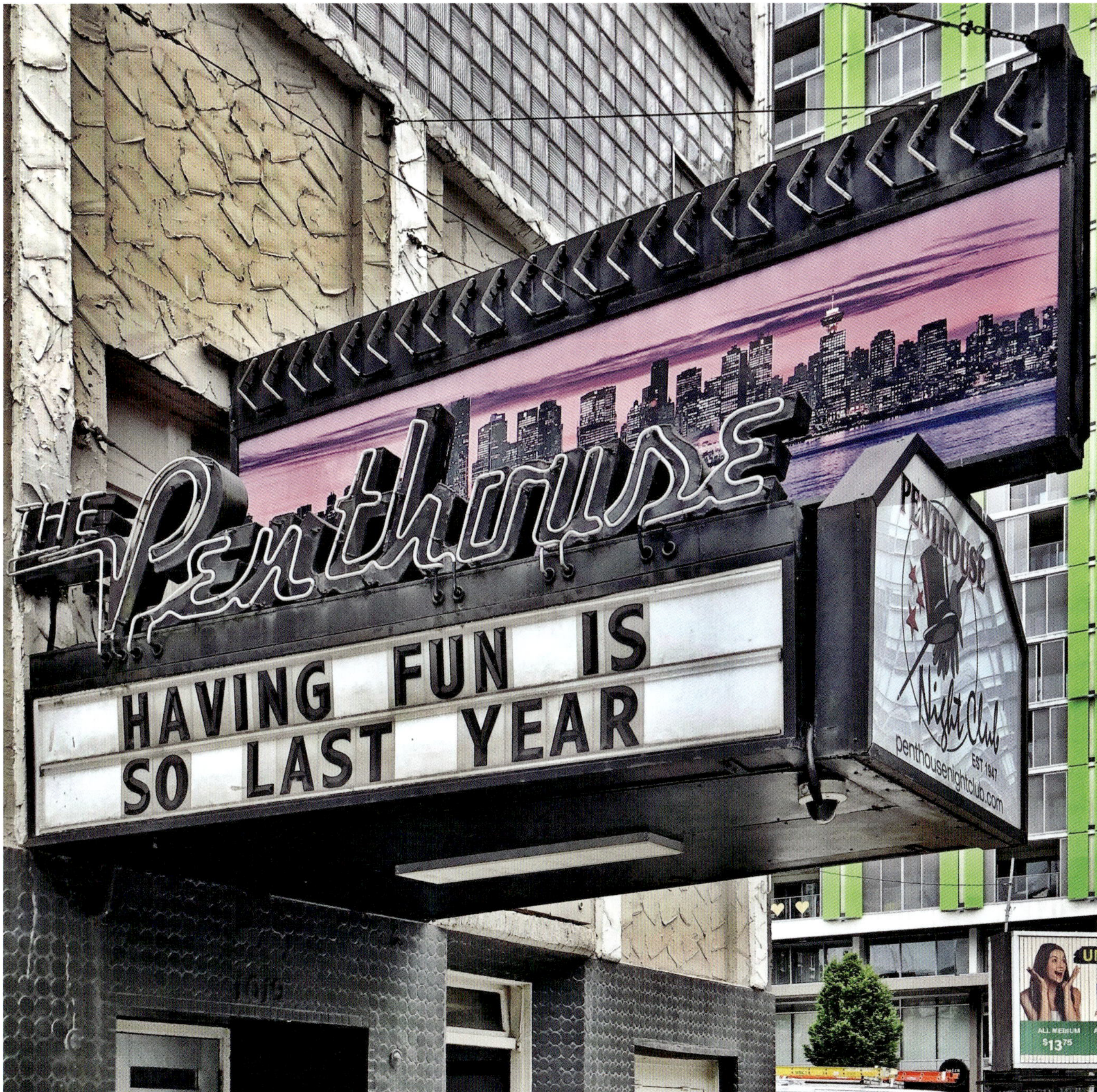
THE Penthouse
HAVING FUN IS
SO LAST YEAR
PENTHOUSE
Night Club
EST 1947
penthousenightclub.com

BETTER SECURITY THAN THE US CAPITOL

A tip of the hat to the Penthouse doormen. On January 6th 2021, the United States Capitol in Washington D.C., was attacked by a mob in an attempted coup, aiming to interrupt the joint session of Congress to formally recount the votes in the US Election from two months prior:

I was at the Penthouse that day just checking out some of the renovations that were going on. We were still closed from the lockdown but getting closer to opening. On my walk home a friend had been texting me that there was a riot happening in the US capitol. As soon as I got in I turned on the TV and sat watching it. It was kind of unbelievable. I hadn't taken my shoes off yet and it just hit me. I put my coat back on and headed down to the club to change the sign. The next day my phone blew up as everyone from the *Huffington Post* to the local newspapers and media all wanted to talk to me.

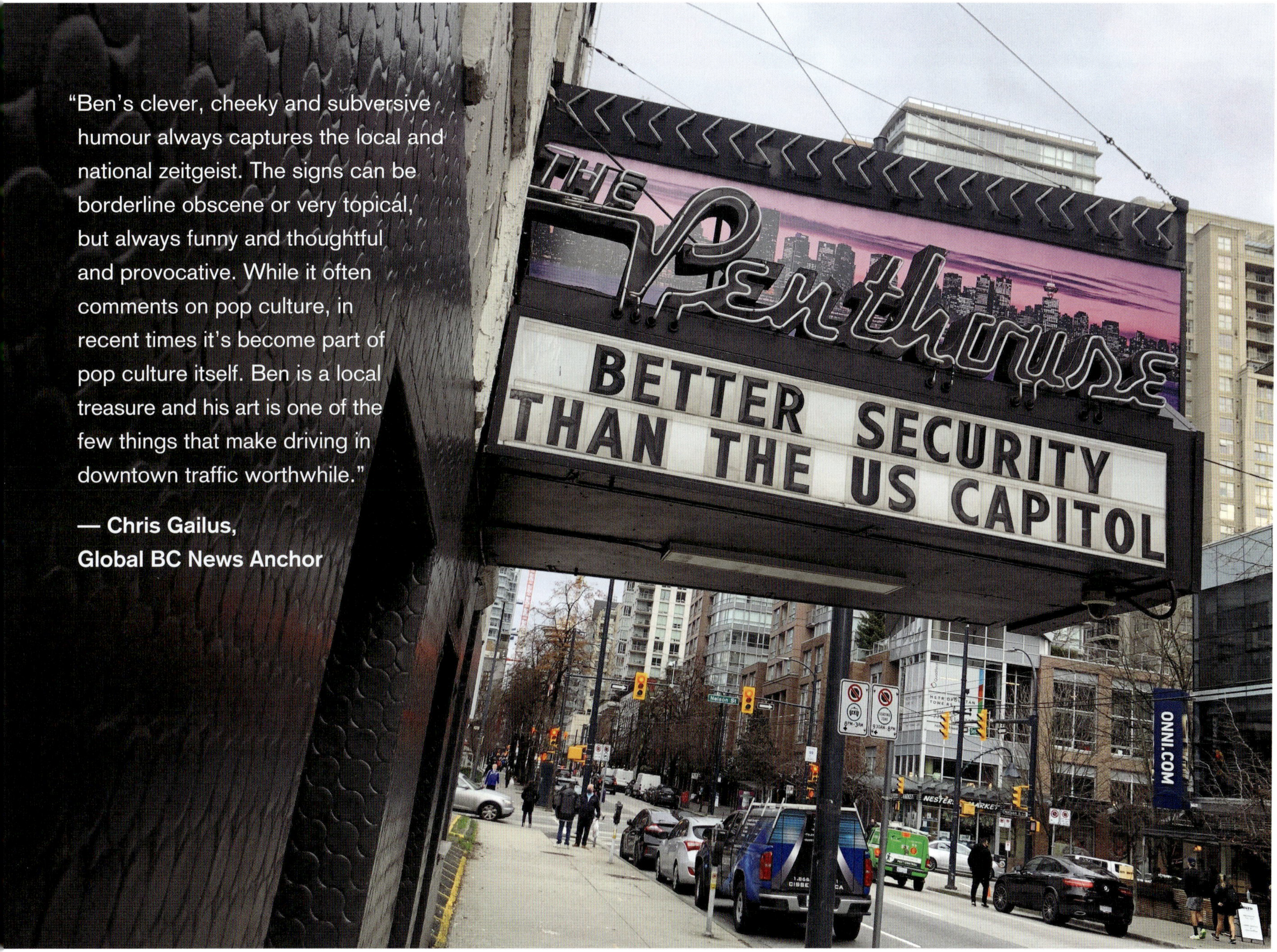

"Ben's clever, cheeky and subversive humour always captures the local and national zeitgeist. The signs can be borderline obscene or very topical, but always funny and thoughtful and provocative. While it often comments on pop culture, in recent times it's become part of pop culture itself. Ben is a local treasure and his art is one of the few things that make driving in downtown traffic worthwhile."

— Chris Gailus,
Global BC News Anchor

I LASTED 6 MINUTES WITH LYNDA STEELE

A day after the interview I thought I'd comment with a new sign.

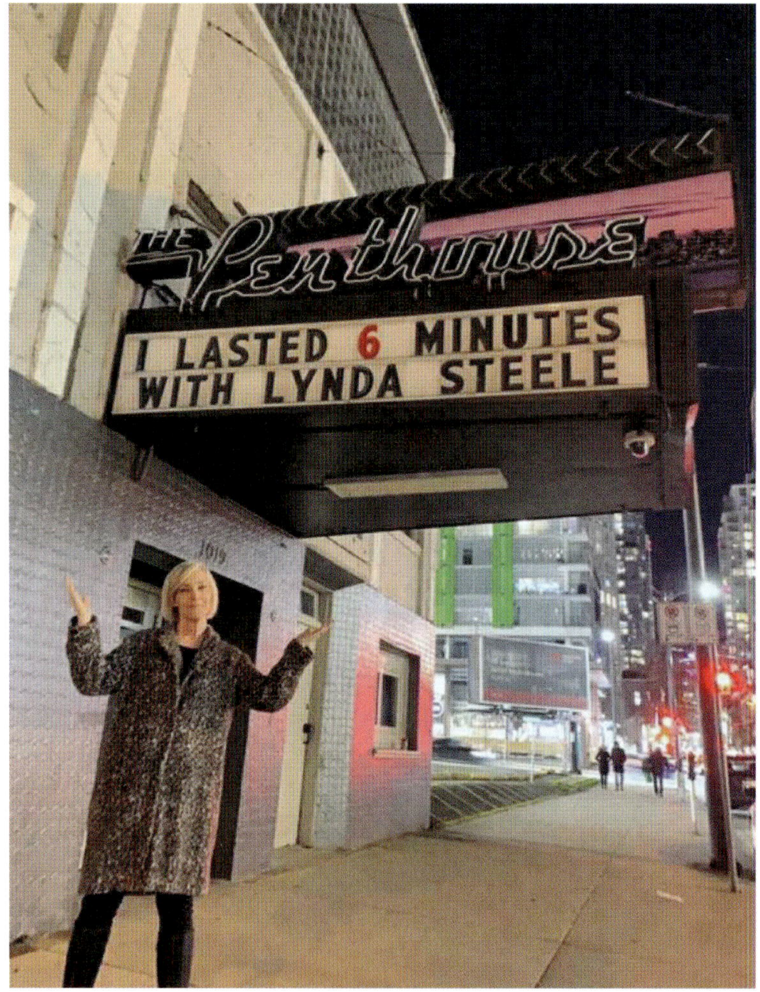

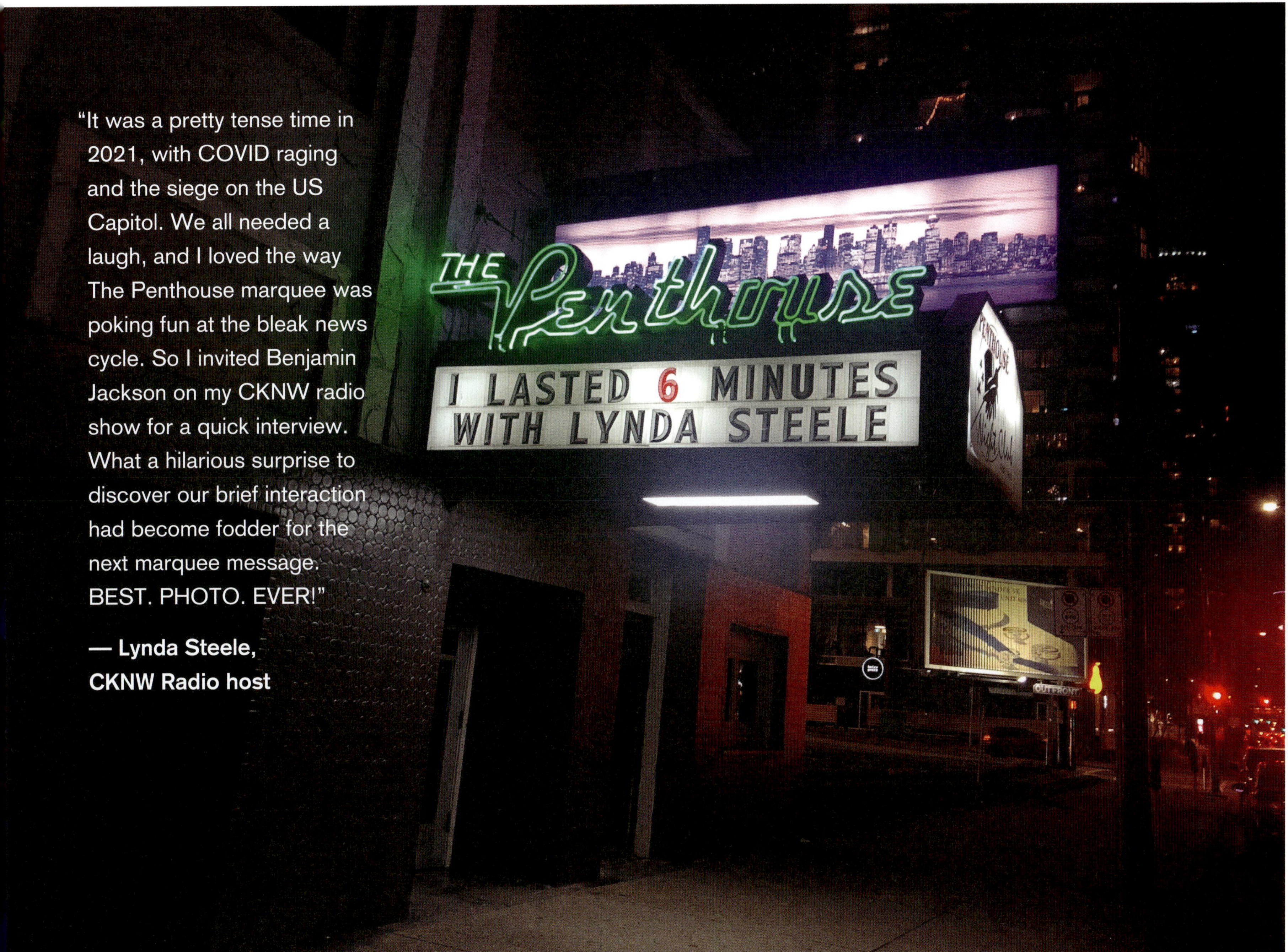

"It was a pretty tense time in 2021, with COVID raging and the siege on the US Capitol. We all needed a laugh, and I loved the way The Penthouse marquee was poking fun at the bleak news cycle. So I invited Benjamin Jackson on my CKNW radio show for a quick interview. What a hilarious surprise to discover our brief interaction had become fodder for the next marquee message. BEST. PHOTO. EVER!"

— Lynda Steele, CKNW Radio host

“OPEN UP SHOPS” – DMX

The marquee has always showed it had love for the streets.

It was around April 2021, that time when people were both tiring of the lockdown, and looking forward to things fully opening up again, and the rapper DMX died. I thought of his track Ruff Ryders Anthem, where the chorus goes, “Stop, Drop, Shut ’em Down, Open Up Shop”, so it was a nod to him. We ended up not opening for another five months. But I suppose we were all just hoping it would end soon.

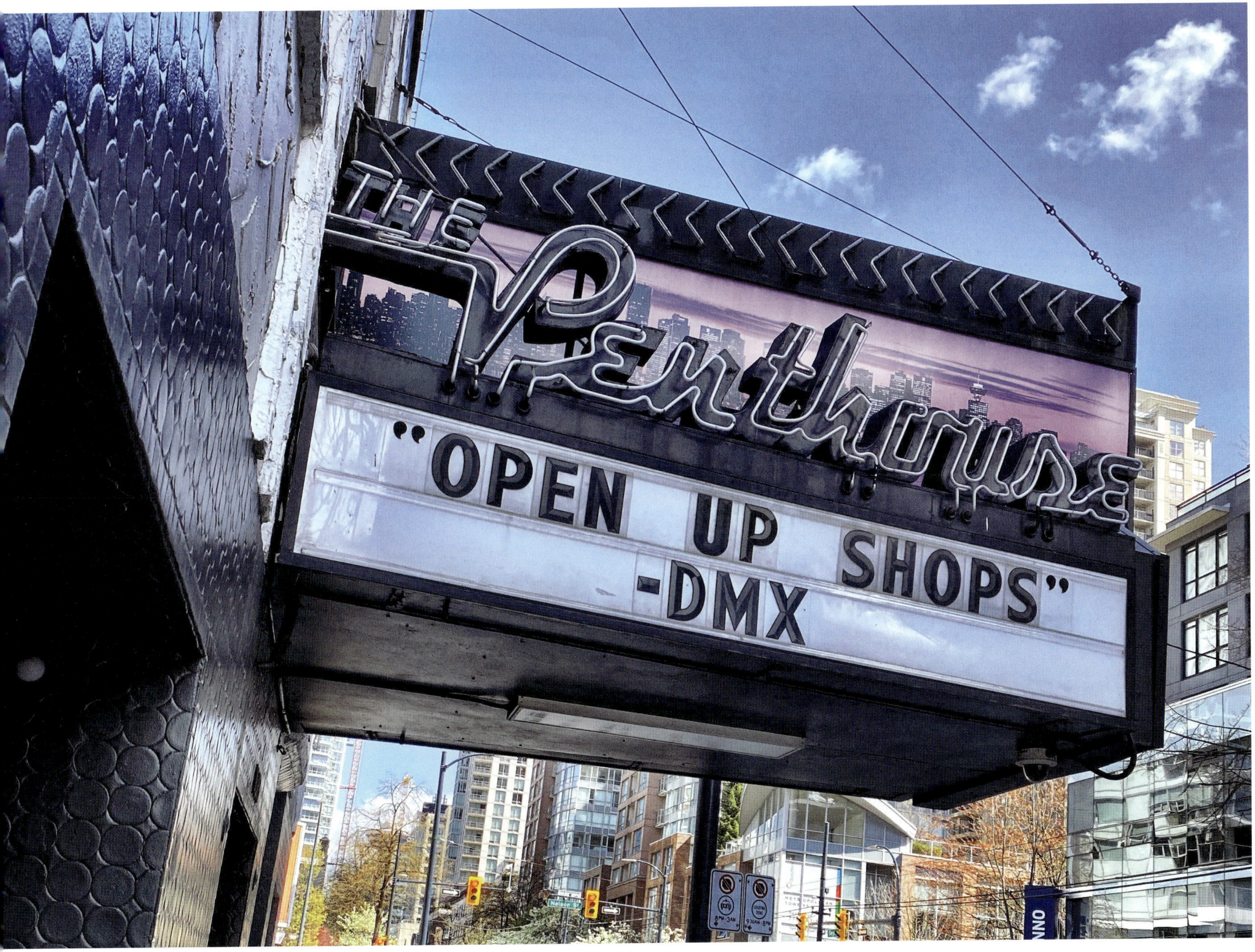
THE Penthouse
"OPEN UP SHOPS"
-DMX

PFIZER NOW MAKES MY 2 FAVOURITE THINGS

In December 2021, the pharmaceutical company Pfizer announced it had developed a COVID vaccine. The corporation also notably had developed Viagra some years earlier. Photos of this marquee went viral, with over 200,000+ views on Google.

We were still in the thick of it, without an end in sight, when Pfizer announced they had an approved vaccine that was going to be available. So that was a glimpse of hope, and I think that's why this one got so much attention. CKNW radio host Lynda Steele, who had noticed the US Capitol sign, interviewed me on her show. I was becoming not so anonymous anymore.

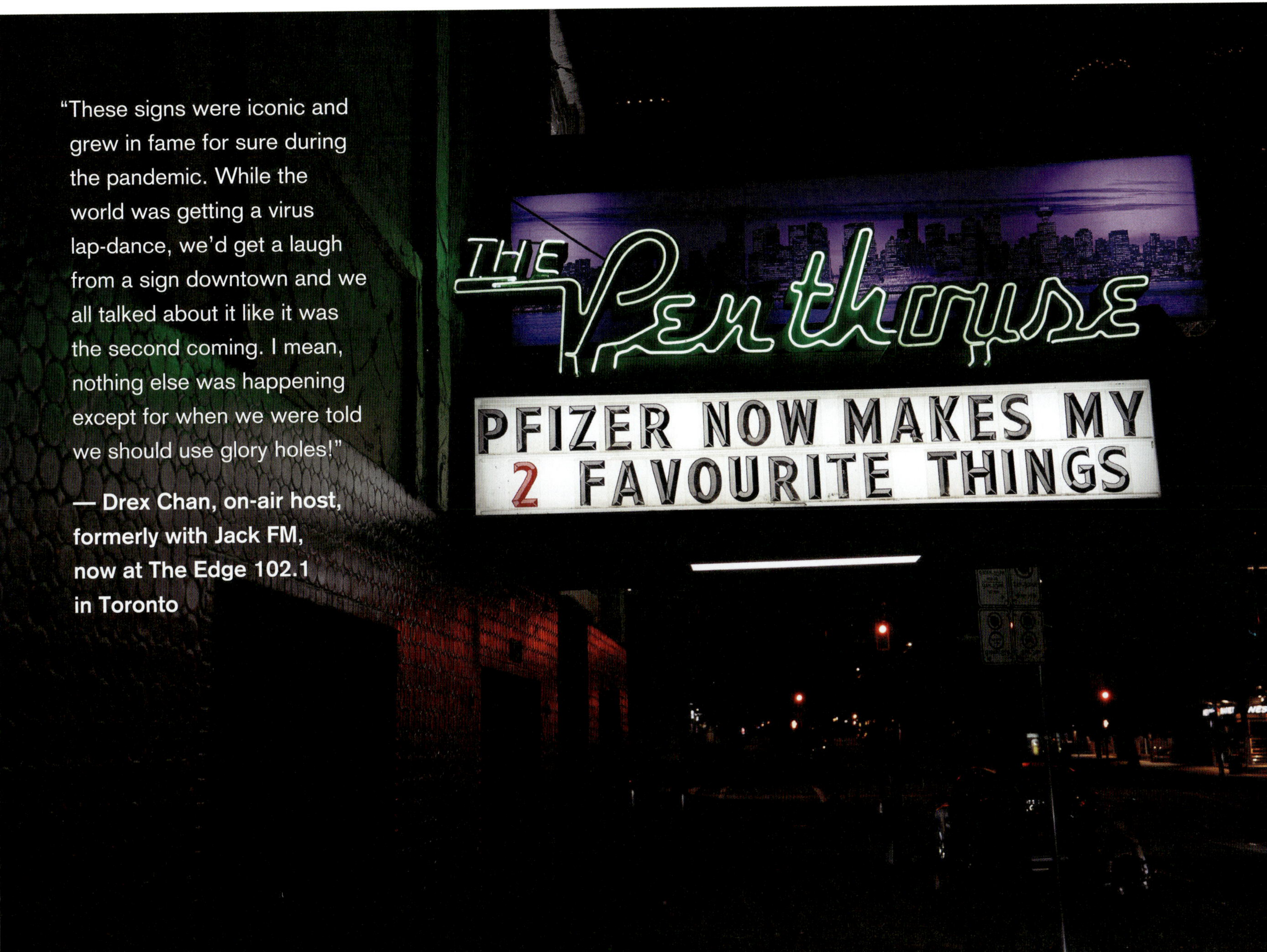

"These signs were iconic and grew in fame for sure during the pandemic. While the world was getting a virus lap-dance, we'd get a laugh from a sign downtown and we all talked about it like it was the second coming. I mean, nothing else was happening except for when we were told we should use glory holes!"

— Drex Chan, on-air host, formerly with Jack FM, now at The Edge 102.1 in Toronto

NO PASS. NO ASS.

The creation of the British Columbia vaccine passports in August 2021, where patrons could enter an establishment if they had the QR code proof of vaccination scanned off their mobile phones, signalled the end of the lockdown, and for the staff at the Penthouse it signalled some hope that the club would reopen again.

We didn't even have a date yet, but we knew the re-opening was coming. The media interviewed Danny [Filippone], and everybody was talking about it. At the end of the news on CBC they wondered "what the Penthouse marquee guy is going to come up with when they reopen", and I suddenly realized I was expected to come up with something! City inspectors were going around the clubs quite a bit back then, so we had to follow the rules implicitly, but that was our way of having a little fun with it too.

“The marquee at the Penthouse has this remarkable ability to capture the zeitgeist much like a polaroid camera. I especially came to appreciate this during COVID. I still have the pictures on my phone from ‘Clothed Until Further Notice’ and months later when it read ‘No Pass. No Ass’. Few images sum up the lows and highs of BC’s lockdown era better.”

—John Ackermann, CityNews Radio 1130 On Air Host

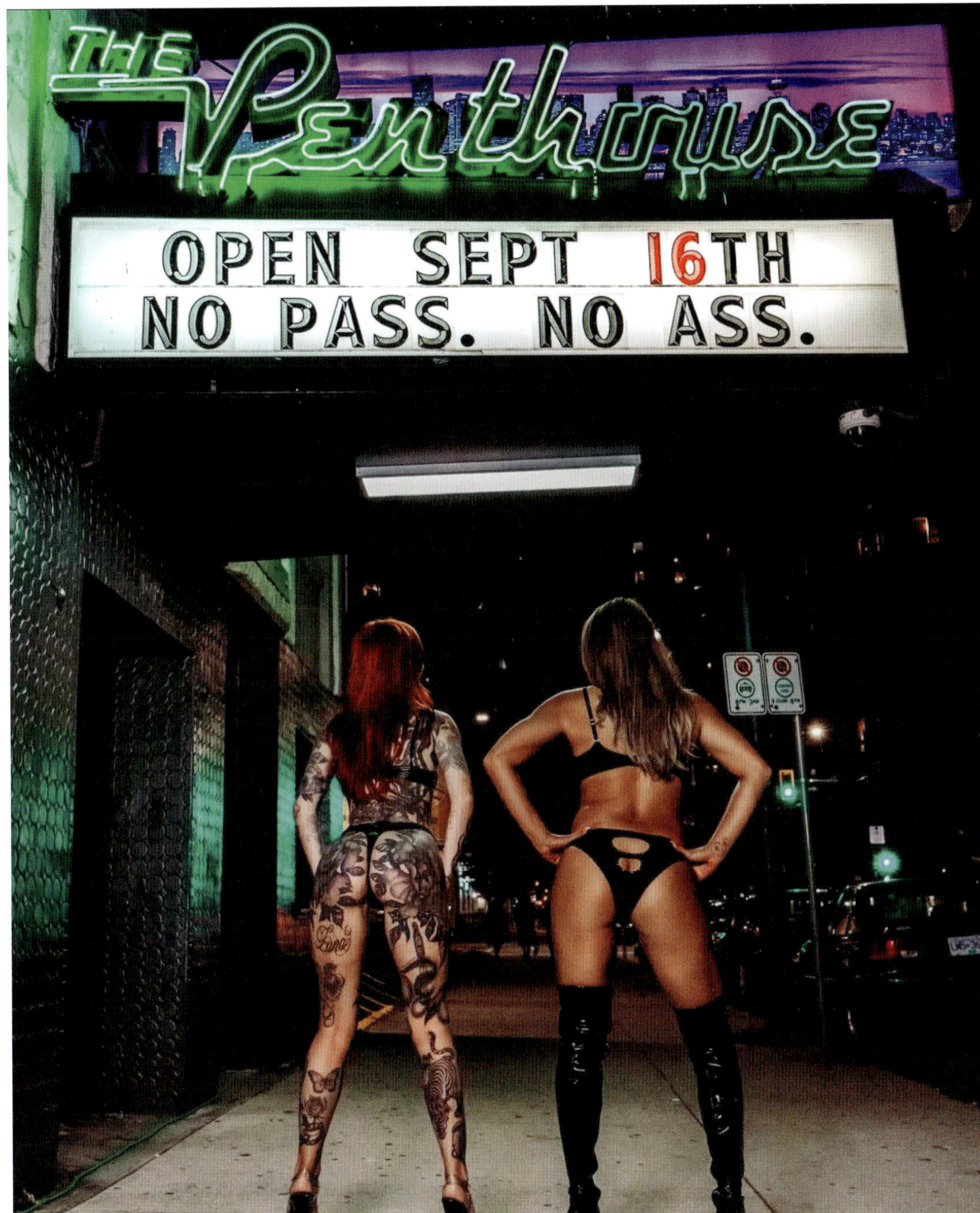

CERTAINLY NOT MAKING A JADA SMITH JOKE

With Will Smith's "Slap heard around the world" in March 2022, the Penthouse marquee decided to play it safe.

I was at an Oscar party that night and watched it live. I left the party before midnight and went down and changed the sign that night. So everyone saw it going to work the next morning.

"The most entertaining corner in the city of Vancouver — and that's just what I've seen from the outside!"

— Sophie Lui, Global BC TV News Anchor

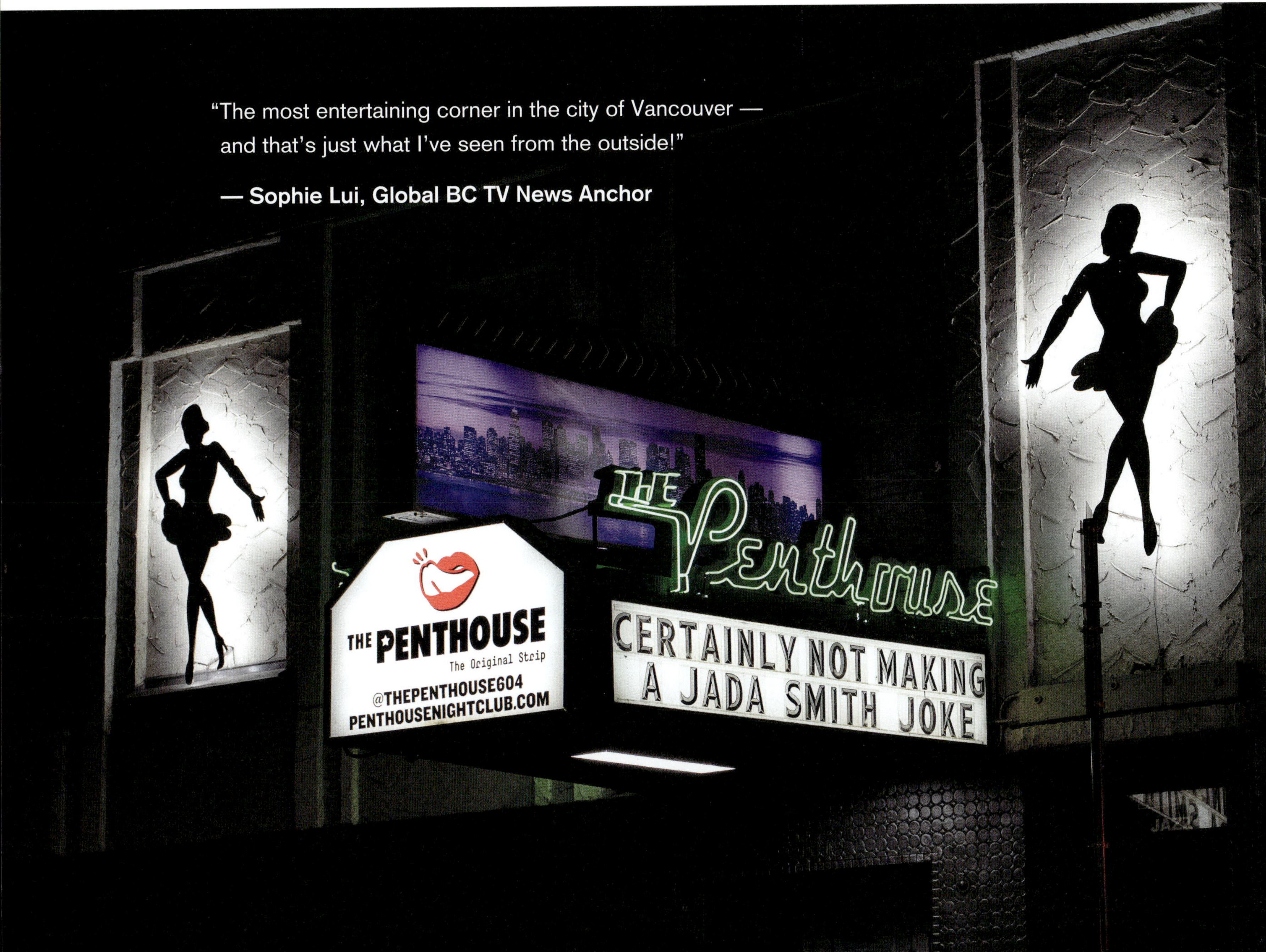

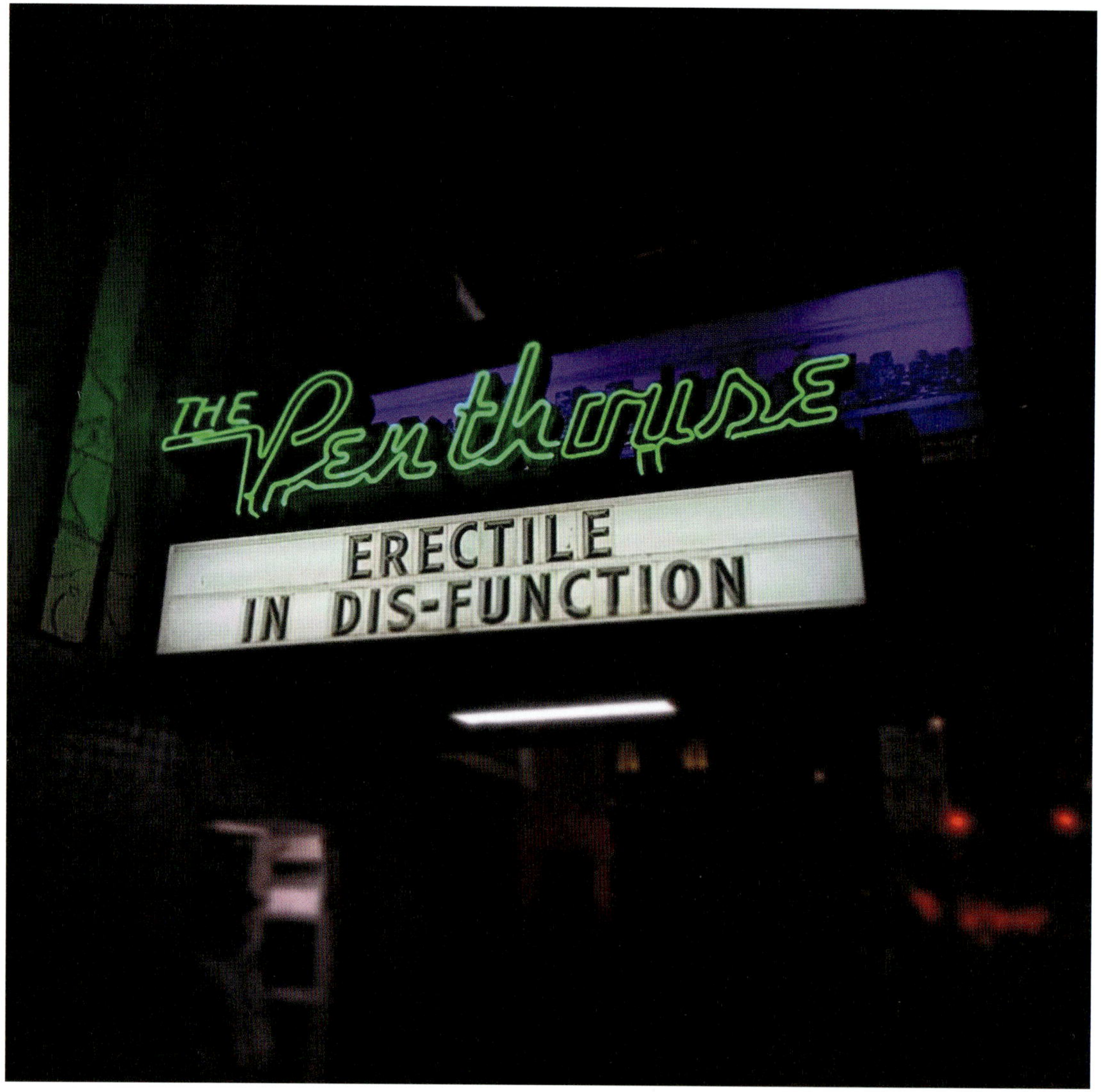
THE Penthouse
ERECTILE
IN DIS-FUNCTION

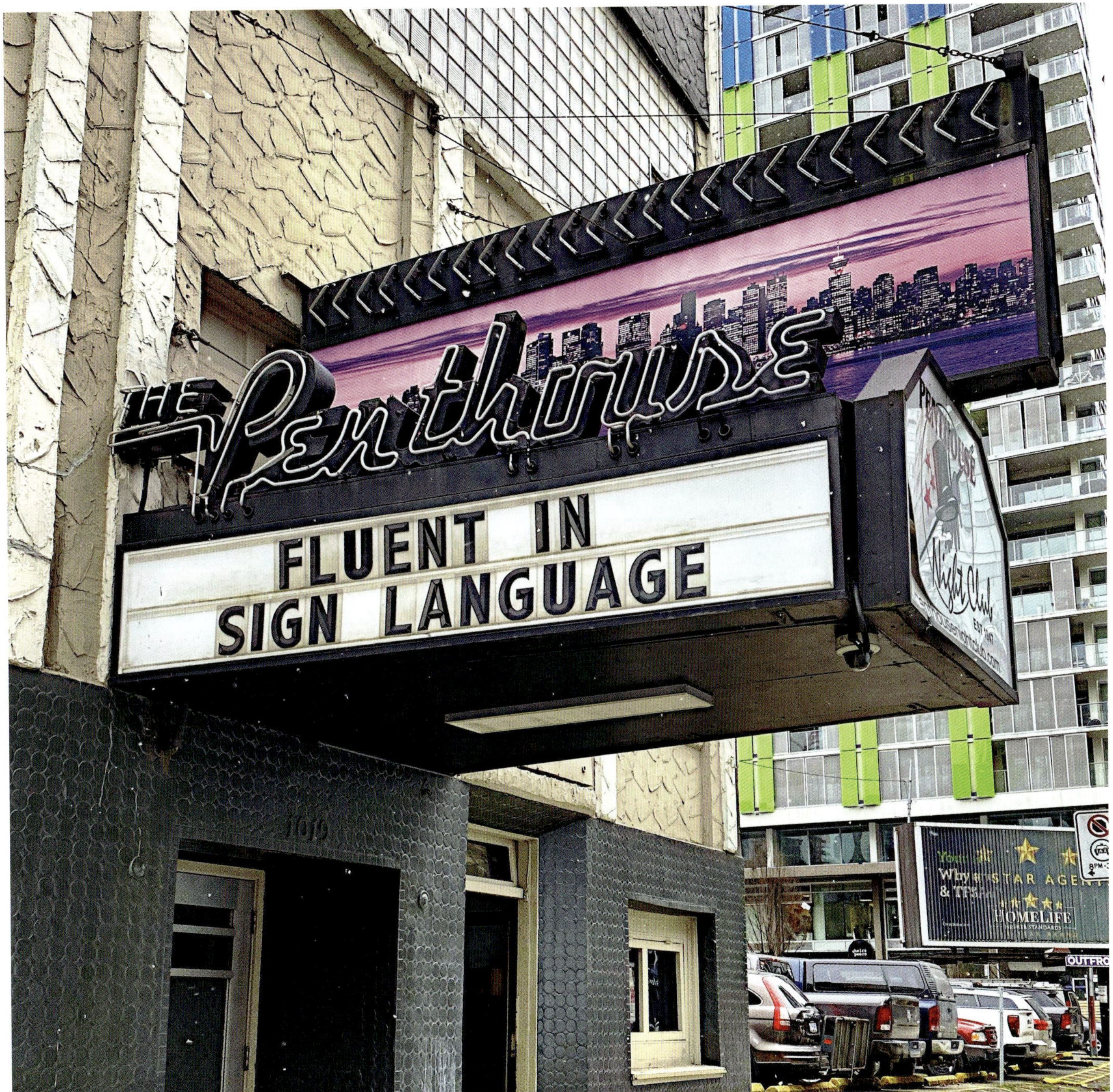
THE Penthouse
FLUENT IN
SIGN LANGUAGE

WE NEVER COVER THE SPREAD

The Super Bowl parties at the Penthouse over the years have been legendary, with the half-time show usually being far more vivid than what's featured on television. Super Bowl LVII in 2023 featured the Kansas City Chiefs vs. the Philadelphia Eagles. The Chiefs won, but perhaps everyone in attendance at the Penthouse won that day?

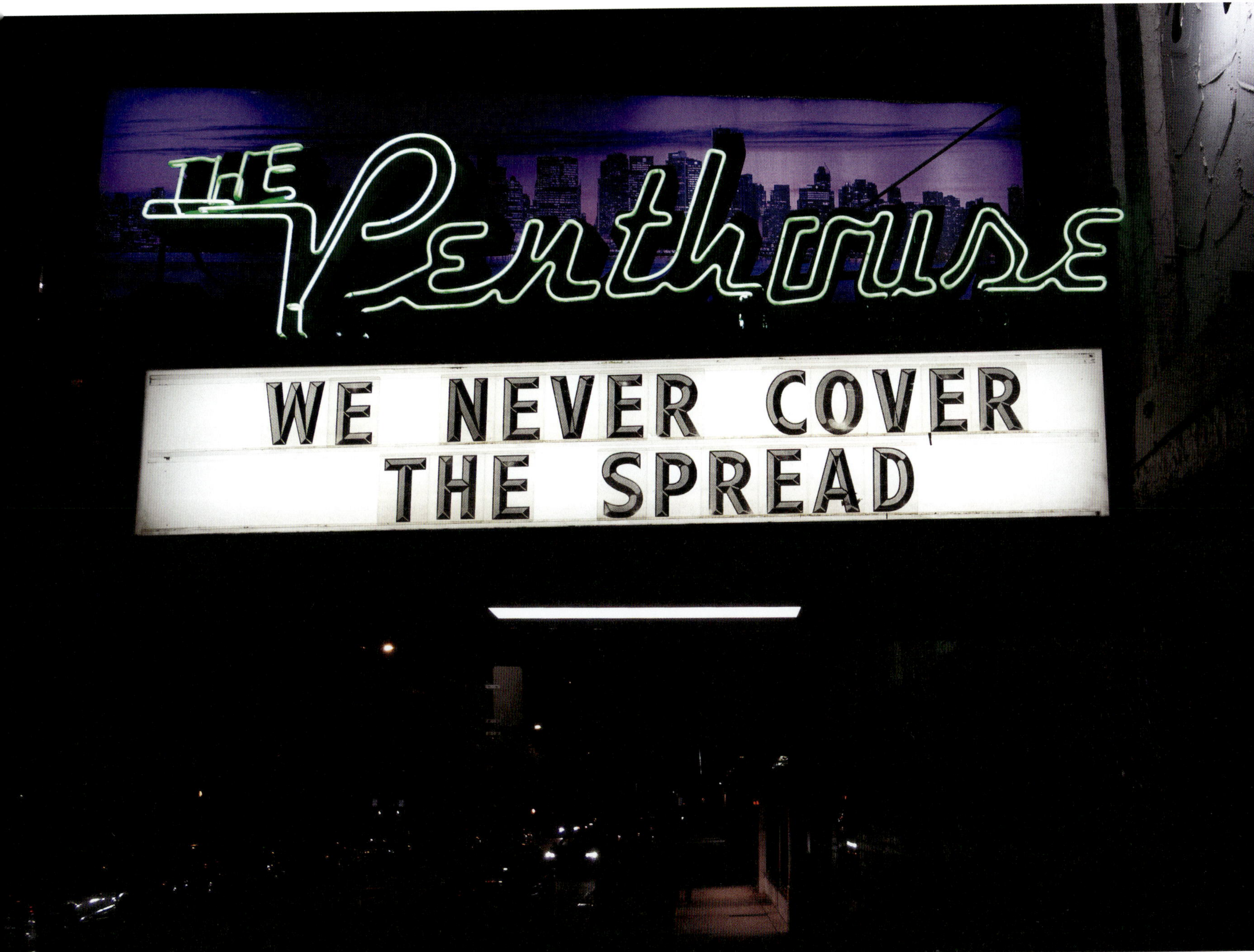
THE Penthouse
WE NEVER COVER
THE SPREAD

GO CANUCKS GO VANCOUVER IN ~~4~~ ~~5~~ 6

History shows that things can sometimes get sticky at the Penthouse.

They didn't do it in four, so we put an X over 4, and they didn't do it in 5, but they did it in 6. I managed to cover up the 4 and 5 with an "X" that I made with duct tape. But the duct tape is still stuck on those numbers and won't come off!

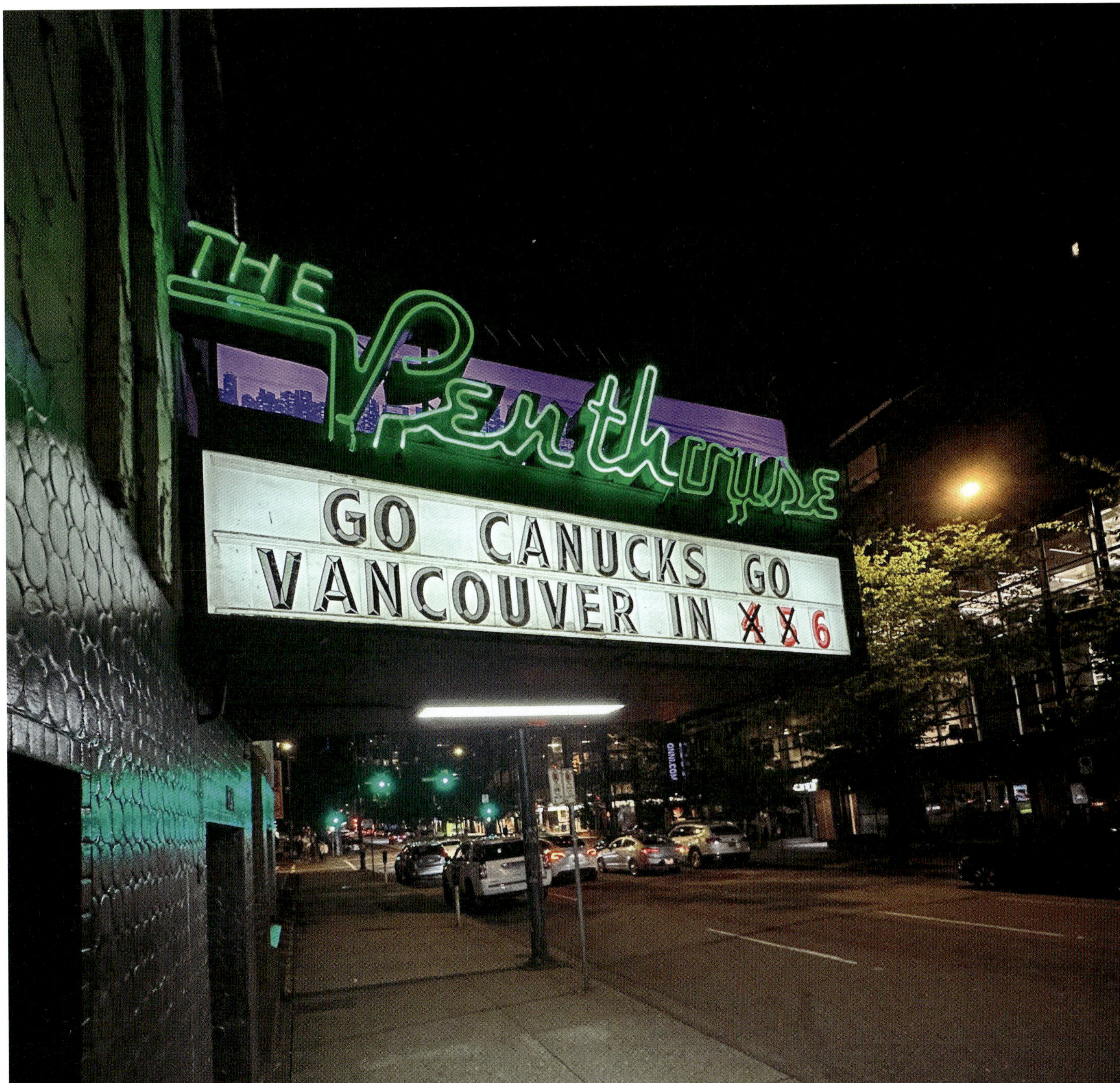
THE Penthouse
GO CANUCKS GO
VANCOUVER IN 456

CANUCKS DRINK FREE (AFTER YOU WIN 1)

At the start of the Canucks 2022 season, with an 0–7 start, and seven straight losses, two in overtime.

This sign went up after they'd had four losses in a row. The Canucks kept losing so I thought we maybe should take it down — like we were adding to the problem. It got shared on social media a lot, particularly on Reddit. Once they finally won a game, I added with letters below it, "Bottoms Up!"

"If you've lived in Vancouver for any amount of time, you have your version of the good old days. For me it was when CFOX was at 1006 Richards Street, with the Bulldog Café across the street, and that crazy lady with all the birdhouses in her tiny yard next to Richards on Richards. You could probably find an unknown singer named Michael Bublé at BaBalu's up the street, just past the iconic Penthouse Nightclub. Who would have guessed the Penthouse would outlast them all. Truly a Vancouver treasure, still relevant and still entertaining."

— Jeff O'Neill, CFOX On-Air Host / The Jeff O'Neill Show

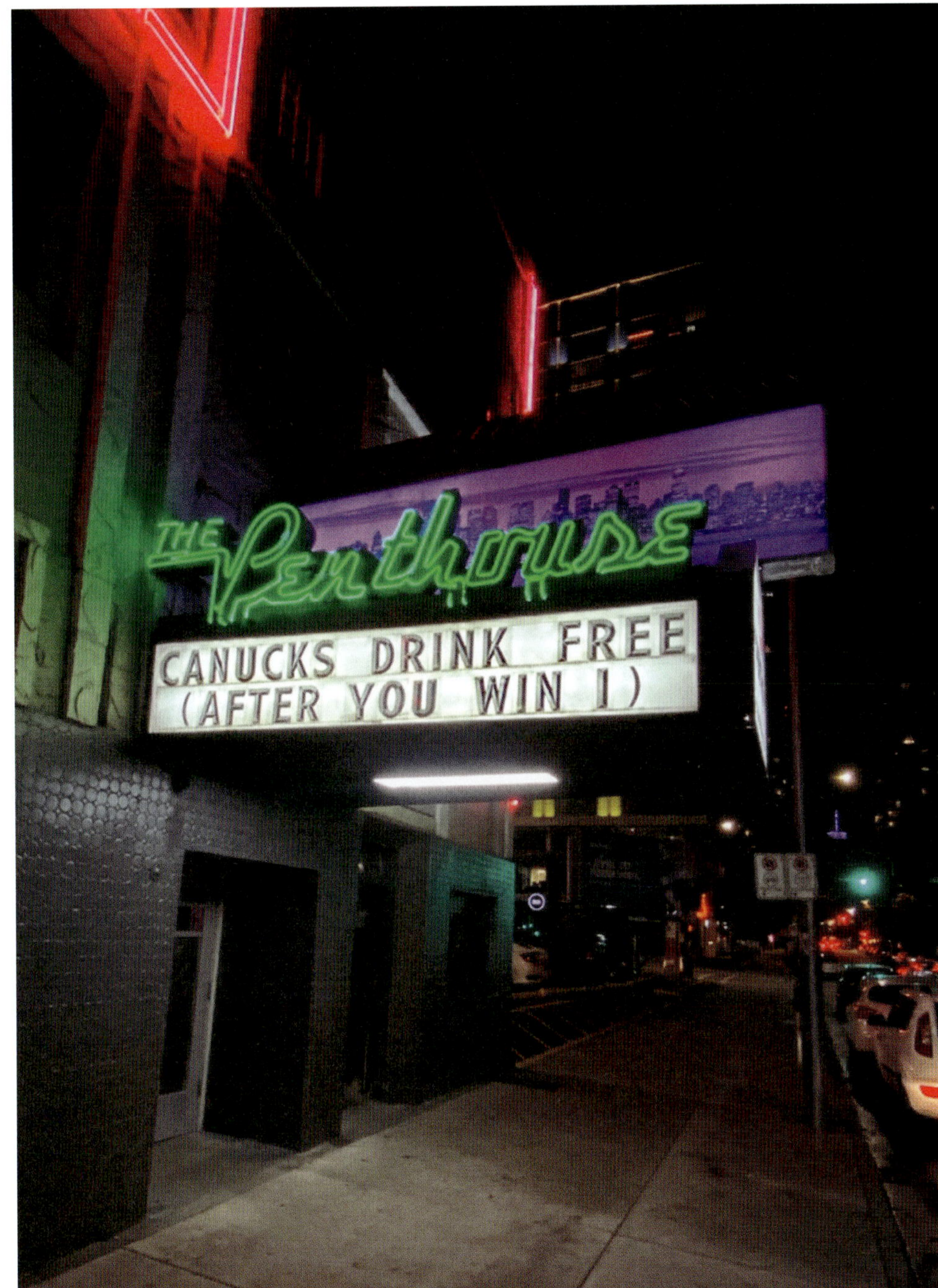

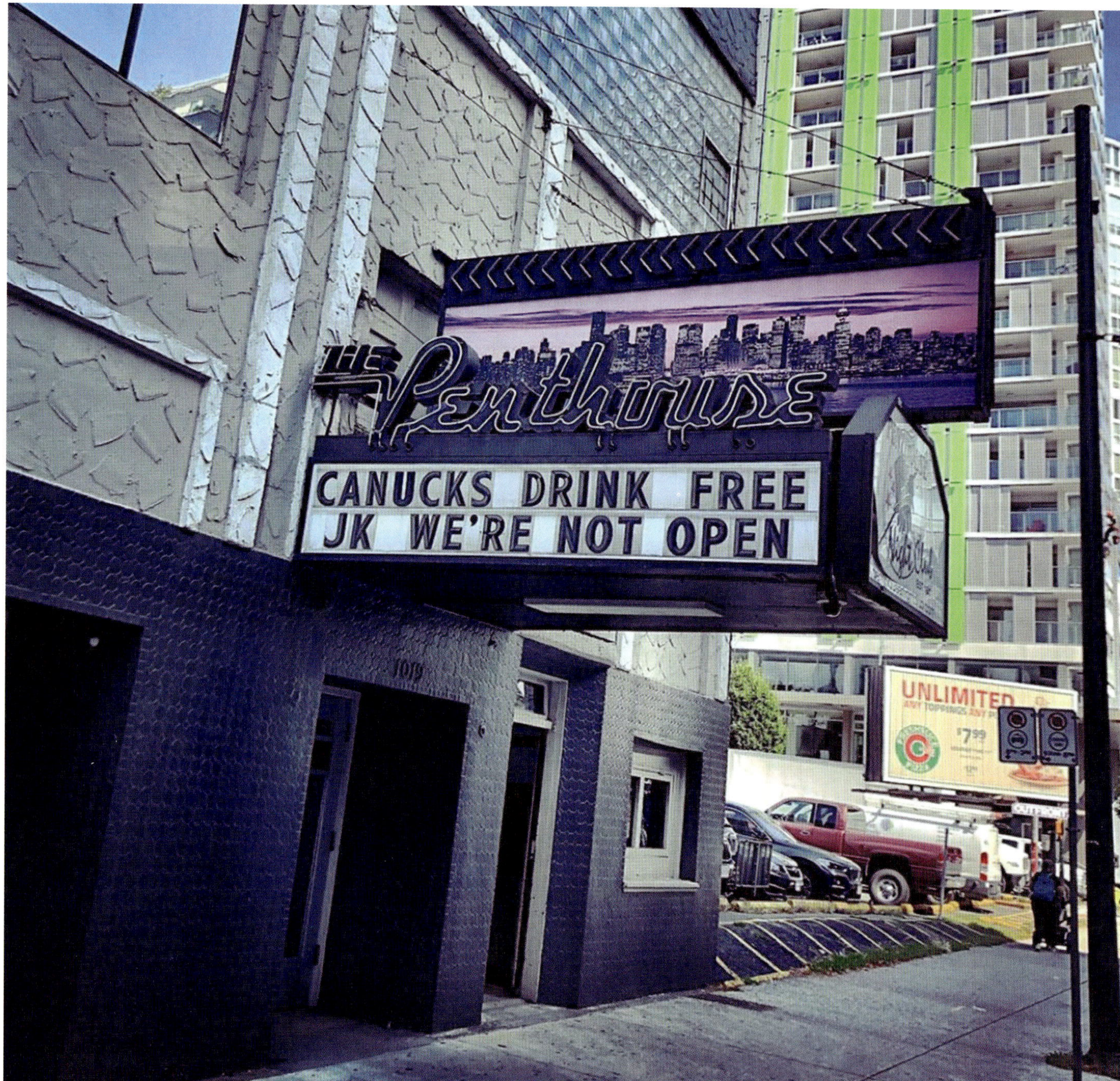
THE Penthouse
CANUCKS DRINK FREE
JK WE'RE NOT OPEN
UNLIMITED

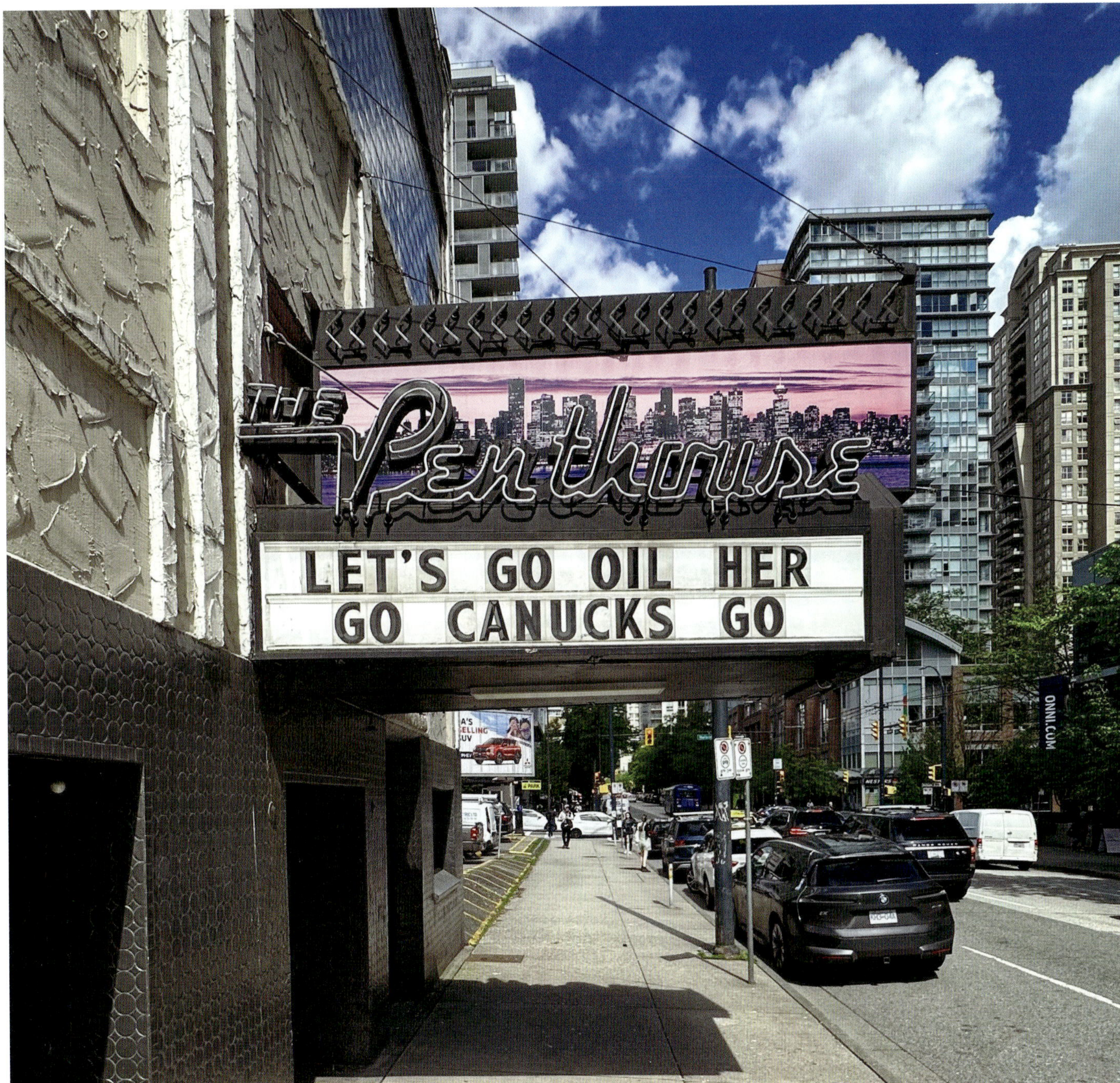
THE Penthouse
LET'S GO OIL HER
GO CANUCKS GO
ONNI.COM

SHE DON'T HAWK TUAH
I DON'T TALK TUAH

In 2024, Haliey Welch ("The 'Hawk Tuah' girl") became an internet celebrity after her onomatopoeia catch-phrase made during a street interview went viral on TikTok. And overnight her phrase seemed to be on everyone's lips:

That one went crazy, and people constantly reposted and shared it. Anything that starts trending that big in the world, I try to get my take on it up on the sign the same day, or as soon as I can. I gather she does a podcast called Talk Tuah now. I'm ready to be a guest on the show if she needs me.

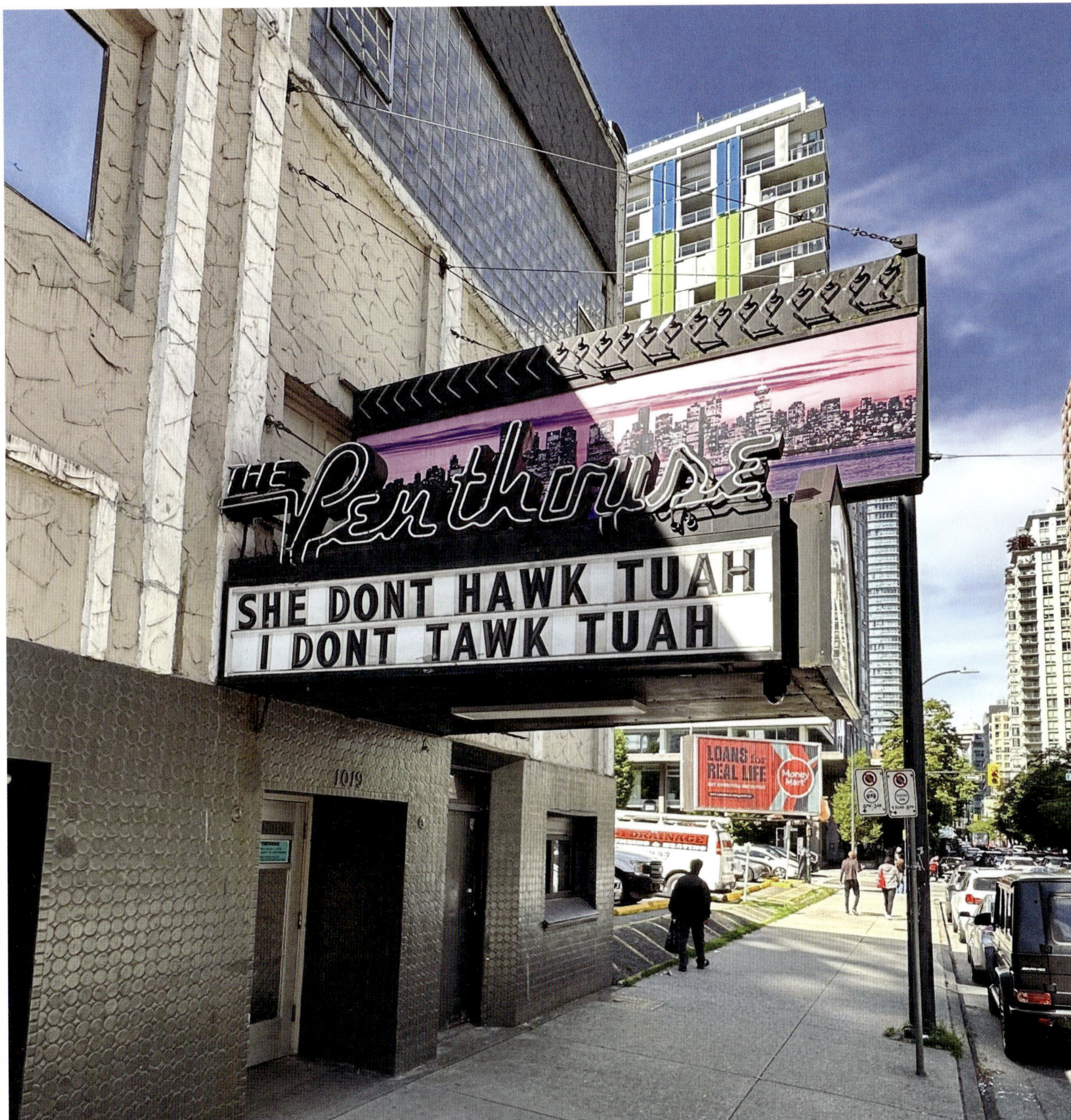
THE Penthouse
SHE DONT HAWK TUAH
I DONT TAWK TUAH
1019
LOANS for REAL LIFE
Money Mart

HIRING BREAKDANCERS
NO EXP. REQUIRED

Breakdancing became an Olympic event at the 2024 Paris Summer Games. The competition came under scrutiny after Australian competitor Rachel "Raygun" Gunn's performance which garnered — rightly or wrongly — some considerable scorn and mockery. But Raygun will always be a winner in the hearts of the Penthouse.

Part of the trick of writing the signs is that there's limited type space. I try to avoid abbreviations, and it can sometimes be tough to choose which word to abbreviate. I couldn't fit in the whole word "Experience". So that was it — and at the time of the competition, I thought it got a good-natured response.

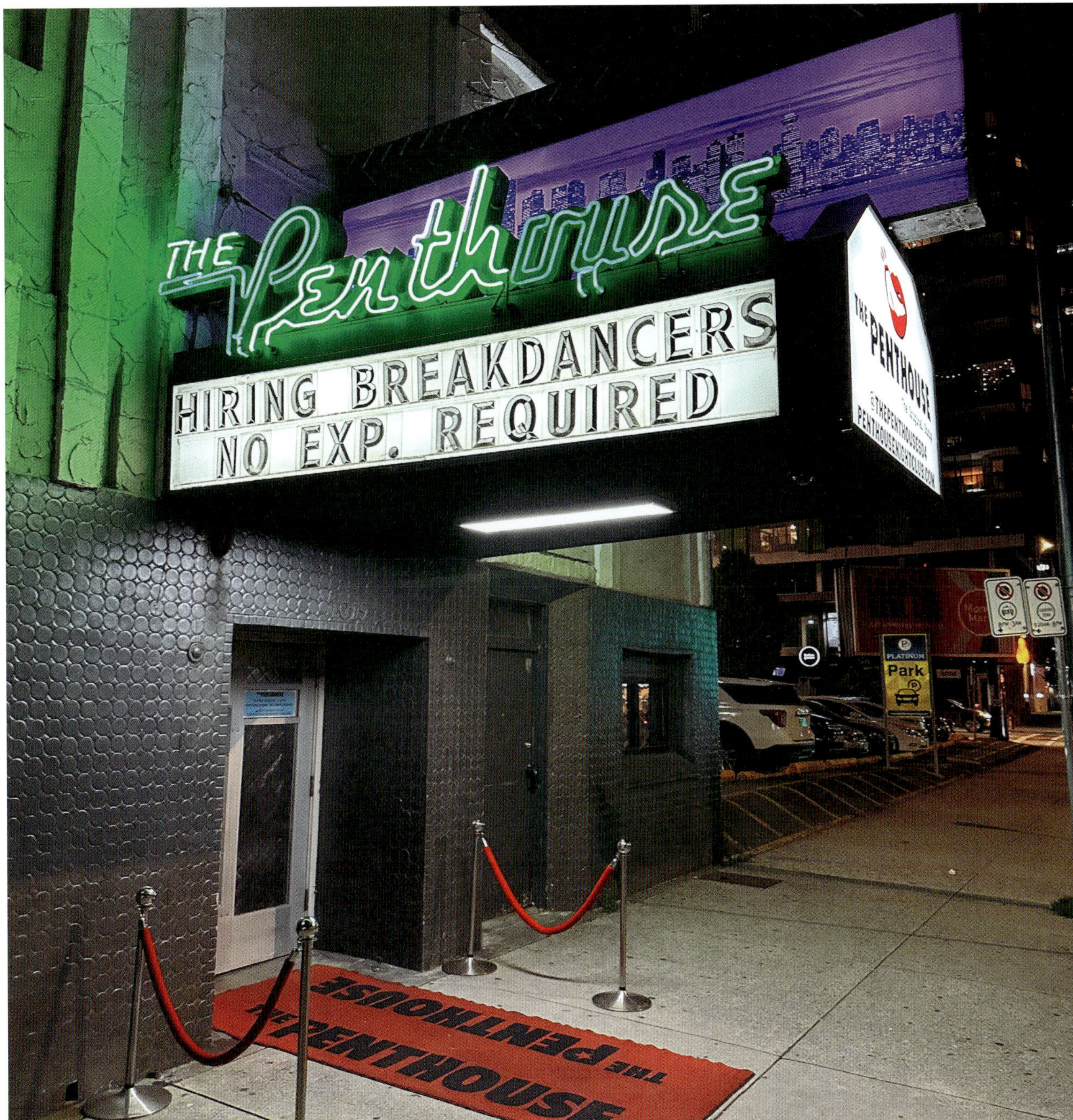

THE Penthouse
HIRING BREAKDANCERS
NO EXP. REQUIRED
THE PENTHOUSE
@THEPENTHOUSE604
PENTHOUSENIGHTCLUB.COM
PLATINUM
Park
THE PENTHOUSE

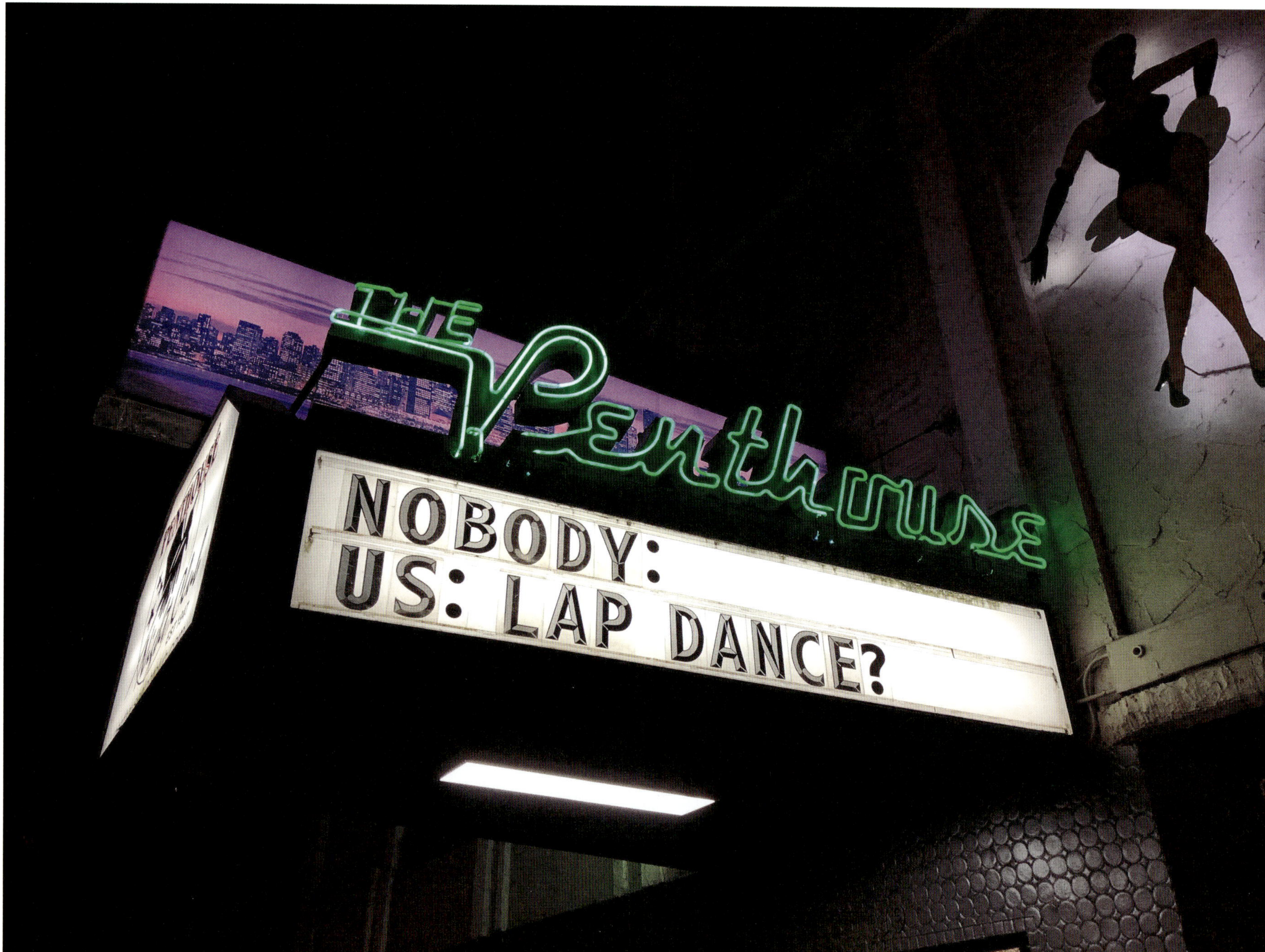
THE Penthouse
NOBODY:
US: LAP DANCE?

“As a lifelong Vancouverite, I’ve been in awe of the historic Penthouse Nightclub and its distinctive marquee ever since I was old enough to drive down Seymour Street. It’s always been a landmark in the Vancouver club scene! But in the last many years, what started out as an inflection point to amuse commuters on a one-way street during the gloomy 2020 lockdown, has turned into a monster — of global proportions! Kudos to Ben the Sign Guy for bringing new eyes around the world to the iconic Penthouse!”

— Joe Leary, the Chat Room at Tyrant Studios host/Sportsnet 650AM

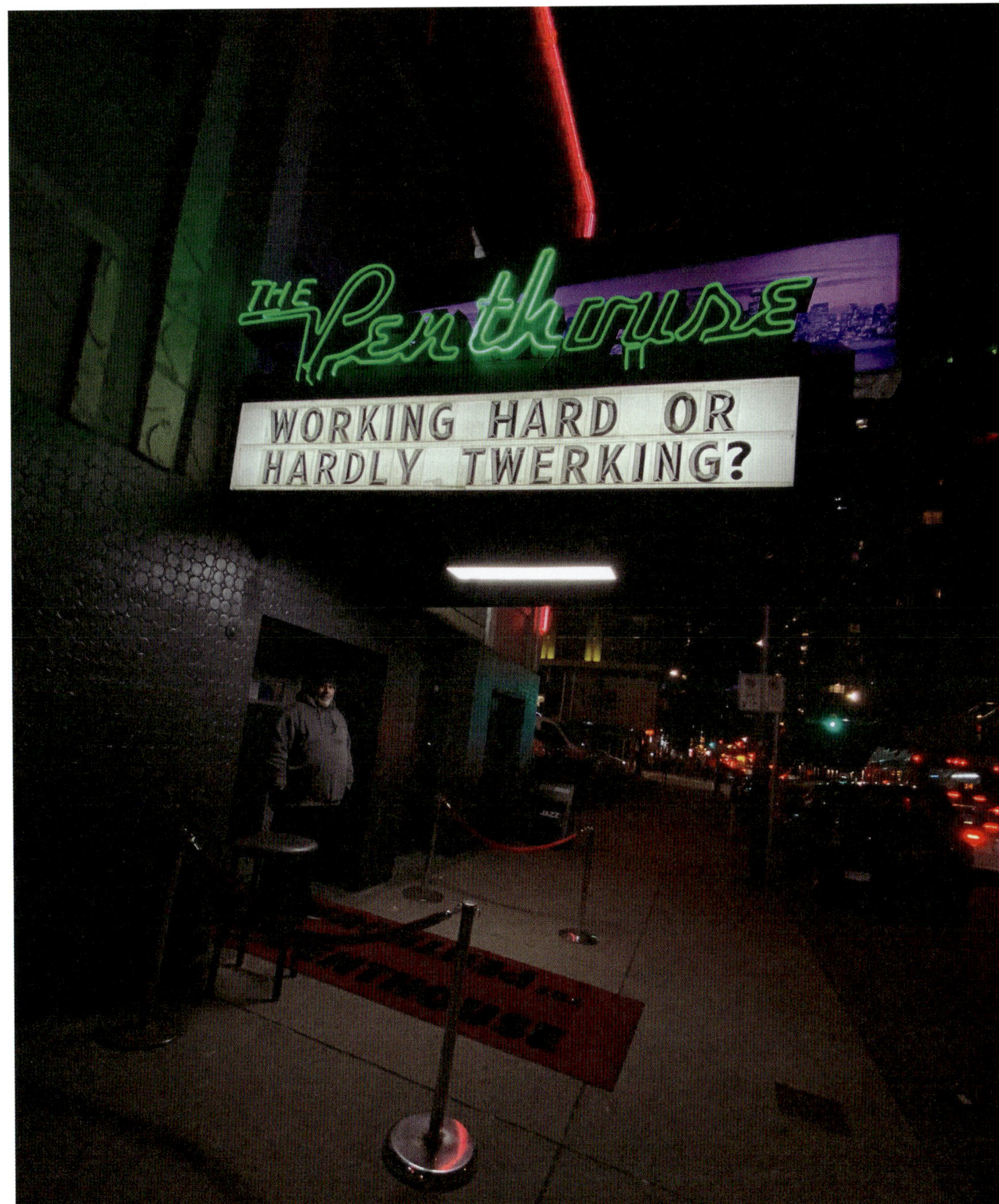

REMEMBER ICQ? NO? HAVE YOUR ID READY

ICQ was one of the world's first popular instant messaging programs, allowing users to chat in real time, which became popular in the late 1990s and early 2000s. One must be 19+ to enter an establishment like the Penthouse, and this sign from 2018 almost helped determine age better than BC approved identification.

Some people stopped me to ask, "I don't get the joke," and I said if you don't remember it, that's why we'll need to see ID!

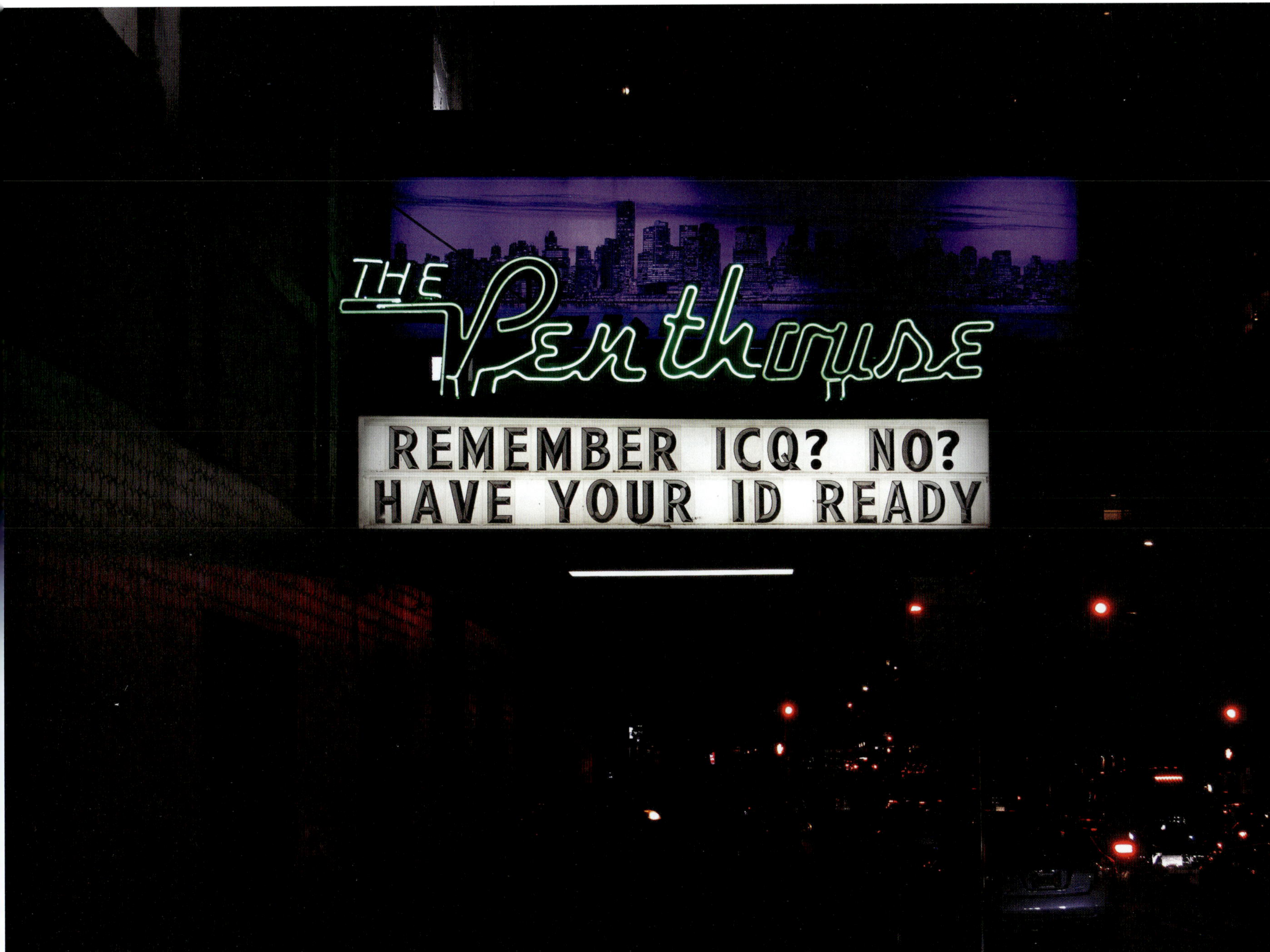
THE Penthouse
REMEMBER ICQ? NO?
HAVE YOUR ID READY

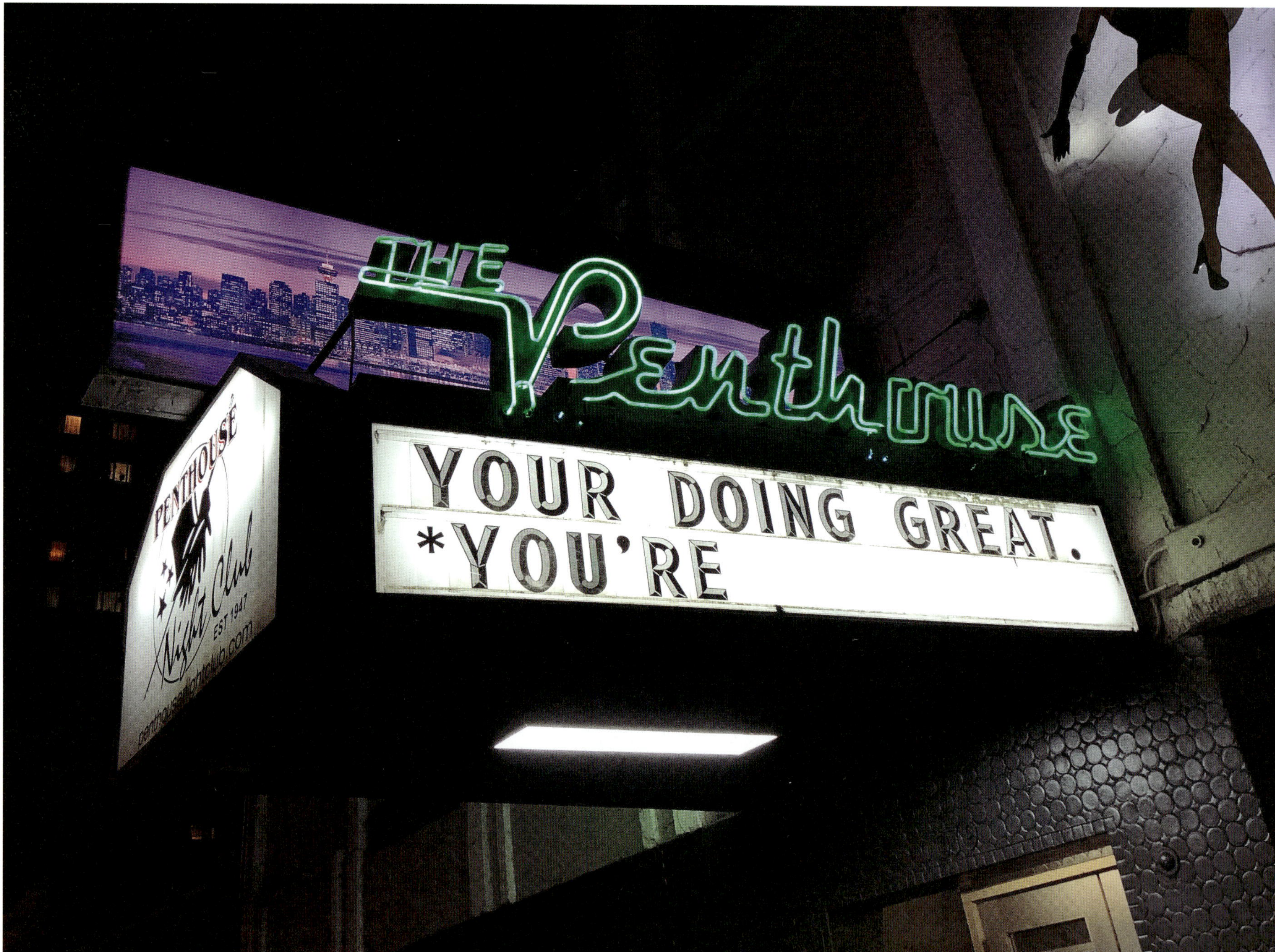
THE Penthouse
YOUR DOING GREAT.
*YOU'RE
PENTHOUSE
Night Club
EST 1947
penthousenightclub.com

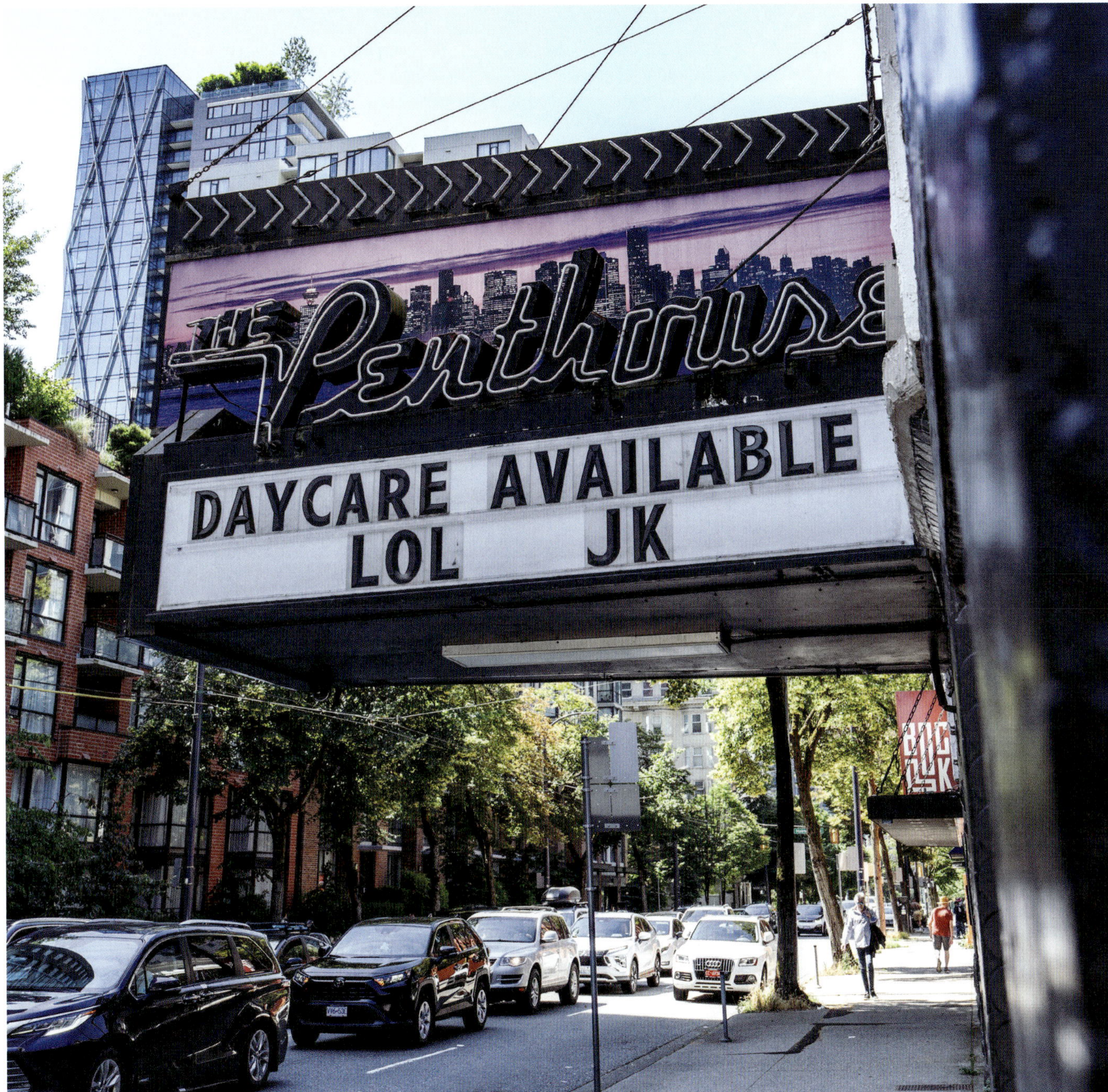
The Penthouse
DAYCARE AVAILABLE
LOL JK

SHE CALLED IN THICC TWERKING FROM HOME

The Merriam-Webster dictionary defines "Thicc" as a slang term that means, "Attractively full-figured; thickset." Used to compliment curvy women or brawny men.

I was heading to the club, thinking about it. I originally had a couple of other versions, and I didn't think any of them were going to fit on the sign. The club's dancers loved this one in particular!

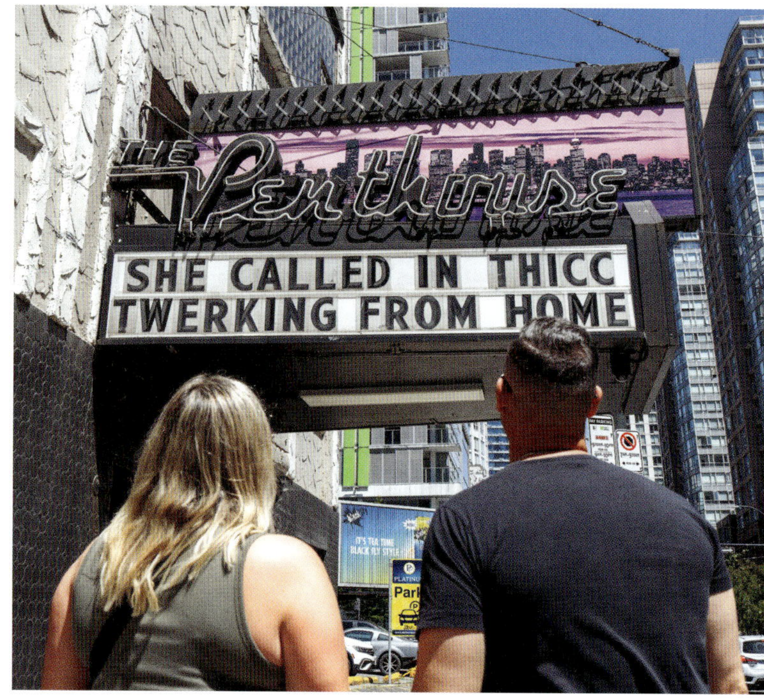

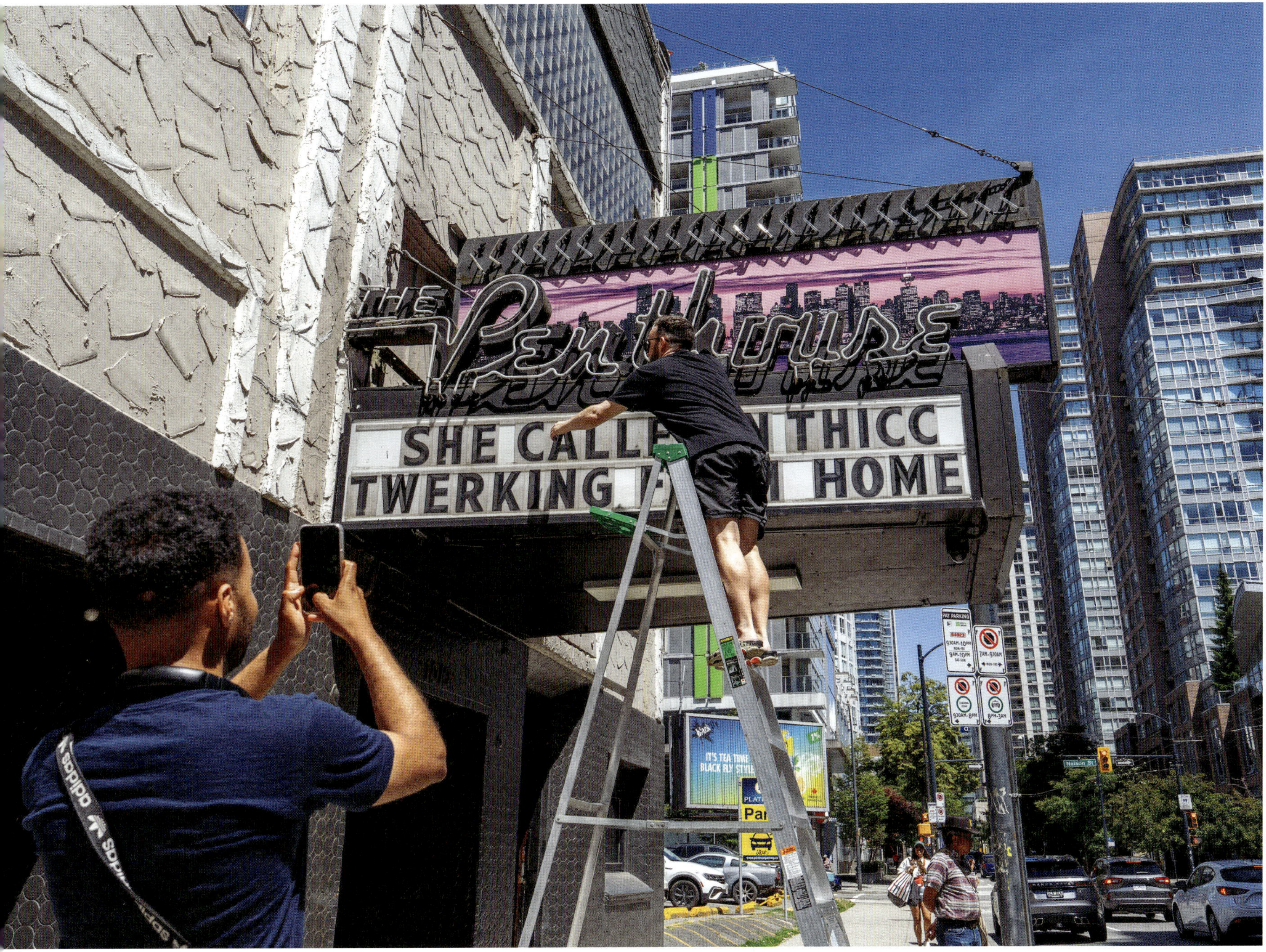
The Penthouse
SHE CALLE
THICC
TWERKING
HOME
IT'S TEA TIME
Nelson St

MAKING LAP DANCES AFFORDALBE SINCE '47

It's almost forgotten now, but in December 2024 a local realtor named Ian Watt, apparently in an effort to raise his profile, put up a billboard down off Expo Boulevard that read, "Ian Watt – Making Yaletown Unaffordable since 2005". Watt caught considerable negative attention for his actions, and claimed he was just "being honest about the economic landscape in Yaletown for young people," and that he was trying to be ironic. When local news media spotlighted the sign, the real estate company Watt worked for quickly had it removed.

Let it be known, however, that The Penthouse has always been a friend to the honest working Joe and Joely, always trying to help the little guy out there.

“The sign is such a trademark of the city these days. I love how much attention has been brought to our House.”

— Molly Malone, Premier Exotic Dancer at the Penthouse

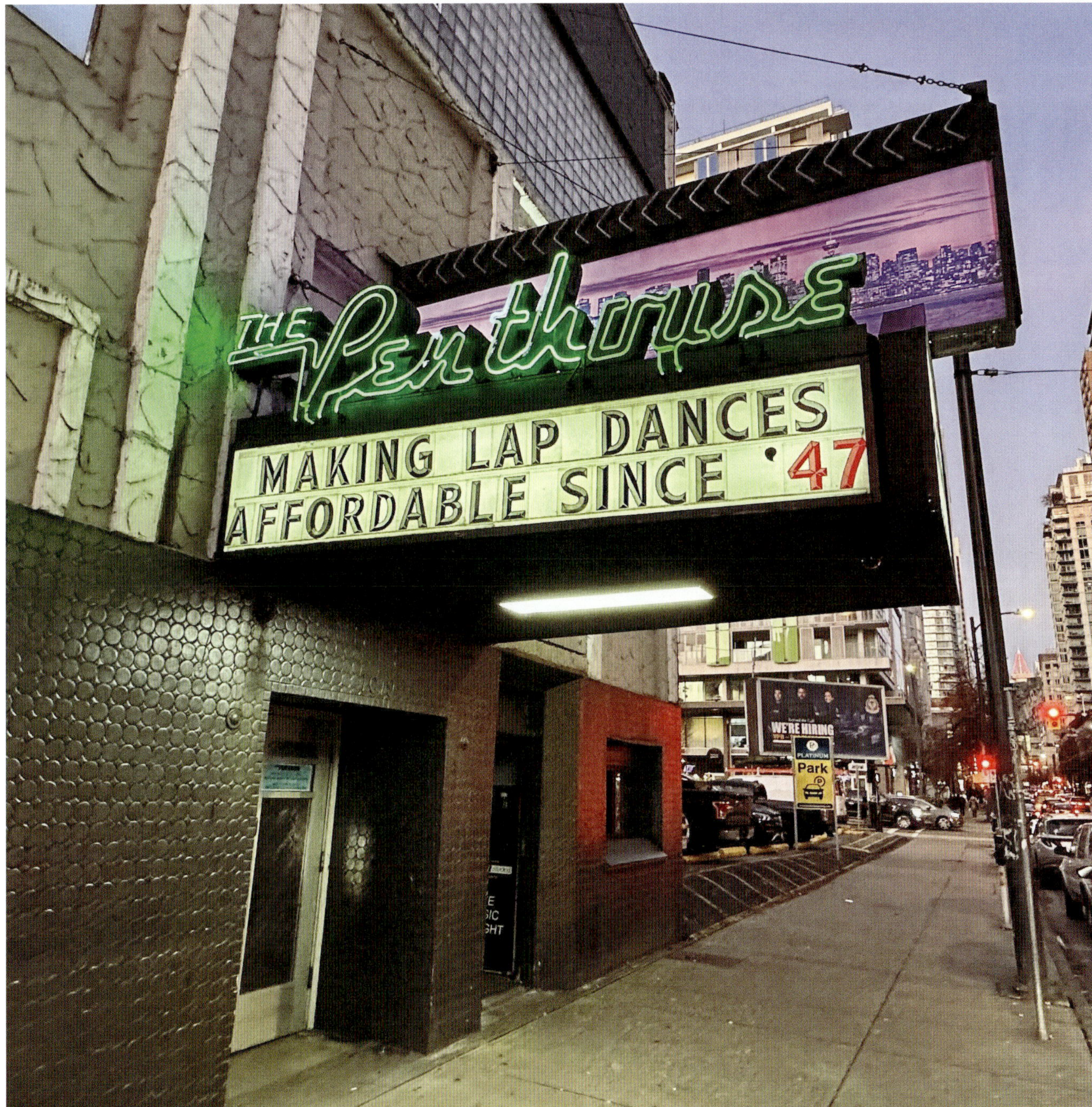

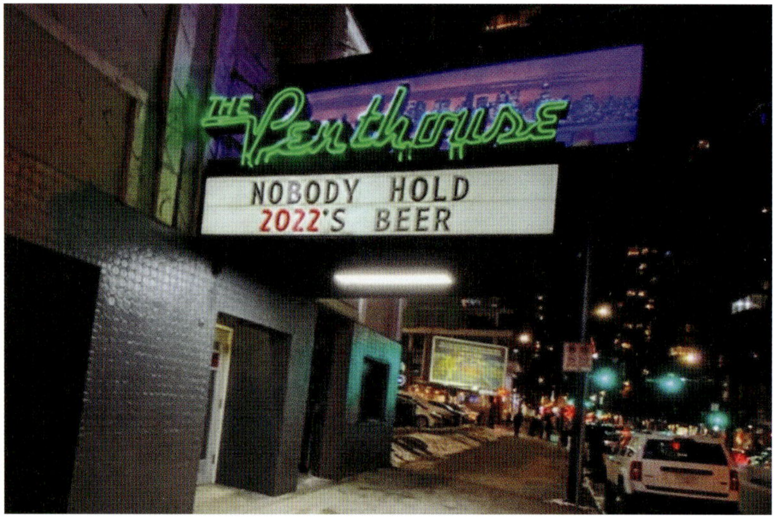
THE Penthouse
NOBODY HOLD
2022'S BEER

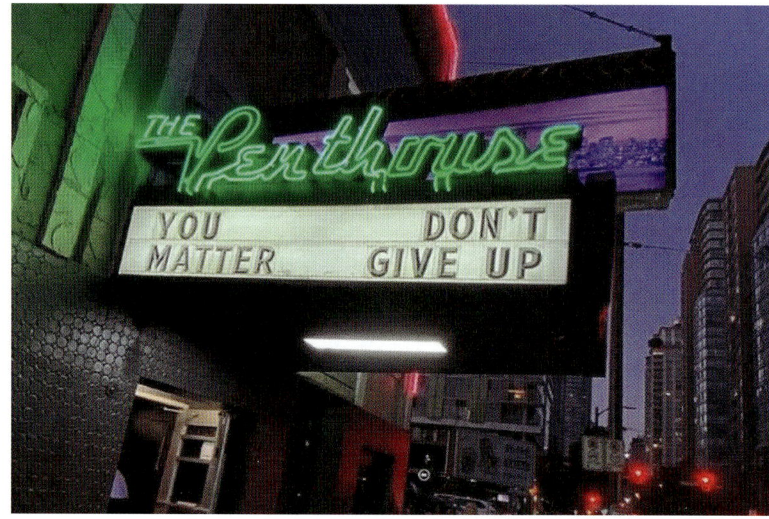
THE Penthouse
YOU DON'T
MATTER GIVE UP

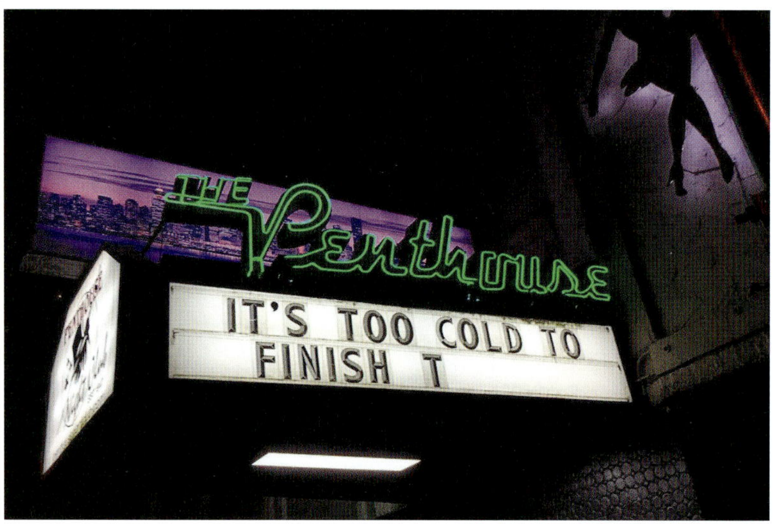
THE Penthouse
IT'S TOO COLD TO
FINISH T

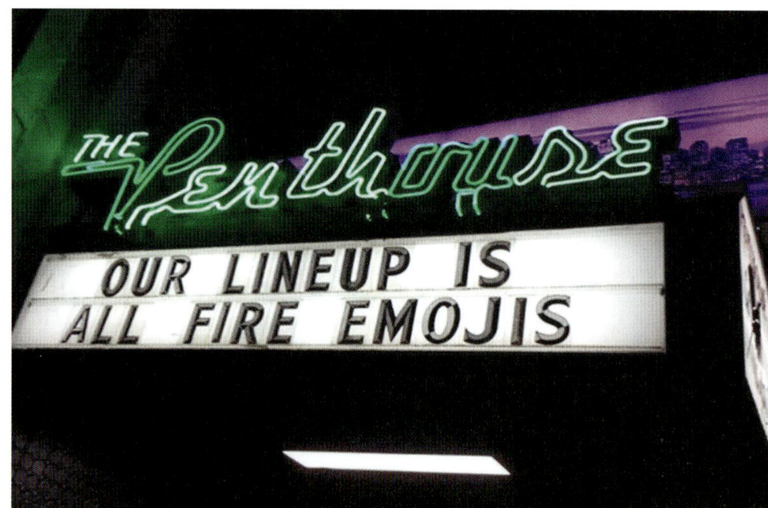
THE Penthouse
OUR LINEUP IS
ALL FIRE EMOJIS

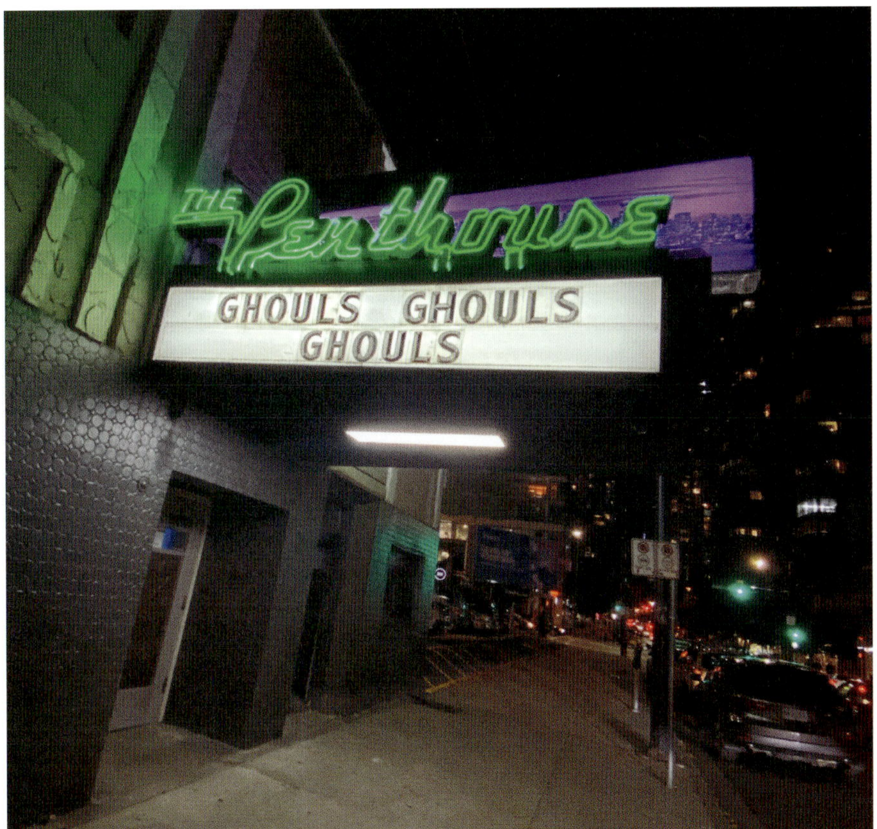
THE Penthouse
GHOULS GHOULS
GHOULS

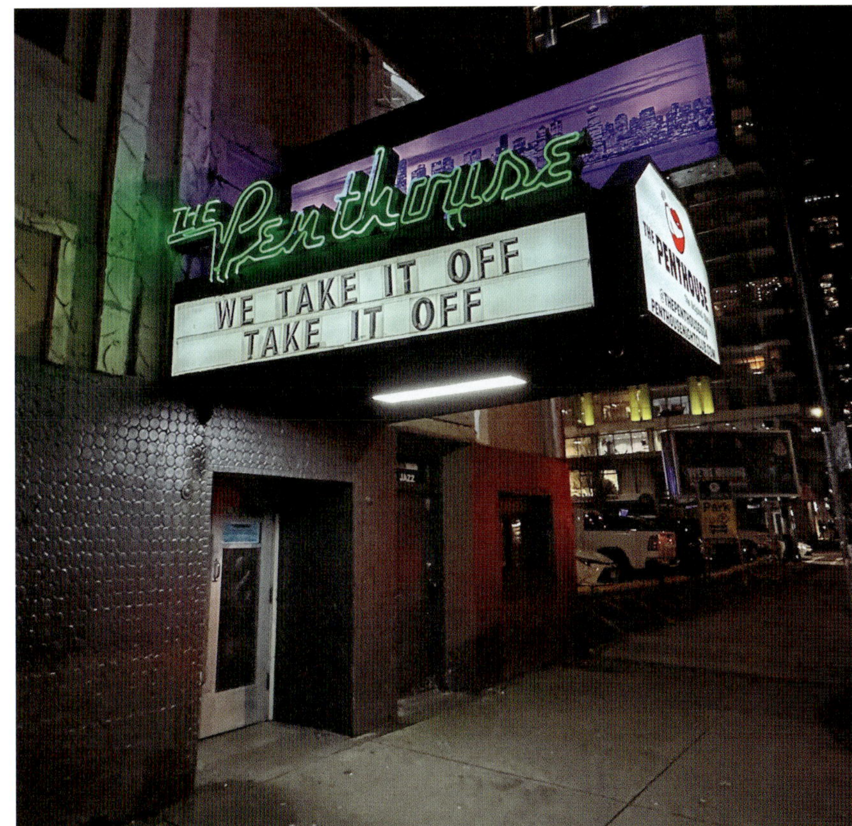
THE Penthouse
WE TAKE IT OFF
TAKE IT OFF
THE PENTHOUSE

AT LEAST SHE WON'T BE AT THE KC GAME

Taylor Swift's "Era's" concert tour — the highest grossing concert tour of all time — concluded with three final dates in Vancouver in December 2024. Swifties from across the planet flew into Vancouver to attend the final concert dates, and the event became the lead story in BC news.

When Taylor Swift first started dating Travis Kelce from the Kansas City Chiefs, she was going to every game. It was obviously big news, and a ratings boost for the NFL — they suddenly had a lot of new viewers on the games. But a lot of regular NFL fans thought the coverage went overboard — I mean, they were following her every move, tracking her private flight in the pre-game show, the route to the stadium — and every time the Chiefs scored a touchdown they cut to her VIP booth for her reaction. Sports fans got tired of it in a hurry — this had nothing to do with the game. If the team scored, why not show the fans in the stadium, or the player's mom in attendance? It wasn't her fault — the media just overdid the coverage of it because it was new.

We're all football fans at the Penthouse, so with Taylor performing that Sunday at BC Place, the sign was just a little nod to the football community and a good-natured teasing of Swift and the Swifties.

But when images of that sign turned up on social media, some of the Swifties who'd flown to Vancouver caught wind of it and thought it was a jab. I even got some angry direct messages from fans who didn't get the joke. But a lot of Vancouverites commented online saying it wasn't a jab, and that the Penthouse marquee makes fun of everyone — even themselves. It was nice to see the public come to the sign's defence. It made me realize how fond people had become of the sign.

I don't know if Taylor ever saw the sign, or heard about it when she came into town.

On the other side of the marquee I had another sign that was a parody of her song "Shake It Off", that read "We Take it off! Take it off!"

I'd like to think if she did see it, and knowing what the Penthouse was, she'd laugh and roll her eyes. She seems like a good sport.

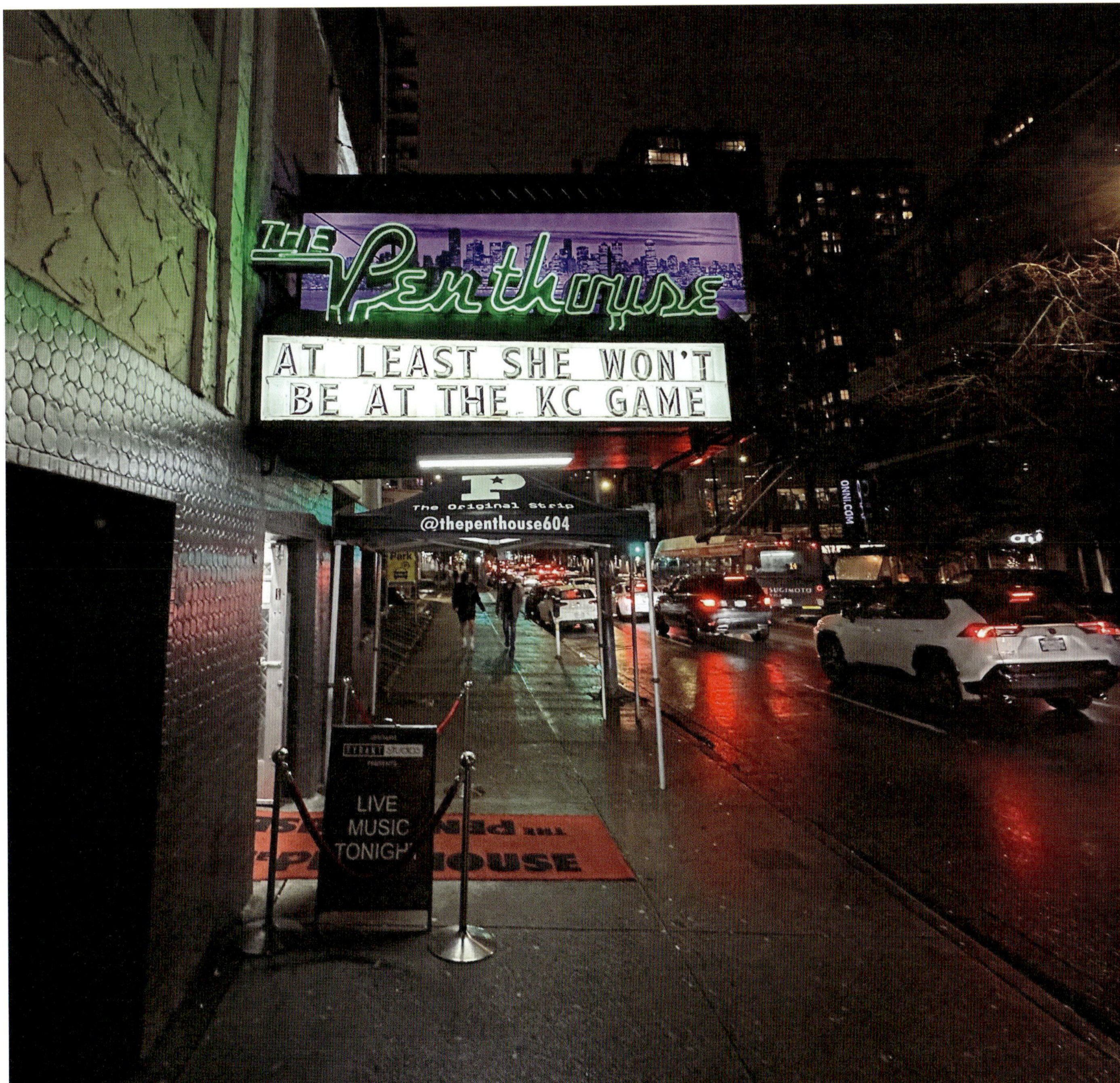
THE Penthouse
AT LEAST SHE WON'T
BE AT THE KC GAME
The Original Strip
@thepenthouse604
LIVE
MUSIC

WE STAND ON GUARD FOR WEED

The Cannabis Act took effect October 17th, 2018 and made Canada the second country in the world, after Uruguay, to formally legalize the cultivation, possession, acquisition, and consumption of cannabis and its by-products. Canada would be the first G7 and G20 nation to do so.

The morning that marijuana was legalized in Canada, I remember Danny [Filippone] called me, "What's the biggest story in the country right now?!", and encouraged me to think up a related sign. But I had to ask him, "Am I allowed to write something about weed?" I brainstormed a lot of different ideas, but it wasn't until around sundown that I thought of that line from the Canadian national anthem. We agreed that that was the one. Pictures of that sign got retweeted by a multitude of cannabis dispensaries that day.

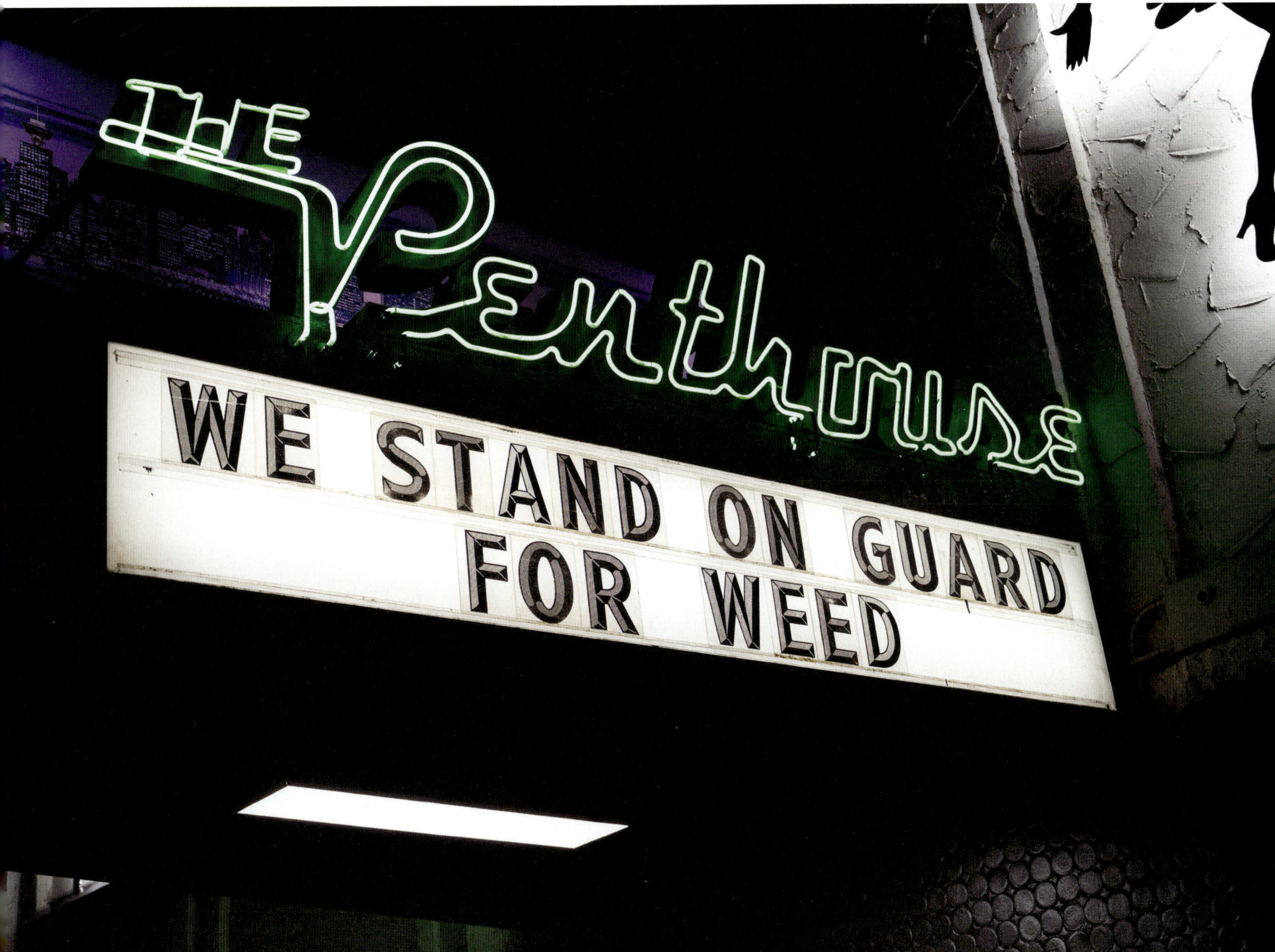
The Penthouse
WE STAND ON GUARD
FOR WEED

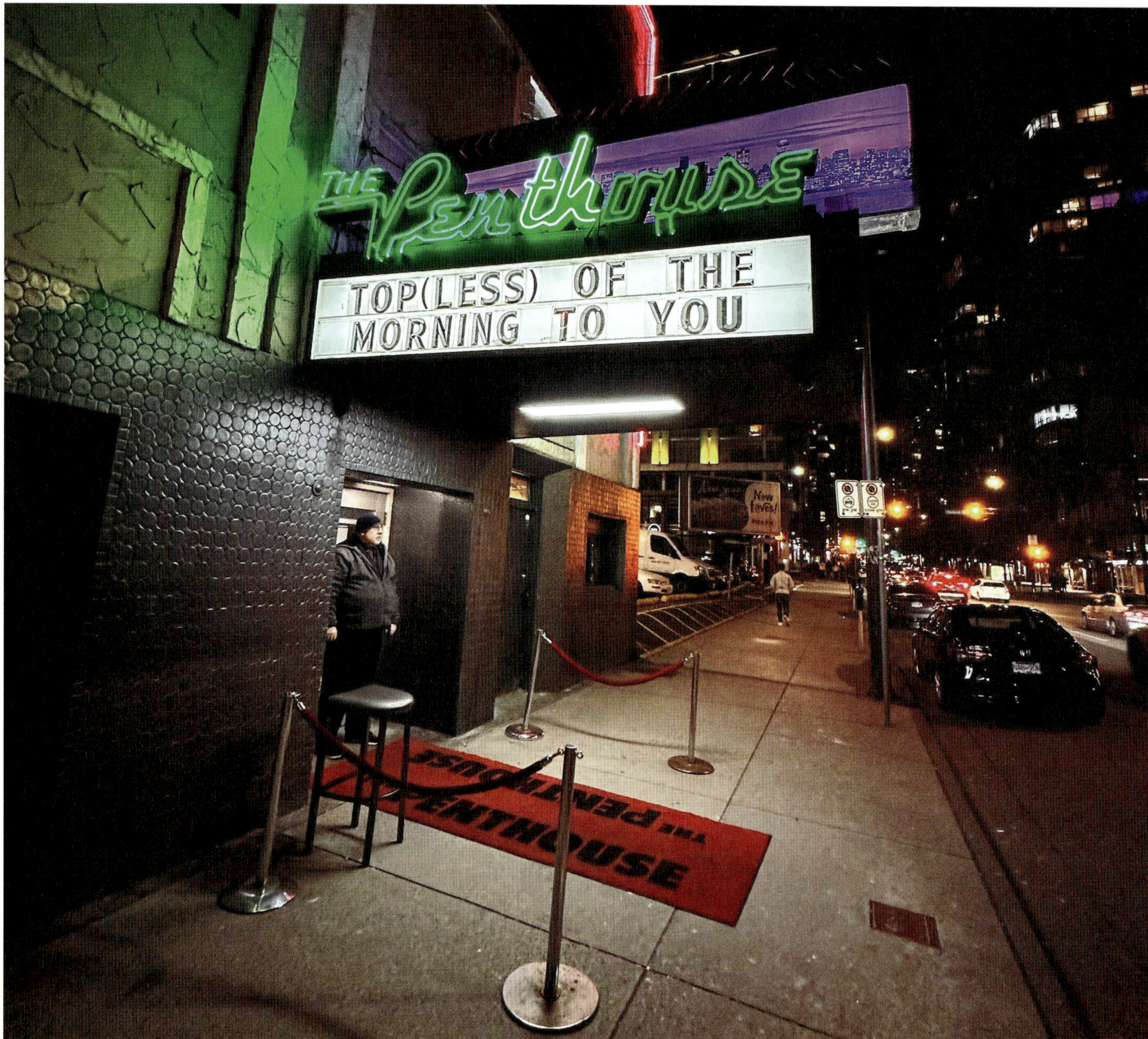

Happy St. Patrick's Day from the Penthouse Nightclub.

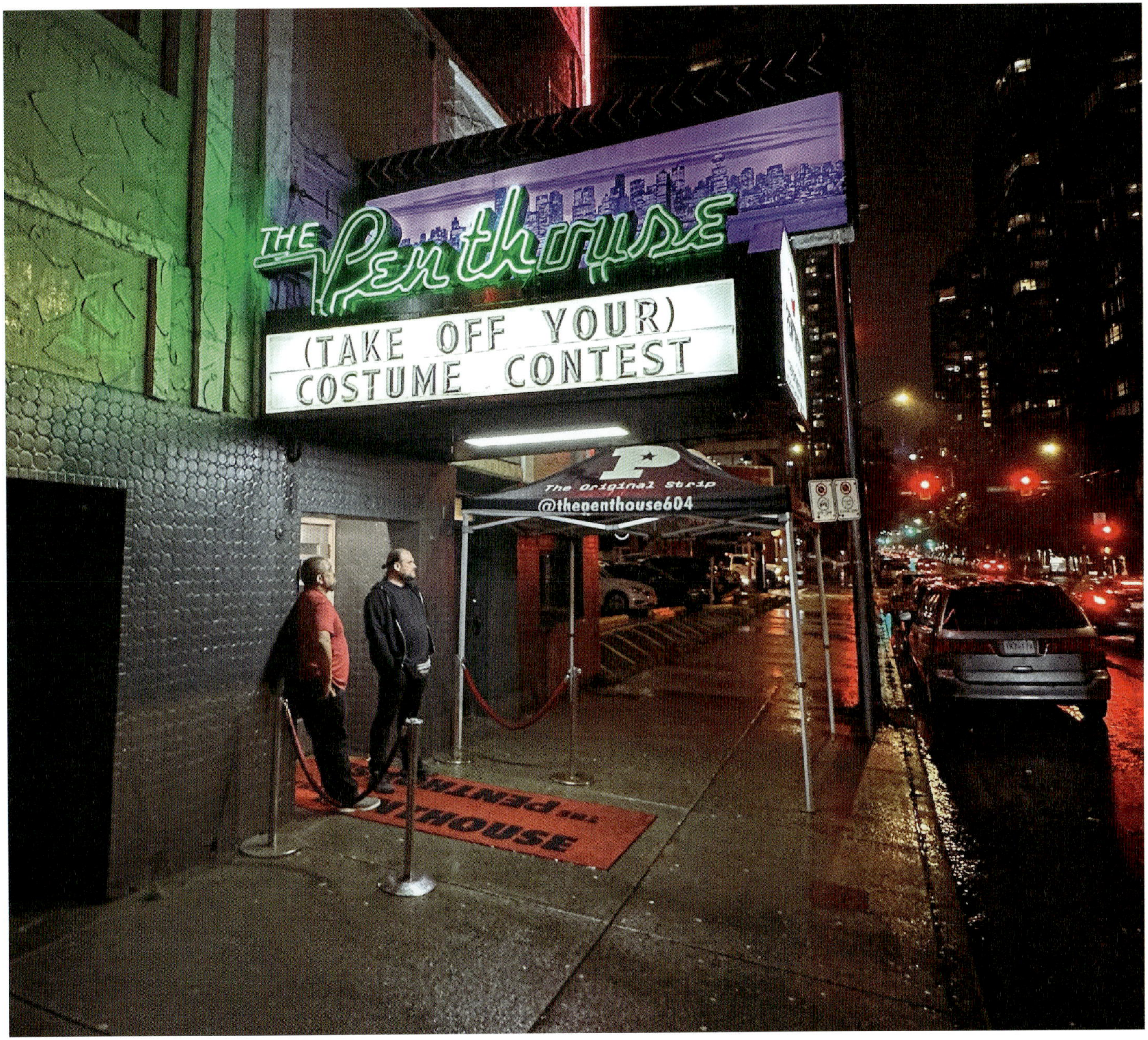

And Happy Hallowe'en from the Penthouse Nightclub, too.

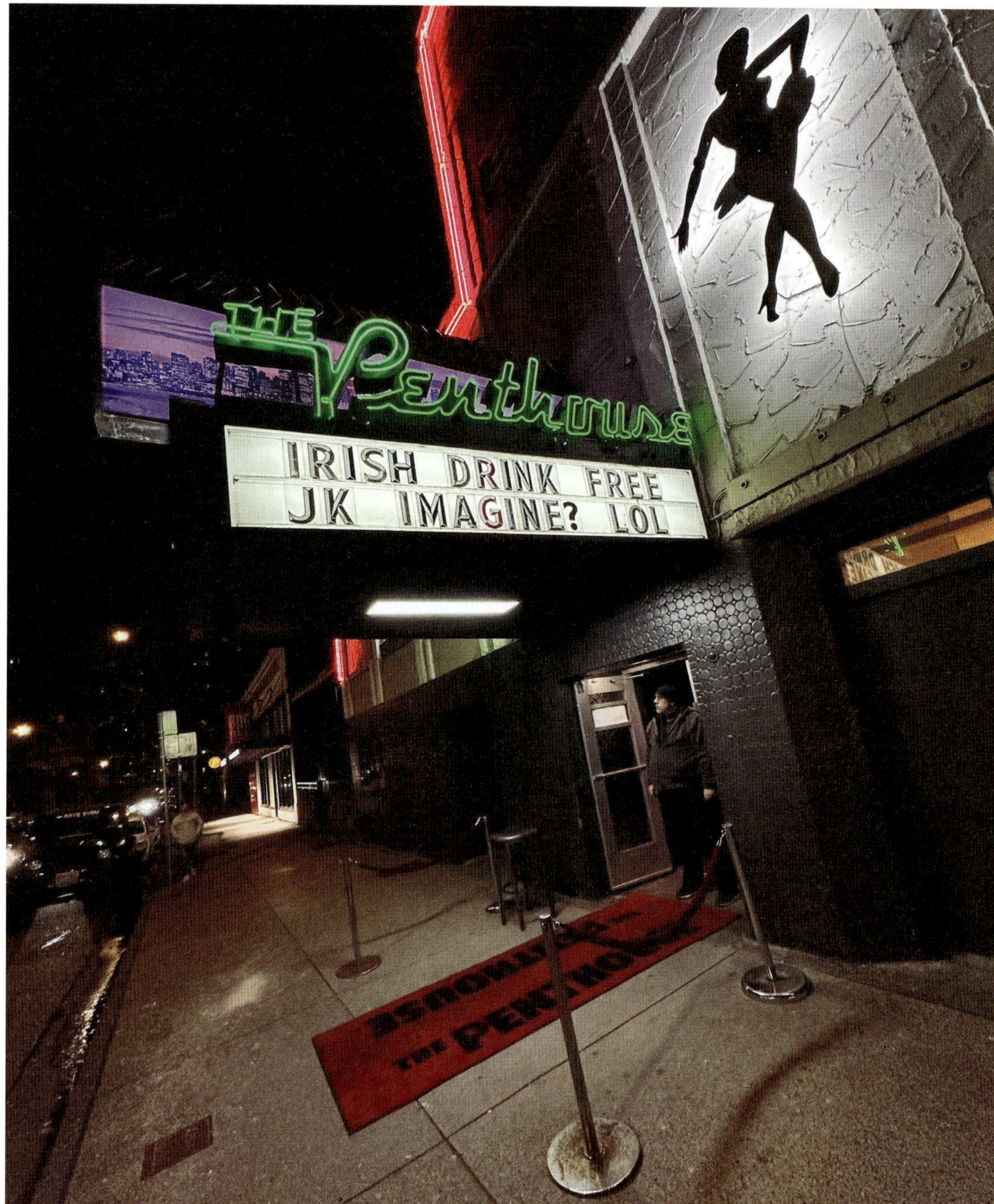
The Penthouse
IRISH DRINK FREE
JK IMAGINE? LOL

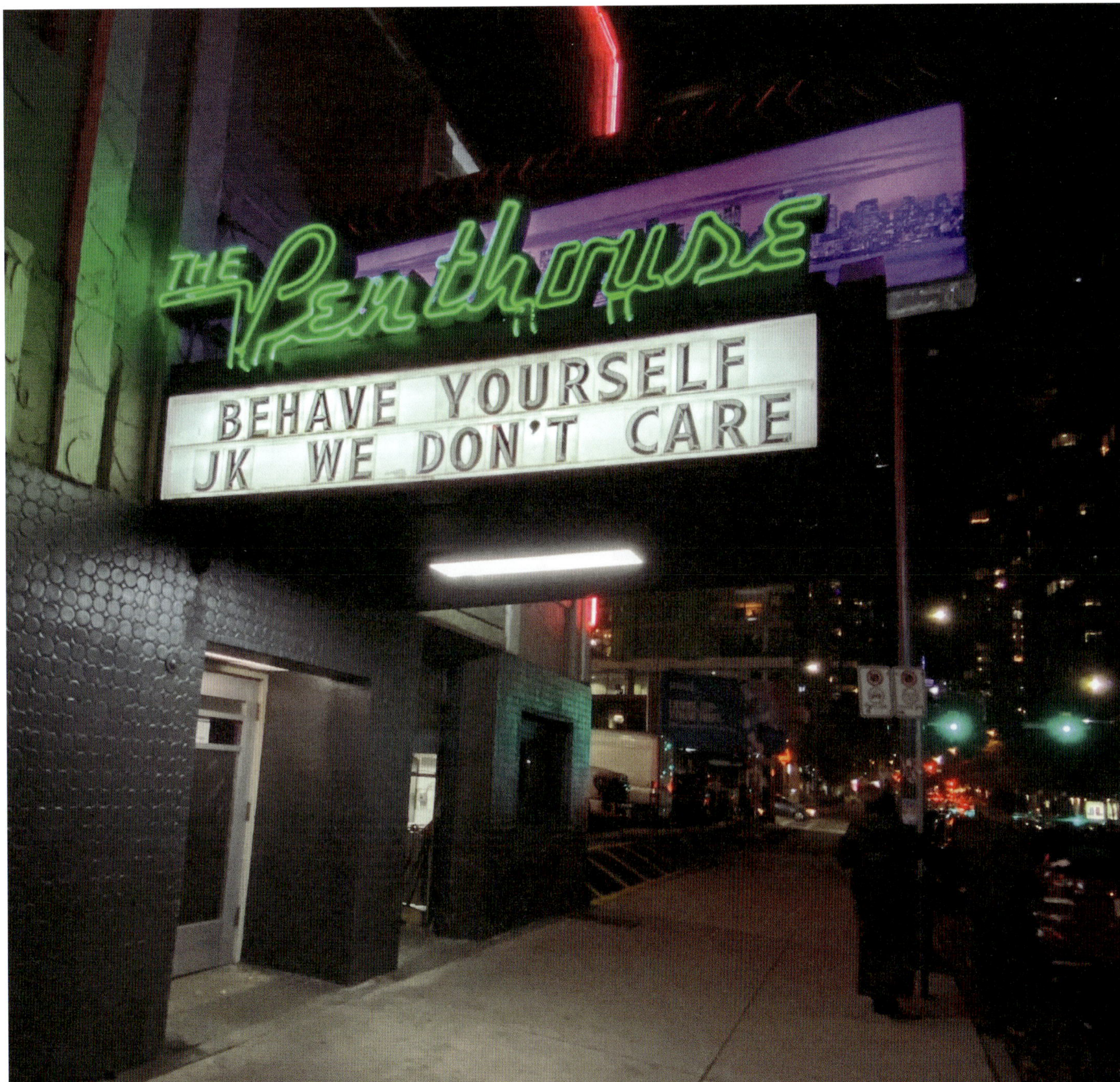
THE Penthouse
BEHAVE YOURSELF
JK WE DON'T CARE

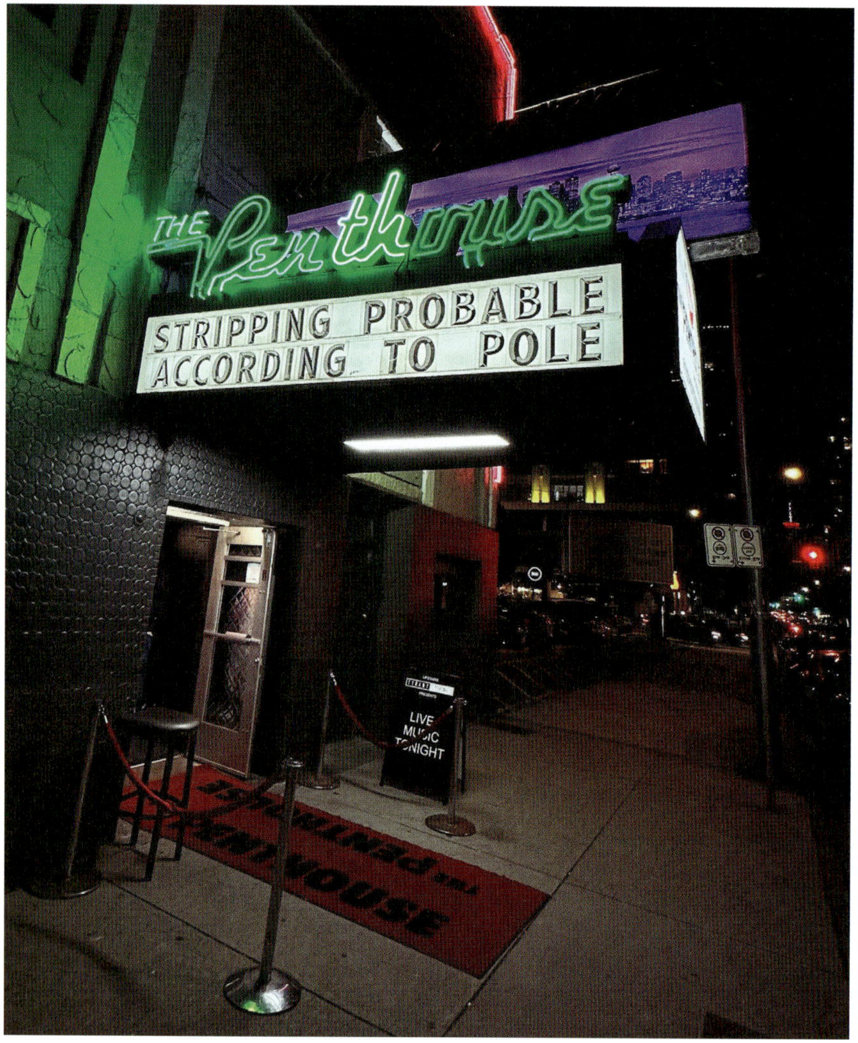
THE Penthouse
STRIPPING PROBABLE
ACCORDING TO POLE
LIVE
MUSIC
TONIGHT

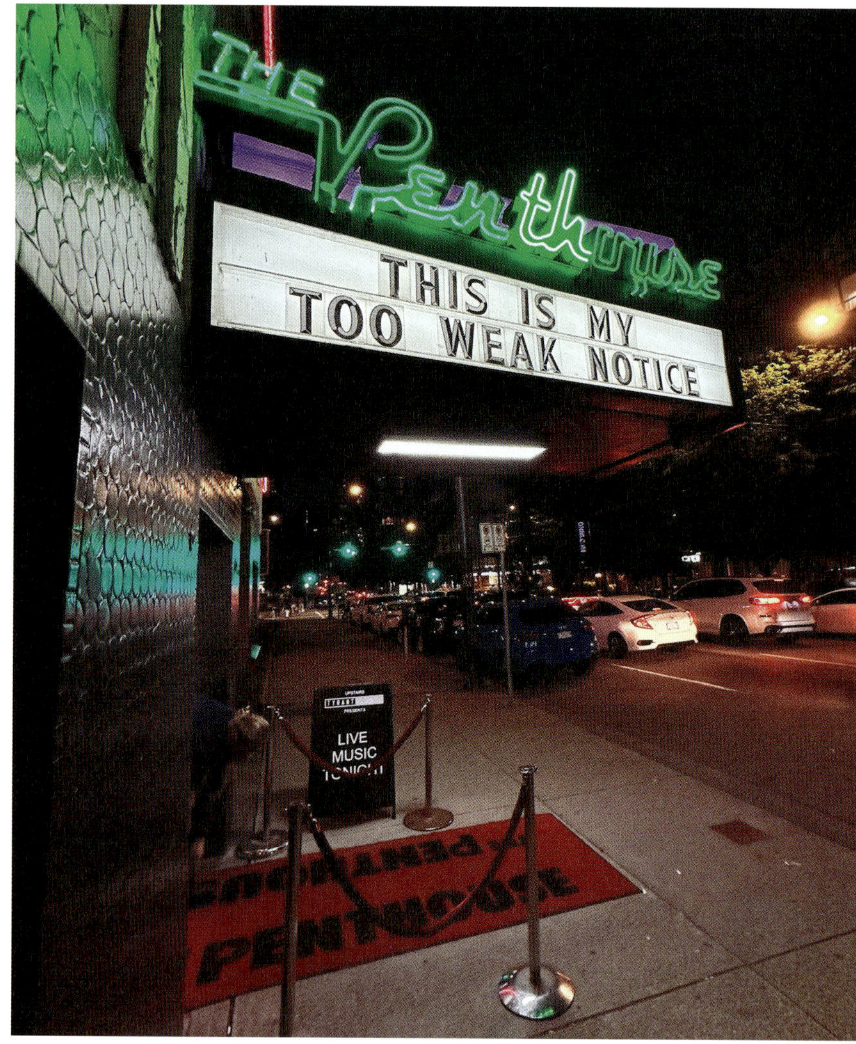
THE Penthouse
THIS IS MY
TOO WEAK NOTICE
LIVE
MUSIC
PENTHOUSE

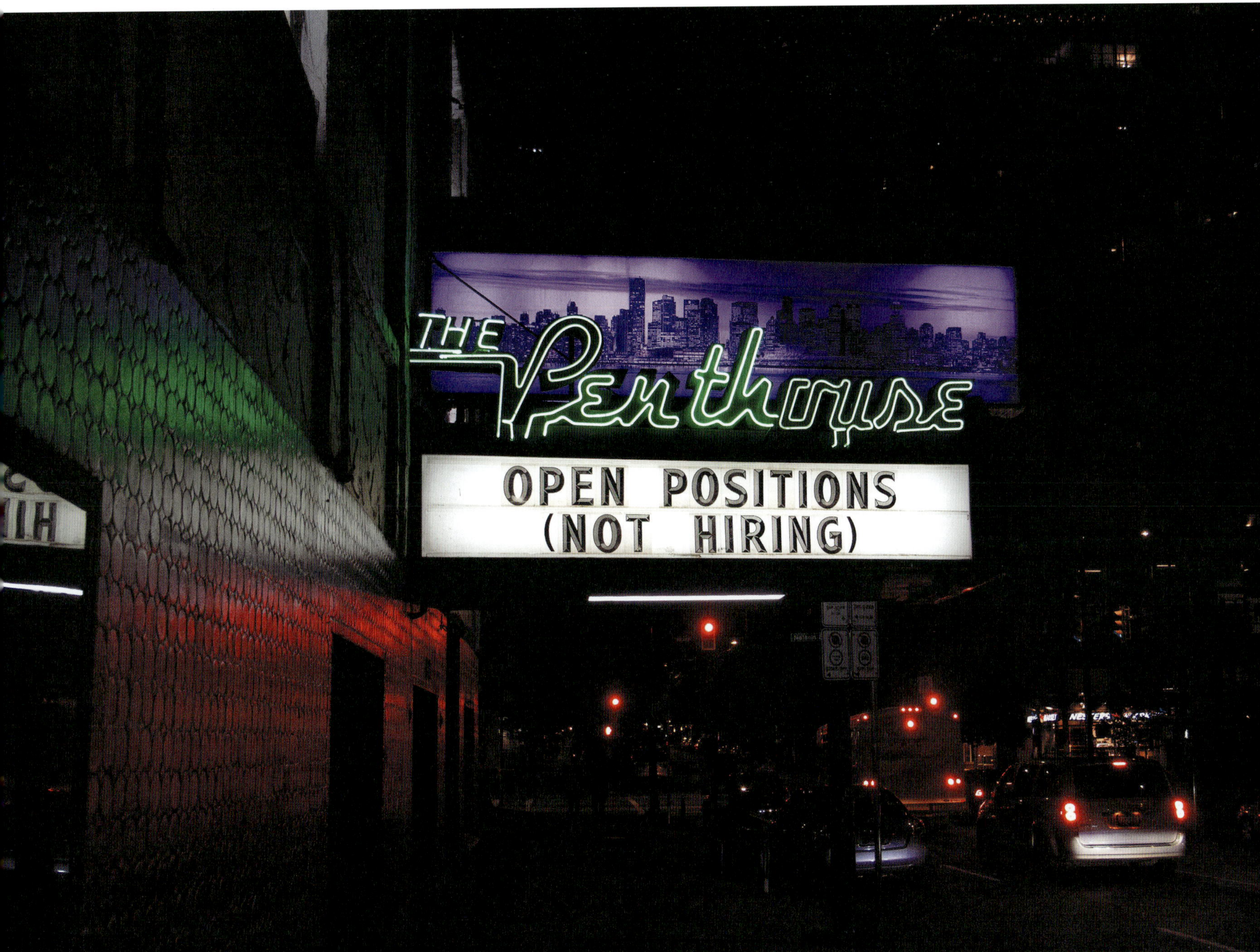
THE Penthouse
OPEN POSITIONS
(NOT HIRING)

F@#K YOU, HORVAT

Bo Horvat served as Captain of the Vancouver Canucks from 2019 until his infamous trade to the New York Islanders in 2023. Once traded, after a Home win against the Philadelphia Flyers in April 2023, a reporter asked him how the atmosphere and excitement of the building ranked for him playing for what was a playoff contender. He replied: "It's been unbelievable. It's a lot better than Vancouver, I can tell you that for free." The Penthouse marquee spoke up for the city that very evening, with the results scoring in overtime the next day.

I was at work when Horvat made the statement, and a lot of people were coming in that night to the Penthouse angry about it. It was a big post-game story. Danny and wife Jackie were in that night too, and Danny couldn't believe it. I said we should actually just put up a sign that reads: "Fuck You, Horvat". There was a lengthy discussion about whether or not we could get into legal trouble for that. Jackie talked us down, saying there was no way we should put that up, but about twenty minutes later I thought, wait, I've got the symbols and we can do a cartoon swear. I said to everyone, 'This has to go up tonight!'

I put the photo of the sign up on twitter that night too and tagged the Islanders with a note, "And I'll tell you that for free!"

The twitter post would garner 632,000 views and multiple stories from local television and radio media who covered the story. Horvat caught a lot of blowback for it, and apologized the next day saying he had nothing but respect for Vancouver and was caught up in the moment and off-guard by the interviewer's question. But a lot of people told me that the marquee and the attention it got was what really pushed Horvat to apologize. Or perhaps the story wouldn't have got the spotlight that it did, and we would have moved on and it would have been forgotten.

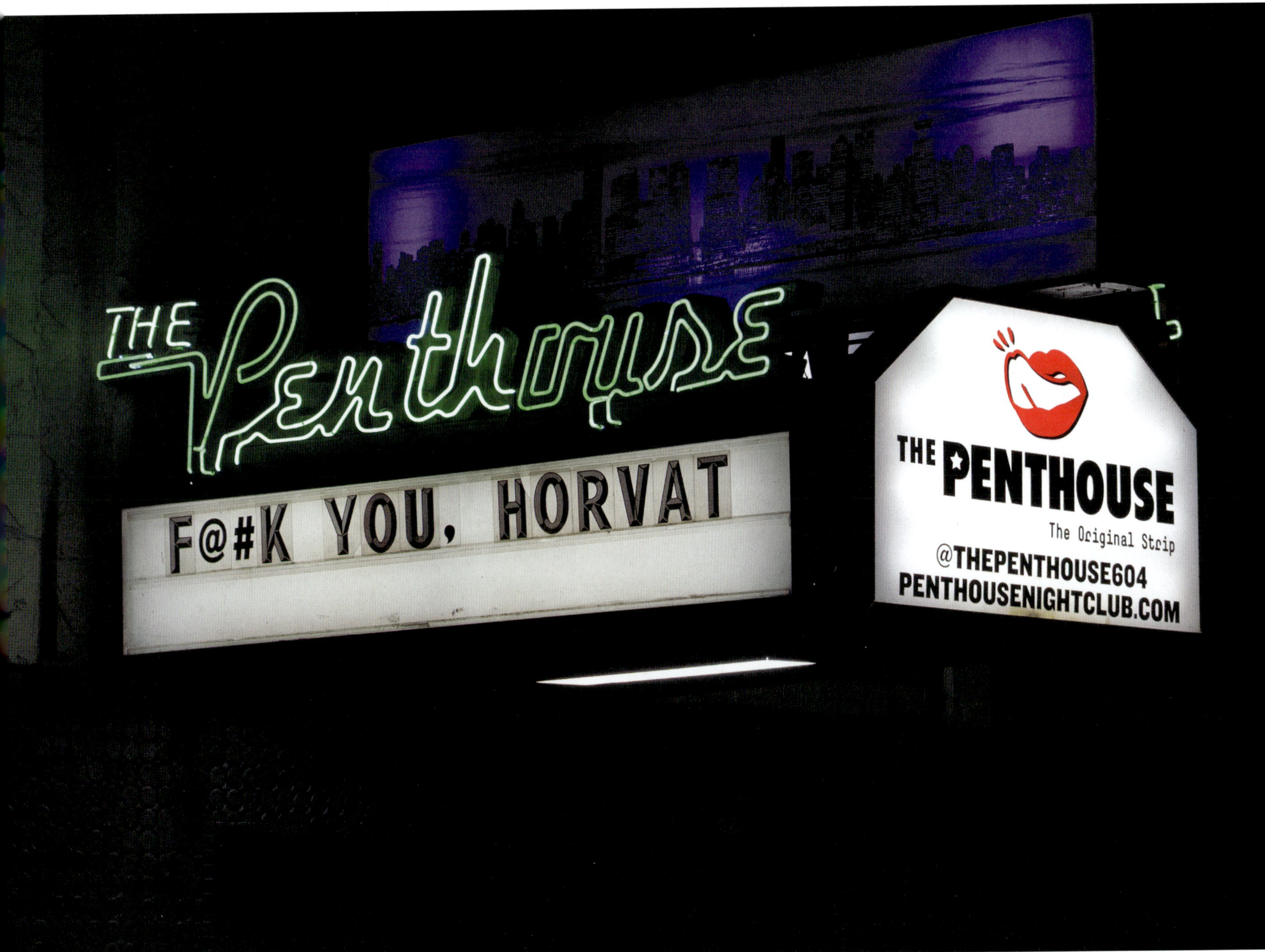
THE Penthouse
F@#K YOU, HORVAT
THE PENTHOUSE
The Original Strip
@THEPENTHOUSE604
PENTHOUSENIGHTCLUB.COM

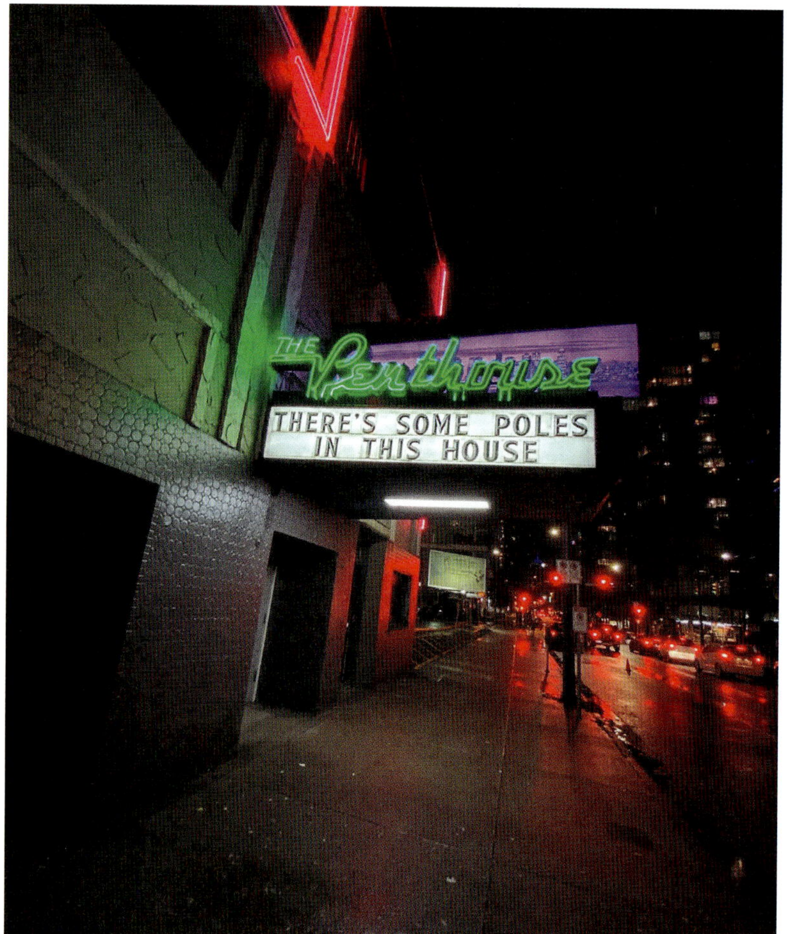
THE Penthouse
THERE'S SOME POLES
IN THIS HOUSE

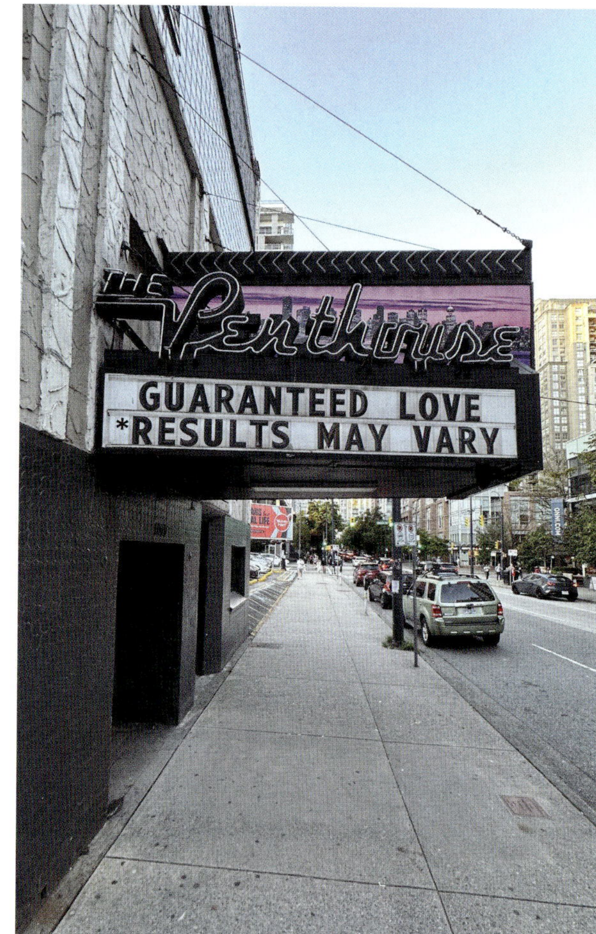
THE Penthouse
GUARANTEED LOVE
*RESULTS MAY VARY

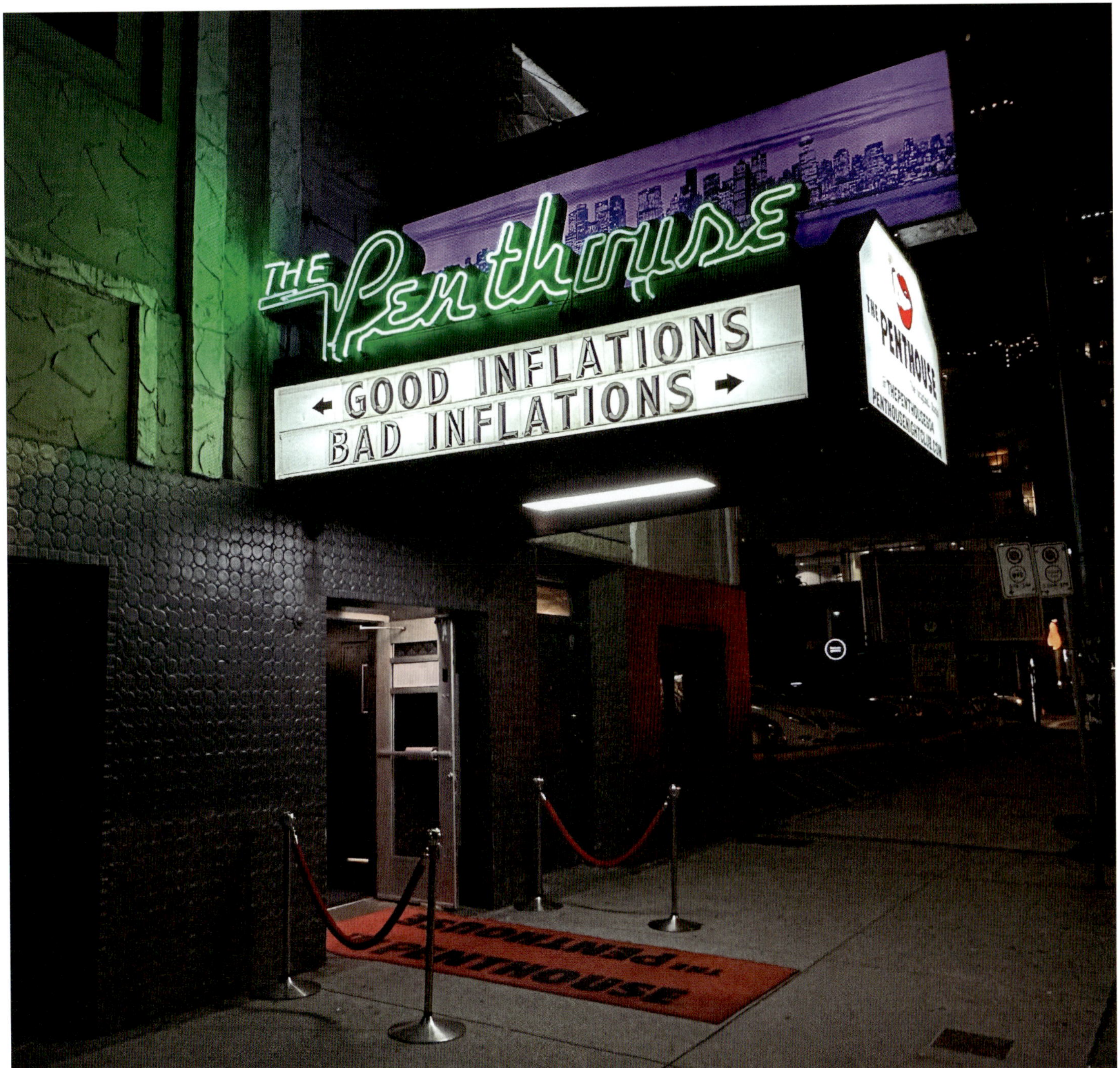
THE Penthouse
GOOD INFLATIONS
BAD INFLATIONS
THE PENTHOUSE
PENTHOUSENIGHTCLUB.COM
THE PENTHOUSE

FOREVER NEIGHBOURS NEVER NEIGHBORS

In January 2025, in the days before the confirmation of the Presidency in the USA, then President-Elect Donald Trump began a series of public statements about how Canada should become the 51st State of the USA.

I'd gone to Toronto for the Christmas holidays, and was in the Air Canada lounge on January 8th waiting to fly back to Vancouver. My flight had been delayed four hours, and the news on the TV's there felt like it was on a repeat cycle, with all these stories. With all these stories of Trump and the 51st state. I was bored waiting for my plane, and started texting Danny back in town about how I wanted to do something about it, and having a few drinks in the lounge thinking I was funnier than I was. I was toying with the wording, "We'll Never Be Your Neighbors" — but that sounded cranky, and it was missing something.

I finally got on the plane, and I was still thinking about it as I took my seat and they were telling us to turn off our phones or put them on airplane mode when it hit me — Forever Neighbours Never Neighbors. I messaged Danny. I remember the flight attendant walking past, telling me to turn it off. Danny said, "That's it!"

I can't sleep on flights, and was exhausted by the time I landed. It must have been close to 4:00 AM when I took an UBER home from the Airport. I live close to the Penthouse and I thought to myself, "I better do it now," so I told the driver to just drop me off at the Penthouse and I went in and changed the sign in the middle of the night. I was half asleep on the ladder! When I got home, I posted some photos of it on Instagram and Twitter before my head finally hit the pillow, and I went to sleep.

Jet-lagged and tired from the previous day, I didn't awake until that afternoon. I had my phone silenced, so when I woke up and saw so many missed calls and texts, I thought somebody had died. I had all these messages about the new sign. Danny had called me dozens of times trying to wake me up, because they were getting all these calls from every TV channel, radio station, and newspaper in town, as well as some out-of-town ones, wanting to talk to me that afternoon. I rushed down to the club where I found cameras and reporters waiting.

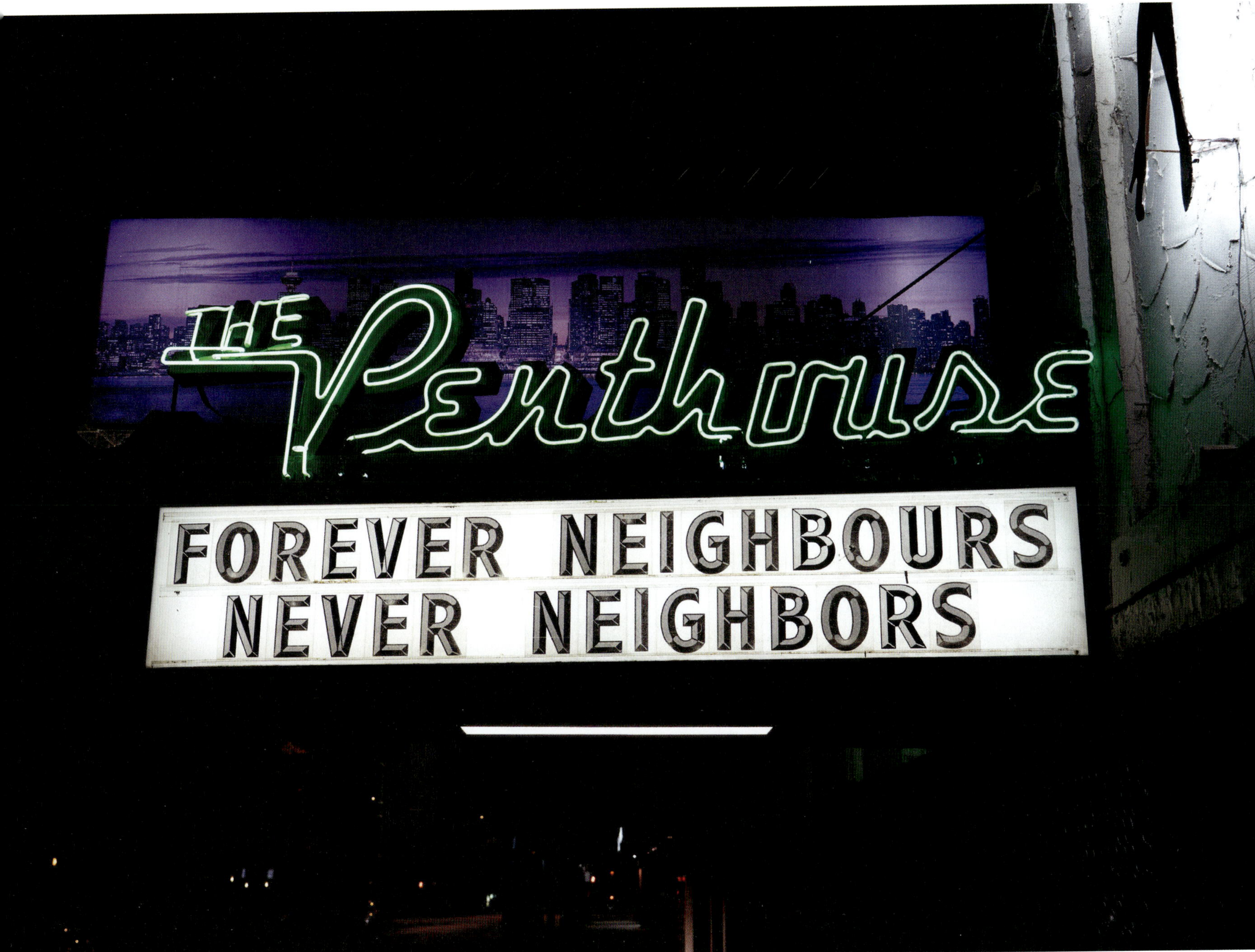
The Penthouse
FOREVER NEIGHBOURS
NEVER NEIGHBORS

The next day Prime Minister Trudeau posted something online about Canadian firefighters helping American firefighters in California, with a tag line 'Neighbours helping Neighbors", and he got a bunch of online flak that he had stolen that line from the Penthouse.

But it was the next day, when Twitter/X suddenly suspended our account with a banner that said it had been done because the post had "violated the platforms rules on hate speech" and then took our whole page down.

I couldn't believe it. I was worried, too. I didn't understand how it had been considered as such. The story of our suspension not only went Canada-wide, but international with media reports from Vancouver to Berlin. It all just blew up after that, and there was another round of media people wanting to talk to me again.

Danny was worried about the stress it was giving me. That X had considered it hate speech was confusing enough, but I didn't want to see the business branded with anything like that. The public started messaging X and Elon Musk himself. I honestly don't know if he ever saw it in the end. It might have just been the X algorithm that flagged it and temporarily suspended the account, but as I say, the whole story just exploded after that. A day or so later, just after an interview with the Jas Johal show on CKNW, I happened to look down at my phone and saw that the suspension had been lifted without any notice or explanation.

We kept the sign up, and it really became a rallying thing at that time. We were half-thinking we ought to copyright it. We ended up making a T-shirt of it, and the Penthouse got thousands of orders from around the country.

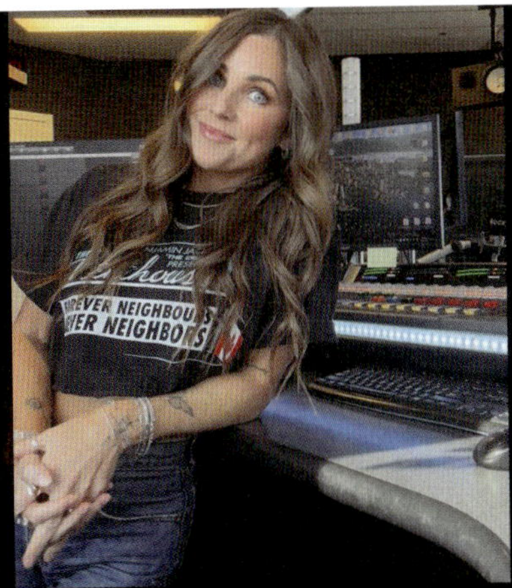

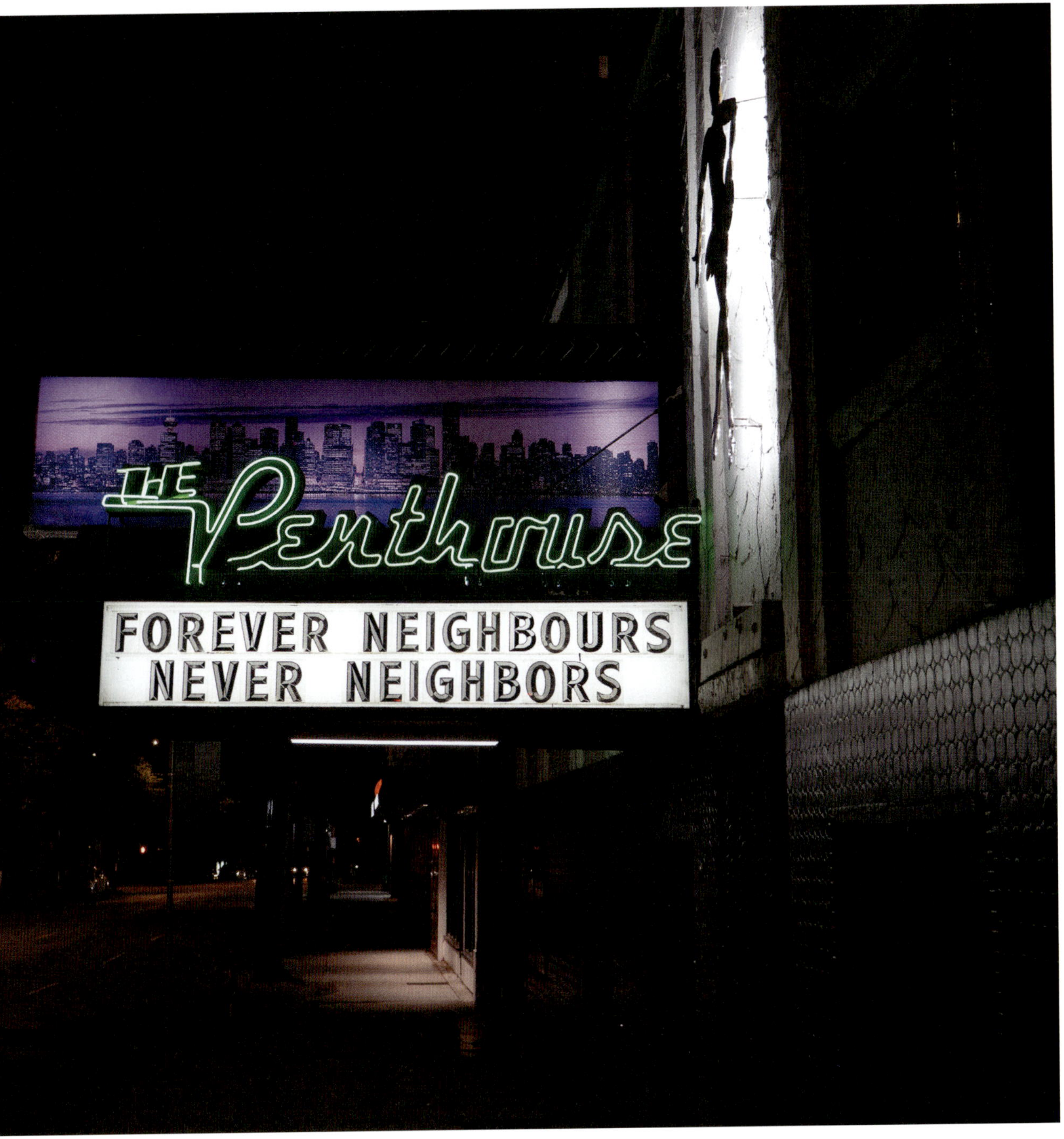

"I always know I can count on the sign to make me laugh. 'The Wreck Beach of Night Clubs', 'No Shoes, No Shirt, When can You Start?', 'Daycare available just kidding'. But my favourite didn't necessarily make me laugh, my favourite said everything that needed to be said. Simple, to the point, and perfectly Canadian. 'Forever Neighbours, Never Neighbors'. I mean, I loved it so much I bought a shirt!"

— Alece Lind Anderson, On-Air Host – CFMI Rock 101

LOST & FOUND: WEDDING RING

One ring to rule them all... And the truth is stranger than friction.

I'd come up with the sign back in 2018. It was probably up for three weeks. But strangely enough in 2025 a man contacted the Penthouse voicemail one Sunday saying he'd lost his wedding ring. Danny and his wife Jackie went down to look for it. They turned on all the lights, scoured every inch, looking everywhere for it. There was no sign of a wedding ring.

We got an email a day later from a different guy who said he'd found a wedding ring at the Penthouse — but it sounded like he was holding out for a reward. Danny replied telling him he ought to just do the right thing and give it back to the guy who'd lost it — but he wasn't really budging. Eventually Danny connected the two guys in an email chain, but with it he attached a photo of that old 2018 sign. It worked, and must have guilted the guy who found the ring, and he returned it to the other man, whose wife never knew anything about it.

"We get contacted all the time about things people leave behind. Mostly car keys, house keys, passports. Gosh, we've got enough left-behind jackets in our lost and found to start a clothing store. Because nobody expects things to be found, there's a little game I often play, going out of my way to return something. I've met people at gas stations, people taking off at the airport for their honeymoon. Nowadays people have "Find-a-phone" apps on their mobile phones and we get contacted with people telling us their lost phone is pinging at the bar. 'Do you recall where you were in the club?', I always ask. 'Oh, well, I was at the bar for a bit, then the front row by the stage.' Almost always their phones are found by one of the VIP chairs when they went for a lap dance, and it (the phone) slipped out."

— Danny Filippone, Penthouse Nightclub owner

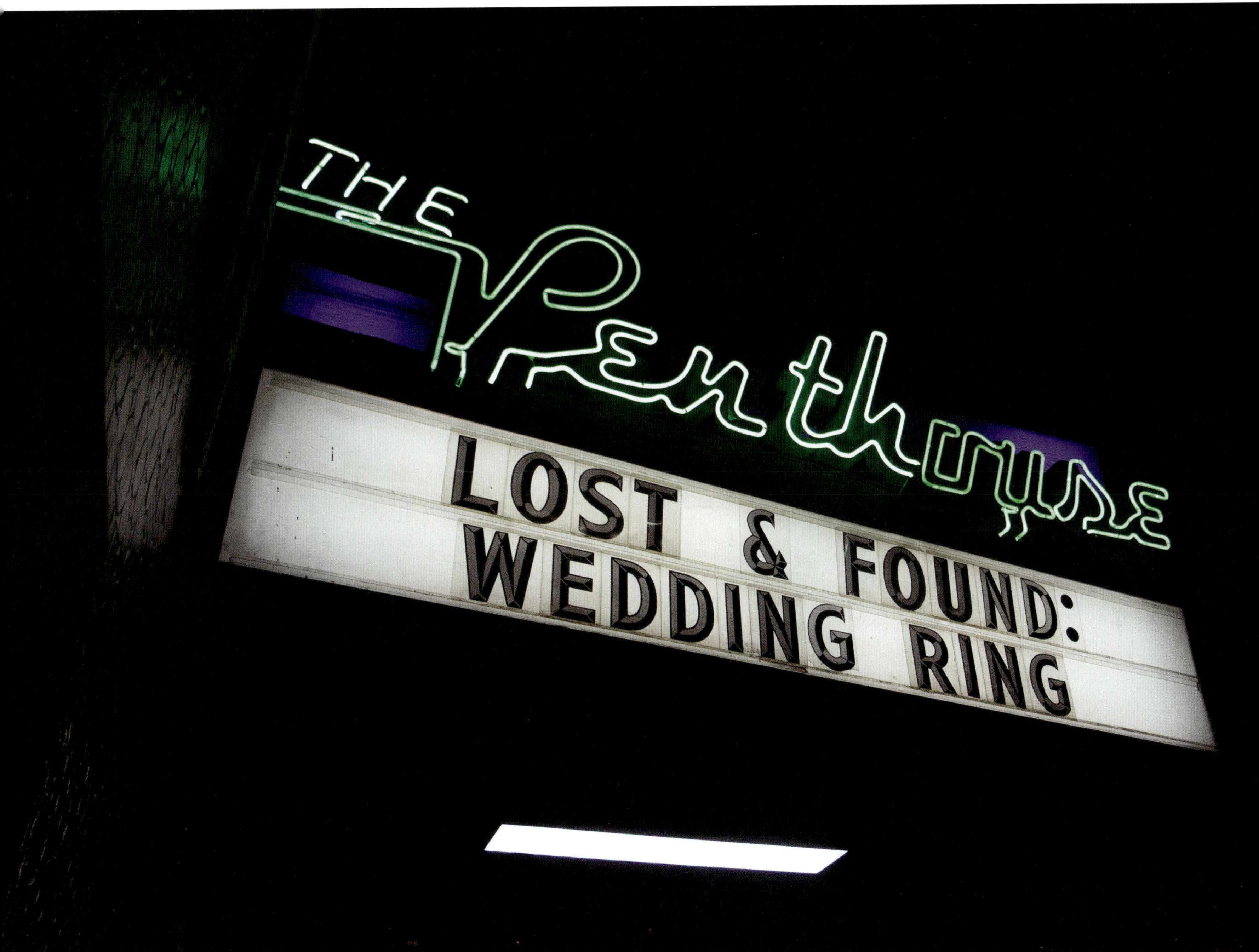
THE Penthouse
LOST & FOUND:
WEDDING RING

RELAX GUYS, COLDPLAY ISN'T HERE

In July 2025, at a Coldplay concert in Foxboro, Massachusetts, two corporate executives were caught in an intimate embrace on the "kiss cam." The viral video of the event featured a comment from Coldplay singer Chris Martin who wondered aloud if the couple was having an affair, as it showed the couple quickly ducking out of view. Their outing resulted in resignations, and the incident became a cultural flashpoint about both workplace relationships and being "caught in public." But the Penthouse and its marquee were there to calm those here in our city — and a photo of the sign's marquee minutes after Jackson had finished it would become one of the biggest reactions ever to one of the marquees.

I originally wanted to write, DON'T WORRY GUYS CHRIS MARTIN ISN'T HERE, but "Chris Martin" took up too much room. I guess I got too fixated on Martin's role in the whole thing and couldn't see around it, but Danny encouraged me to just use "Coldplay" instead, and a friend of mine agreed, so I put it up around lunch the day after the show had happened. I went home, and planned to come back to work that evening and get a picture of it at night — I think the marquee looks better at night with the lights. But some guy driving by took a clip of it, literally hanging out his window, and posted it. By the time I returned to work it had been seen 10,000,000 times, and by the end of the weekend 22,000,000 times on Instagram. The internet itself beat me to the punch. The sign went viral before I'd even had a chance to take a picture of it.

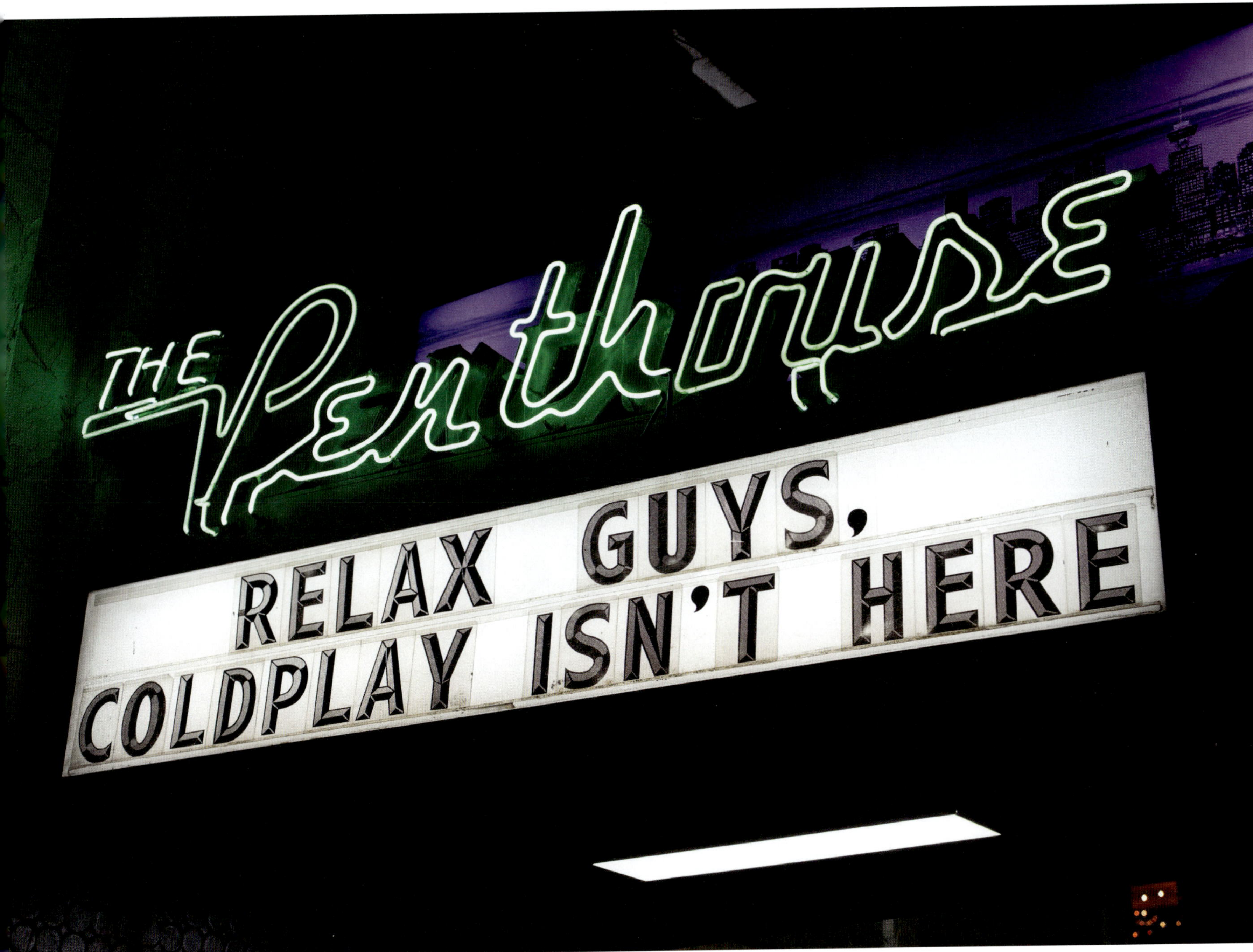
THE Penthouse
RELAX GUYS,
COLDPLAY ISN'T HERE

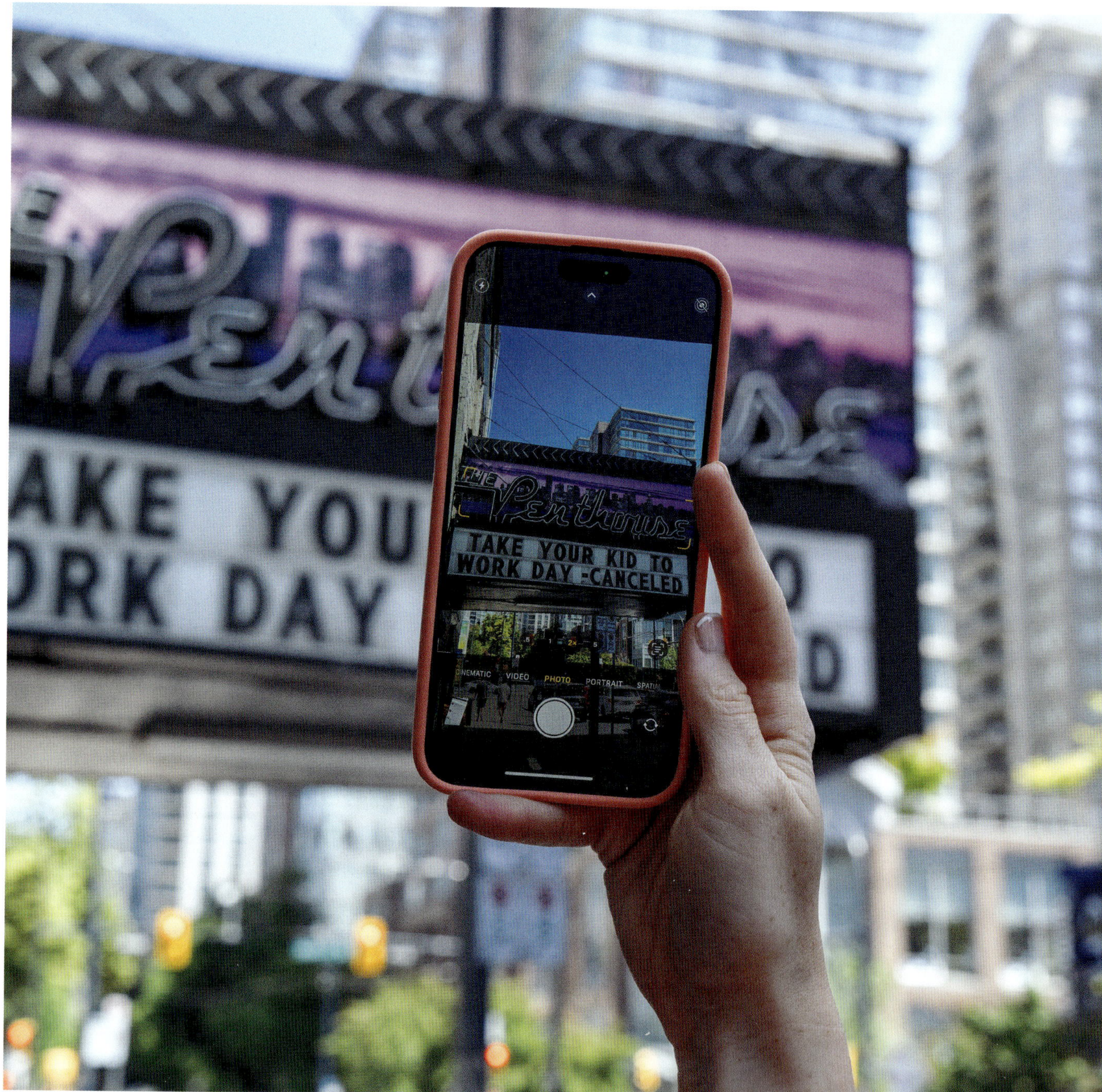
The Penthouse
TAKE YOUR KID TO
WORK DAY -CANCELED

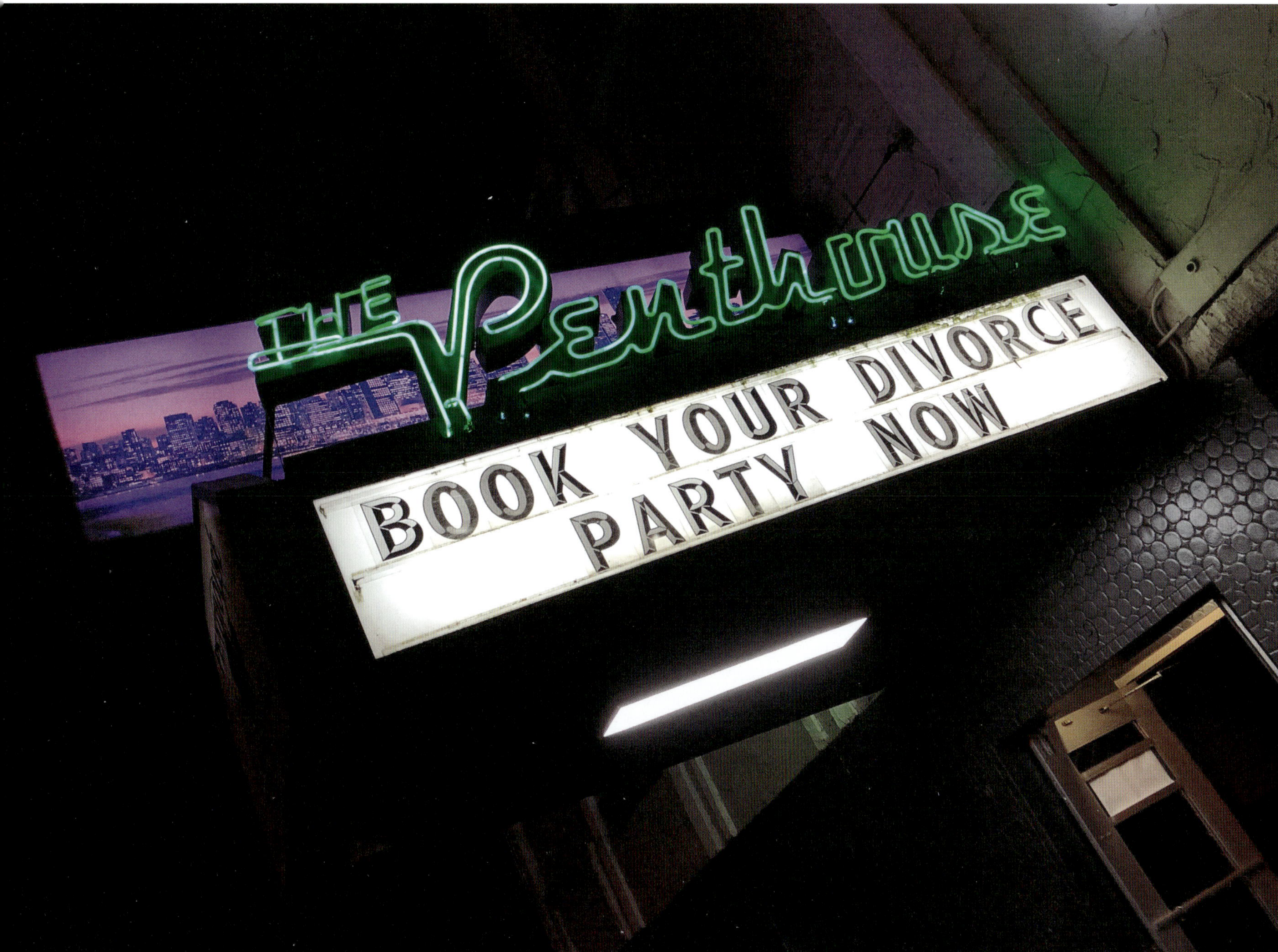
THE Penthouse
BOOK YOUR DIVORCE
PARTY NOW

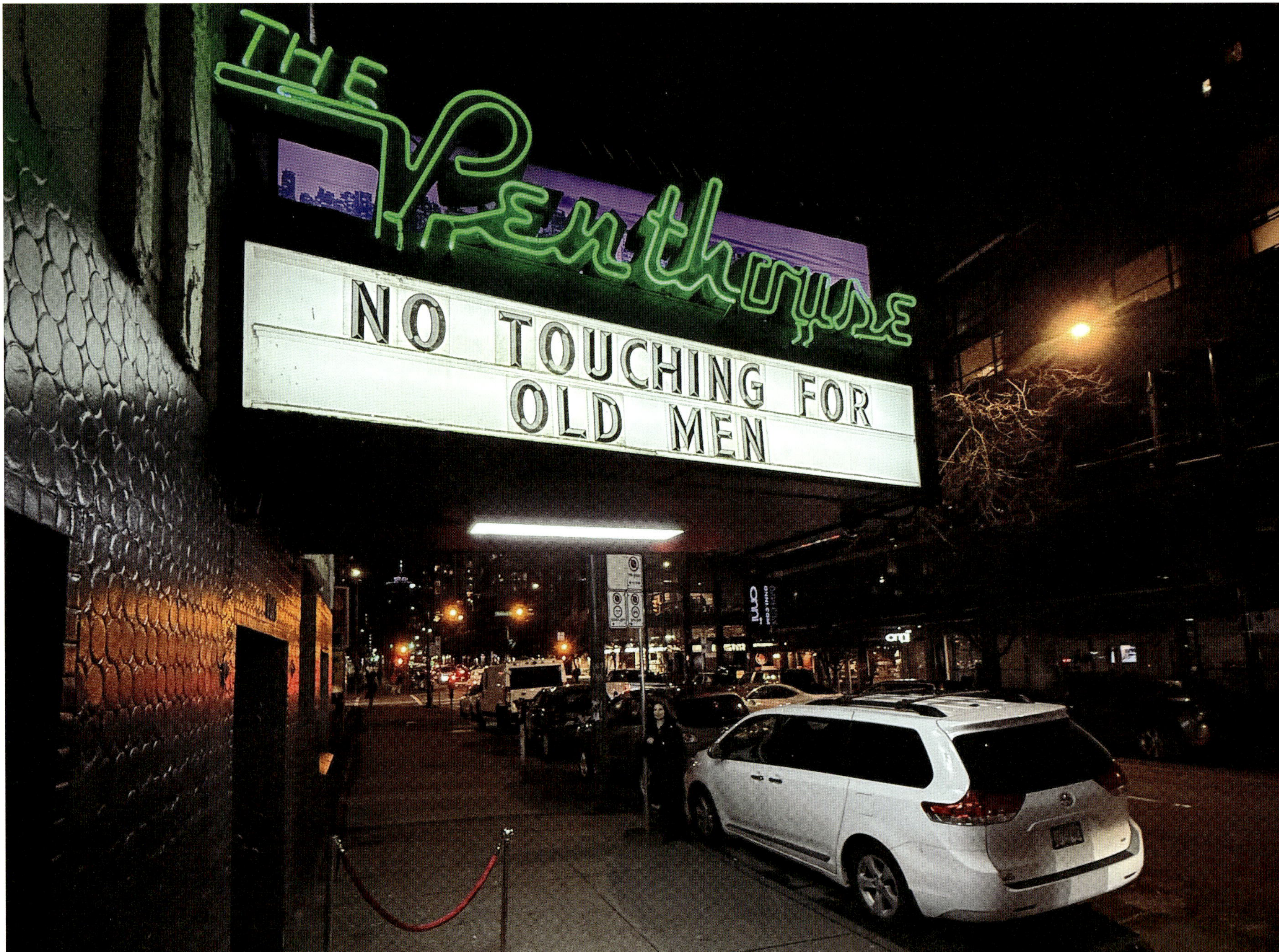
THE Penthouse
NO TOUCHING FOR
OLD MEN

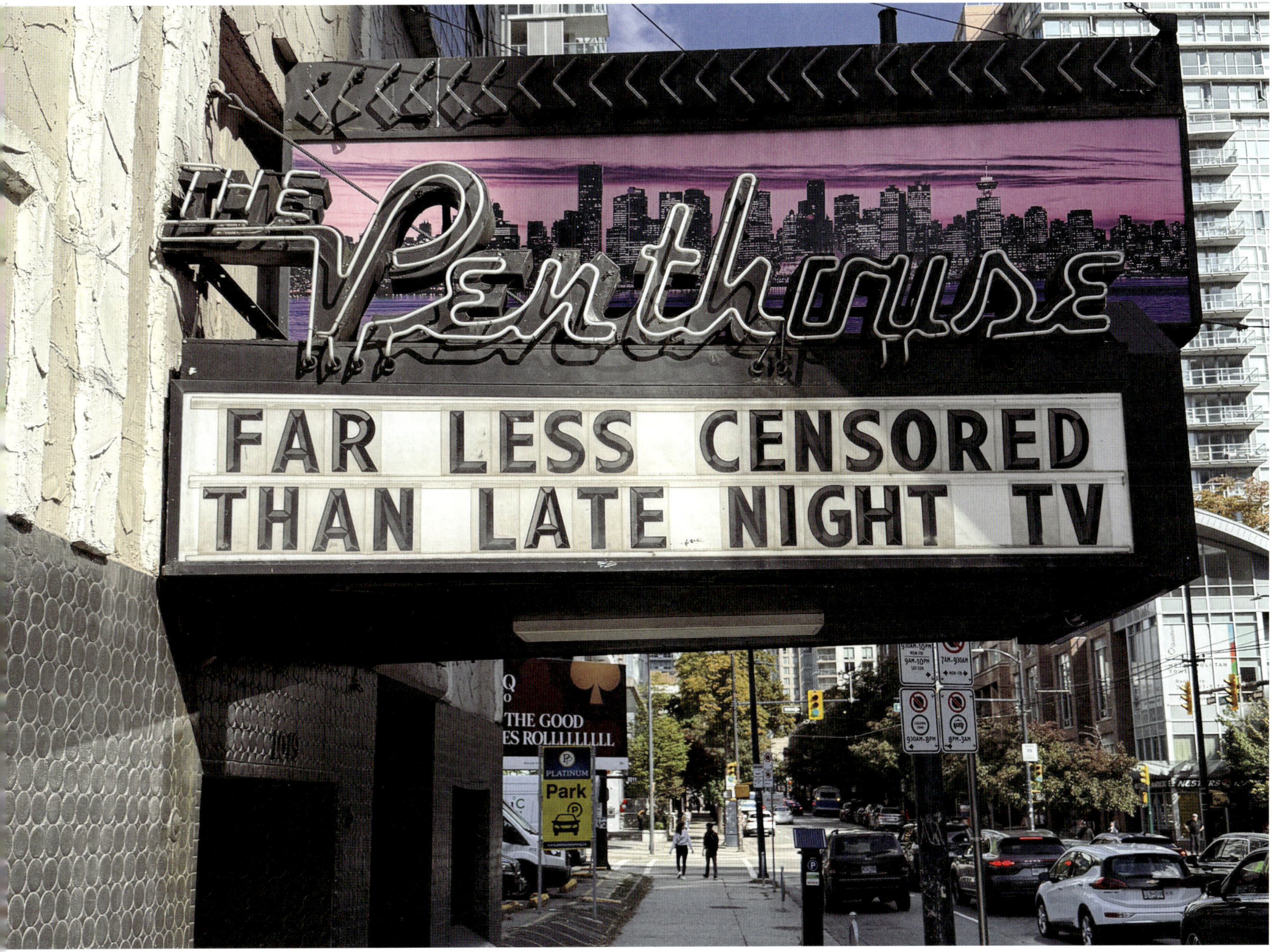
THE
Penthouse
FAR LESS CENSORED
THAN LATE NIGHT TV
THE GOOD
ES ROLLLLLLLLL
PLATINUM
Park

MARQUEES ARE JUST MEMES WITHOUT PICS

The Penthouse has always had its own sense of philosophy. This marquee message would garner 540,000 Google views.

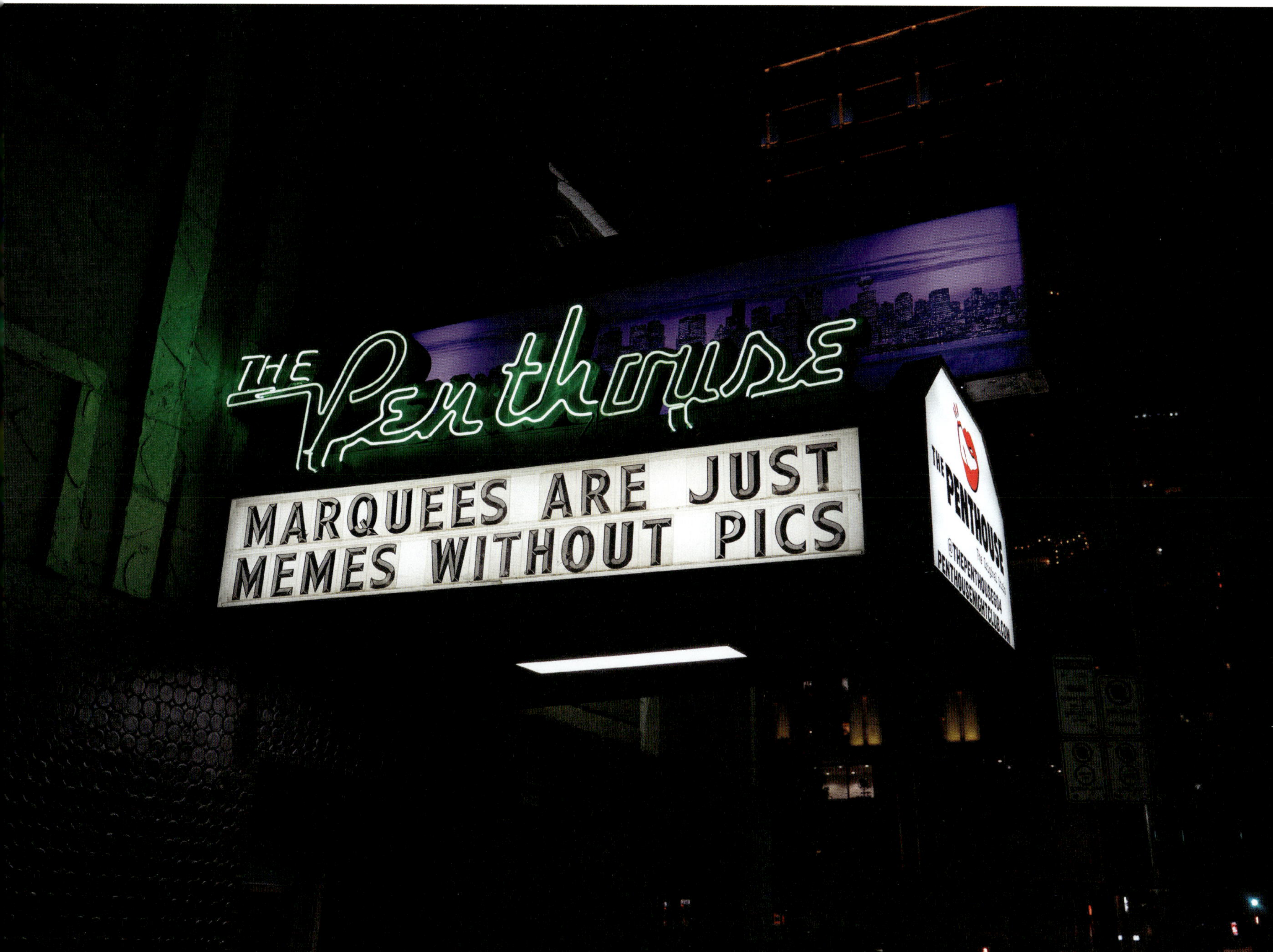
THE Penthouse
MARQUEES ARE JUST
MEMES WITHOUT PICS
THE PENTHOUSE
@THEPENTHOUSE604
PENTHOUSENIGHTCLUB.COM

AFTERWORD

THAT A FEW PLASTIC ALPHABET TILES have successfully navigated to our contemporary politically-correct waters, happily skipped by our sensitive and irascible world of media argue-tainment, where millions of those of every political stripe, woke or asleep, from around the globle, have double-taked, guffawed, blushed, scratched their heads, or tut-tutted to the Penthouse marquee is not so much a testament to those plastic tiles, or what the Penthouse stands for itself, but the irrepressible mind of Benjamin Jackson.

If marketing companies and advertising executives were looking for a mind that could likely come up with the kind of mottos and maxims that would be beloved and remembered for years to come, they might find that brain gregariously bartending behind the bar at the Penthouse Nightclub. But the Penthouse's setting of cocktails, music, and dancers on poles probably seems a lot more invigorating than sitting in a boardroom with a marker and vision-board from 9:00 to 5:00.

Vancouver doesn't enter the national or global realm of pop culture too often. Our media is often over-shadowed by images from New York or Toronto. We might see movies and TV shows where we recognize our own city street — but Vancouver never plays itself. When we see another of Ben's outrageous or funny signs, online or in the news, we're reminded that the sign is one of us. It's from Vancouver, and from Seymour Street. It's like spotting the face of a friend we know in a crowd of people. That's the Penthouse marquee.

The Penthouse has stood on Seymour Street in downtown Vancouver for over eighty years; much longer if history might have counted when the first illegal cocktail had been poured there. It has a remarkable history to itself that I wrote of in *Liquor, Lust, and the Law*. I imagine it won't be around forever; nothing stays the same in Vancouver's ever-changing downtown core. But, because of the last decade, Benjamin and the marquee seem like they've got a few more messages to give us before it's last call. And the city is ready for them.

Because it's no longer just the Penthouse's sign — it feels like it's become Vancouver's sign. Some nights it's the joke. Other nights it's the punchline. Sometimes it's just a picture to easily tap a "like" on by the light of your phone. Sometimes it's just a smile that makes you glad you got out of the house and headed down Seymour Street that night to take it in for yourself and stop inside. On a good night, whether it's raining on Seymour, or the wit and street is dry, the sign is perhaps even Vancouver's unspoken conscience.

It's A Sign of the Times.

— Aaron Chapman (Historian/Author)
Instagram: @ThatAaronChapman, X: @TheAaronChapman

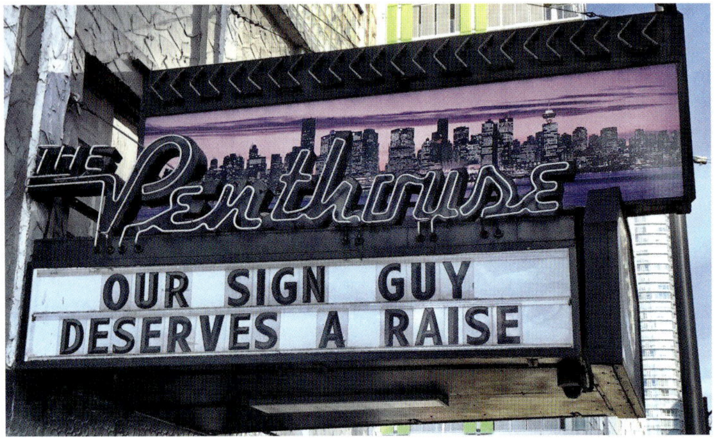

Thank you from Benjamin Jackson:

Many thanks to all the exceptional dancers who I've had the pleasure of working with over the years. This book could not have happened without your inspiration and support. I've said it before and I will say it again, sex work is real work.

I can't forget Gids, Andrew, Georgie, Krystal, and all of the amazing staff at The Penthouse Nightclub, you guys are the best in the business.

To all the individuals who honked from their vehicles while I was on the ladder, who stopped to share kind words or even request a photograph, your support makes my day every time and never ceases to be appreciated.

My incredible mother, Carol, her husband Vlad, my beautiful sister Melody, the kids Hali, Aries, Beckham, and my cousin Hal. Words cannot express how much you mean to me. Family is everything, and I wish Aunt Linda were here to celebrate with us.

The boys: Scott, Stephen Pezzente, Matty (Ace), Handsome Jeff, and my brother Ian — thank you for everything. I love you guys so much.

My love, Tiny Baby Niki, you are my heart. Kat, DH, Jordana and Morena, your support means the world to me. My dear friends Mellisa and Sheebs, thank you for always being there. Grace Kelly, not a day goes by that I don't miss you. Thank you for always keeping me on my toes.

The Filippone family: Danny, Jackie, Justin, and Cam. I'm so grateful to have you guys in my life, and honoured to call you my friends. To Aaron Chapman, it's been an absolute pleasure sharing this journey with you, brother. I can't thank you enough for all of your hard work. Brian and Derek at Anvil Press, thank you for your support. None of this would have been possible without you.

Finally, I express my deepest gratitude to the beautiful city of Vancouver, which I am proud to call home. Thank you!

– BENJAMIN "THE SIGN GUY" JACKSON

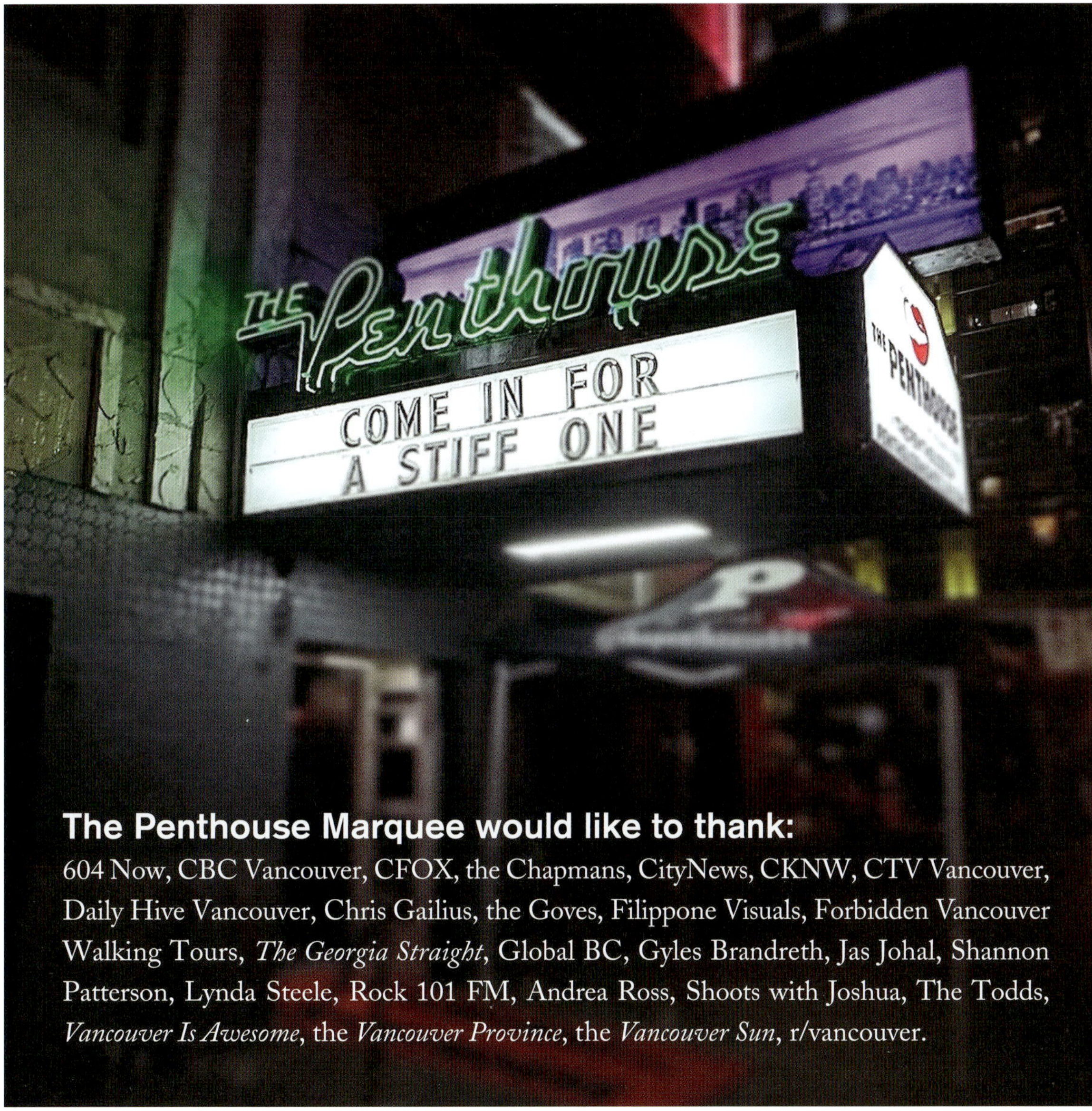

The Penthouse Marquee would like to thank:

604 Now, CBC Vancouver, CFOX, the Chapmans, CityNews, CKNW, CTV Vancouver, Daily Hive Vancouver, Chris Gailius, the Goves, Filippone Visuals, Forbidden Vancouver Walking Tours, *The Georgia Straight*, Global BC, Gyles Brandreth, Jas Johal, Shannon Patterson, Lynda Steele, Rock 101 FM, Andrea Ross, Shoots with Joshua, The Todds, *Vancouver Is Awesome*, the *Vancouver Province*, the *Vancouver Sun*, r/vancouver.

MAKE YOUR OWN SIGN!

It's your turn to become the Penthouse Sign Guy or Gal, and make your own Penthouse marquee! Make a copy of the tiles and you're ready to go — you don't even need a ladder or have to worry about passing pedestrians on Seymour Street bumping into you as you work.

Here's a few tips from Benjamin "The Sign Guy" Jackson, himself:

> "The Penthouse Nightclub marquee has 40 characters total, with 20 per line. I've got about 5 full alphabets, and a short collection of symbols that includes a hashtag, question mark, along with Facebook, Instagram, and the old X/twitter bird symbol. The tiles can sometimes fall and break — so be careful! Nobody said this would be easy. Oh, and you may want to photocopy this alphabet page so you don't need to take the scissors to the book or lose any letters down the back of your VIP chair. And, hey, if you're making a dirty sign — keep it clean out there, or at least funny."

Think you came up with a good one? Post your pics with the #ASignOfTheTimes #MyPenthouseMarquee — and we'll look out for them. Maybe you'll even become guest Penthouse marquee signwriter for the day?

— Benjamin Jackson (Author/the Sign Guy!) Instagram @benzoylecgonine

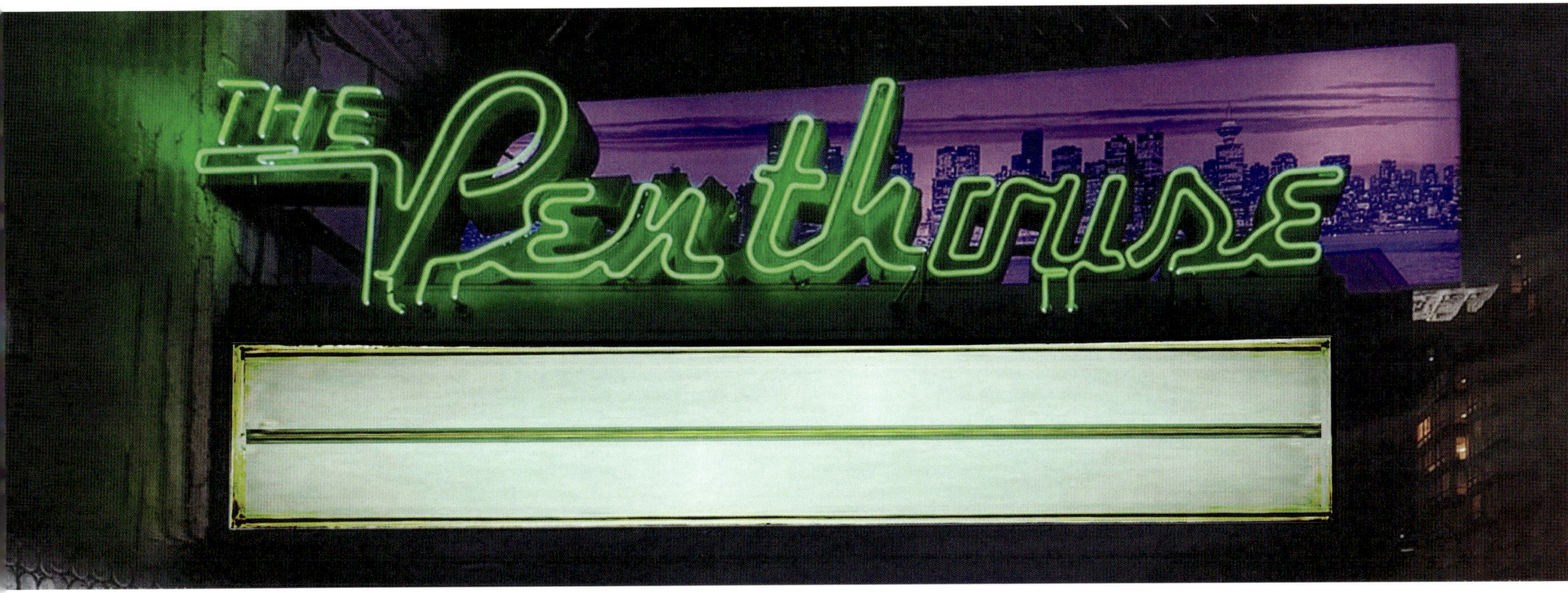

A A A B B B C C C D D D E E E F F F G G G

H H H I I I J J J K K K L L L M M M N N N

O O O P P P Q Q Q R R R S S S T T T U U U

V V V W W W X X X Y Y Y Z Z Z ! @ # $ % &

: ; ' ' " " / ( ) - ?

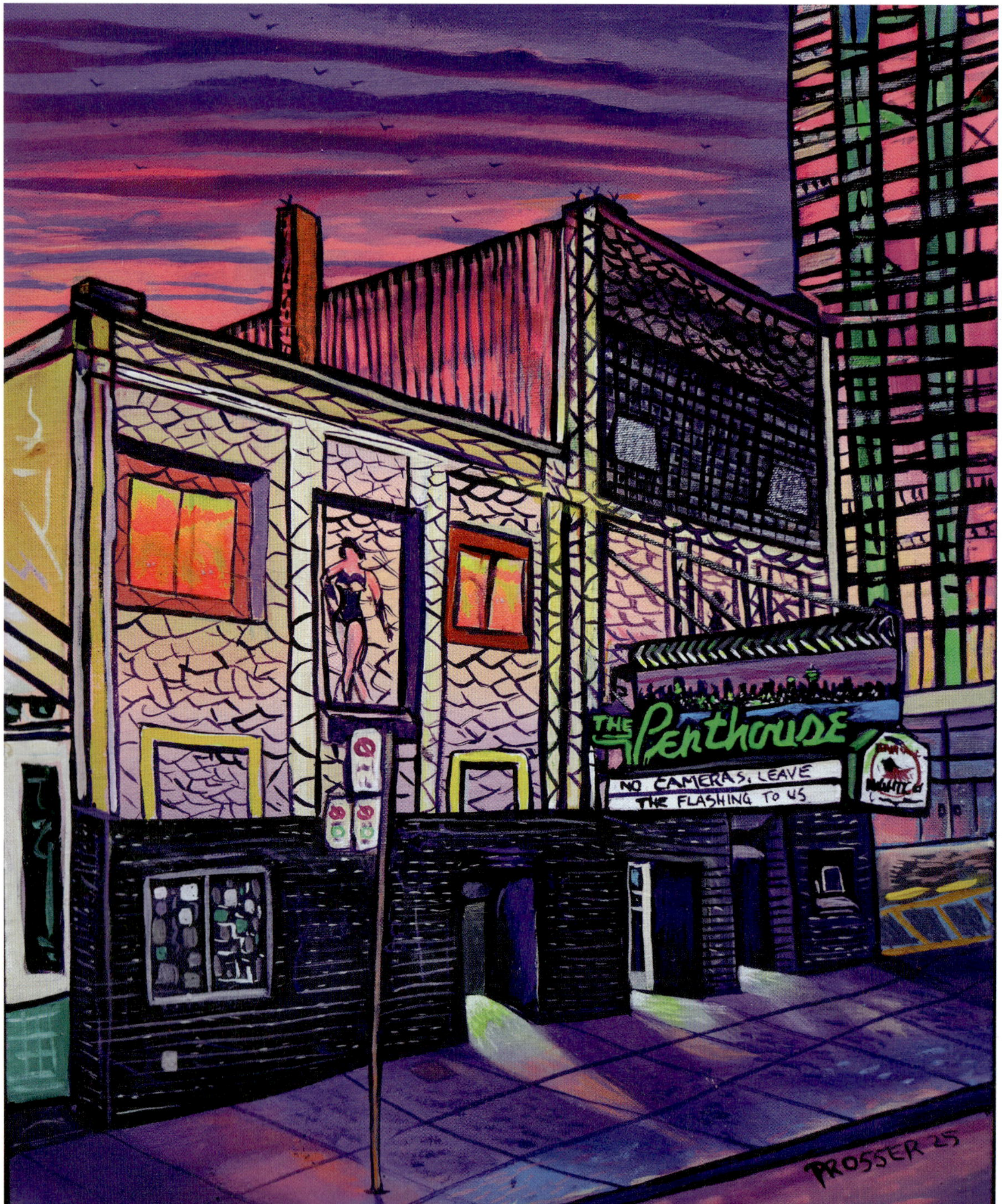

Painting by Mark Prosser.
ProsserArt.com